C000124971

"As a Baptist pastor I never really
says about animals. Reading *Do Dogs*
world! This is a must read for anyone '
Cox, Aslan's Place, Hesperia, CA.

"*Do Dogs Go to Heaven* answers questions most of us probably have, but
dismiss. Jean Holmes has taken time to study a subject at which many people
scoff. Her candid approach, combined with humor, makes this an enjoyable
journey. When I have to part with a pet, it is gut-wrenching. Jean gets to the
meat of answering questions such as "Do animals have souls and spirits?"
There are many other questions Jean addresses. This book will stimulate
you to come up with a conclusion for yourself. Enjoy!" – Rev. Linda Budd,
Senior Co-Pastor, Open Bible Fellowship (now Rivergate Church), Tulsa OK

Quotes from readers of *Do Dogs Go to Heaven?*:

"I, too, like your mother, have asked the question and never felt like I
got a thoroughly believable answer. ... the Biblical backing of my beliefs are
imperative. ... I am quite comfortable with your conclusion and terrifically
joyous about it!"

"...what a comfort your book has been to me, personally."

"I cannot begin to tell you how much your book means to me."

"Thank you for this delightful book. It was so good and comforting. I
lost 2 dogs ... and this book helps to heal."

"I'm really enjoying your book, laughing in parts and pondering in
others, very good!"

"I loved the book and so has everyone else to whom I have given it."

"...my husband and I . . . came to Christ by reading your book right after
we lost our golden retriever. He has read that book so much, he knows it by
heart.... your book has done so much for me and my husband ... You have a
beautiful way of putting His Word in layman's terms."

"...a great book not only in respect to the subject but also to the Bible
itself. I probably learned more about the Bible reading this book than at any
other time in my life. *** Probably the most powerful thing though was the
author's description of animal sacrifices in the Old Testament. When... I first
read the Bible, I was horrified that God would ...require animal sacrifices. ...
I now understand...."

"Thank you so much for taking the time to research and write this
wonderful book. .. Thank you again for this bit of peace for a very heavy
heart."

DO DOGS GO TO HEAVEN?

Eternal Answers

for Animal Lovers

Jean Holmes

JoiPax Publishing
A division of JoiPax, Inc.
P.O. Box 701252
Tulsa, OK 74170-1252

www.joipax.com
e-mail: jean.holmes@joipax.com

DEDICATION

I dedicate this book, Do Dogs Go to Heaven?
Eternal Answers to Animal Lovers, revised edition to:

To the Living God, our Creator, and Jesus, His Son -
Who loves all His creation and
Has eternal plans for the good of all.

To the animals who have loved us, taught us,
cared for us, and protected us - even with their lives; and
Who patiently await our enlightenment.

To my witty, wonderful Mom,
for her courage in asking a question which
every animal lover, wants to know.
Who loved all God's creatures without fear and
Who taught me to love and seek truth, and
To joy in both the sunshine and the rain life brings.

To my father, the veterinarian, known as "Doc" to all of us.
My shy, quietly brilliant mentor, who first assured me
There is a heaven for dogs.
Who lived rightly without boasting.

To my parents who now enjoy heaven,
and who now know the answers.

To all who love animals and who need to know
about their eternity.

ACKNOWLEDGEMENTS

This is to acknowledge the wonderful help and encouragement given to make this revised edition a reality. All who have prayed and believed with me through many challenges and delays -- including former readers, my church and pastors, my Tuesday prayer group, my retreat "sisters" and others, so this book could be in print once again. Also, many thanks to Deborah for her excellent proof reading.

~*Jean Holmes*

CONTENTS

PREFACE TO REVISED EDITION

Animals are such agreeable friends;
they ask no questions, they make no criticisms.
~George Elliot

This book came about because my Mom asked the question which is the title, "Do dogs go to heaven?" During her lifetime, Mom had many friends — a lot of them were dogs. Mom's question strikes a nerve in animal lovers. Heaven for us means our animals will be there, too. This book is written for adults, like Mom. It does not treat Mom's question as something "just for children." It is a thorough study of her question which took years to research and write.

The first edition put 5,000 books in print. People's reactions were often dramatic. While I did not write the first edition as a grief book, many told me it gave them great comfort for the pain of losing a beloved animal. That delights my heart. It is great when anyone experiences God's comfort and finds hope. In this edition, we add a few suggestions to readers on overcoming grief.

Mom went to heaven in 1988. For her, the question is settled. Mom now is with her beloved Lord and her animals. But Mom's question launched me on a quest to find true answers. Not just glib, pat, surface answers, but answers with substance. In the 1990s, the search became a fire in my bones.

I determined to find an answer – one based in Scripture and substantiated by research and evidence. There are some "hard" questions about the role of animals here and in the hereafter. I wanted the answer, even if I didn't like the answer. I wanted the full truth. And I knew I would find it. God has always given me answers when I asked in faith. [See James 1:5].

THE IMPORTANCE OF ANIMALS

Animals play tremendous roles in our lives – and have done so since the dawn of creation. From aardvarks to zebras, elephants to trained mice, animals enrich our lives. Animals provide companionship, do work, become food and clothing, and are vital players in the diverse interconnected ecologies of our world. Pets give us unconditional love and faithful companionship. Animals as diverse as reindeer, elephants, oxen, horses, camels, llamas, cats, and dogs, have worked with us and for us. Today a variety of animals are serving in therapy roles. The videos of animals doing funny or wonderful things circulate the globe now on the Internet or television shows. History is replete with examples of animals who have been friends, rescuers, healers, and calming influences.

The whole world is full of animal lovers. The pet industry in the U.S. alone, is a multibillion dollar industry. Americans currently have over 61 million dogs and over 75 million cats. Brazil is second in dog and fourth in cat ownership. China is second in cat and third in dog ownership. Russians have 9.5 million dogs and almost 13 million cats . France and Italy have over 9 million dogs and 8 or 9 million cats. South Africa and Thailand have millions of dog owners, too. (This does not count birds and other pets.) Some of the oldest breeds of dogs and cats come from Asia and Egypt. Since time began, animals and humans have shared bonds of affection.

Modern animal behavior studies show animals display intelligence, moral choice, and some even use tools. "Moral choice" includes honesty, responsibility, bravery, loyalty, love, and grief — as well as their opposites. Play and humor are evident. Animals have acted, even died, heroically or sacrificially for others. Animals solve complex problems, use tools, and communicate. Some have complex social structures. There is increasing medical evidence of animals as human healers. We humans study, exploit, revere, fear, love, laugh at, hate, document, film and write about animals both domestic and wild.

QUALIFICATIONS

What are my qualifications to write this book? My heritage, my experience, and my training have all prepared me. Most important, finding an answer has become a kind of "calling," driving me to pray, research, observe, and work until Mom's question had a well-documented answer.

I have been surrounded by animals from infancy. My parents, my older brother, and I are all animal people. Mom was an incredible woman, and a great Mom. Mom had poise and pluck, grace and wisdom. Mom also had a tongue as sharp as her mind – although Mom chose to use her tongue to love and protect. Where ever Mom was – in the house, the barn, or outdoors, she made life – even its challenges and hurts – fascinating and often funny. Mom was fearless and adventurous. I gained a great deal from her, not the least of which is my intense love of and admiration for animals. Mom is the reason for this book. (Thanks, Mom!)

My late father was a brilliant veterinarian. Doc graduated from Ohio State University with honors. Doc had a large and small animal practice in Indiana, during my childhood. Through Doc, I was exposed to a wide variety of animals — some tame, some wild.

Mom enjoyed all creation. From her, I learned to view nature, in all its grandeur, with awe and wonder. Mom also taught me how funny nature can be. Understanding and respecting all living creatures was a requirement in her presence. Mom taught me that each animal had its own unique personality, its own strengths and weaknesses, its own purpose and value. From her and the animals, I learned that the God of Isaac (Isaac means laughter), has filled his universe with hilarious, joyous things.

My parents modeled intelligent curiosity, responsible caring service, dedication, and a love of excellence. Mom was especially patient, gentle, and just — although she could be a "she-bear" when protecting others from harm. My parents showed me a passion for truth and integrity, for justice and right actions — even when it kills you. While my parents were far from perfect, I saw in them the basic moral values which make a person a good citizen of this world and the next. Caring for animals is part of that citizenship. Caring was a requirement. Cruelty was not an option.

Mom enjoyed raising pedigreed Dachshunds. Mom also saw that my brother and I had plenty of other animals and learned to take care of them. My family had dogs, cats, pigs, cows, rabbits, geese, ducks, horses, a parakeet and even a pet crow.

I come by the love of animals naturally. I cannot remember being without one or more pets. Horses were my first love and filled my childhood days. I read about animals and listened to others' experiences with animals. I still enjoy learning about everything, from science to art to music to farming. Throughout my life, I've learned to remain curious and ask questions. Logic and other mental and emotional disciplines were part of my education.

I practice law in Tulsa, Oklahoma. As an appellate practitioner, I research and write briefs for courts. I am accustomed to gathering evidence and legal authorities. Having practiced for years in a variety of practice areas, my skills in research are well honed.

An important qualification is that God, our Creator, is real to me. I know Him experientially. I know God exists and He loves me. I love God with all my heart, soul, mind and strength (even if not perfectly). I also have the Fear of the Lord, in the Biblical meaning. The Fear of the Lord is the key to obtaining God's wisdom. [See Ps. 111:10; Prov. 1:7; 9:10; Isa. 11:2-3]. The truths in this book which are God's were given to me because of these things I firmly believe.

For years, I explored the world's religions and philosophies searching for the living God. For decades, I have had a personal relationship with the One God, Jesus [or Yeshua] of Nazareth. Jesus is my Lord and Savior, my best friend and confidante. The promises that the Holy Spirit (Spirit of the Lord) will guide me into all truth and will teach me all things, are real to me (many times over). [John

14:26 & 16:13; 1 John 2:20, 26.] An avid student of the Bible, I try to find Christian and Jewish sources in every search for truth.

Last, but not least, I love animals — especially ones who have been my friends, companions, and teachers. Mom's question became my question, too.

The views expressed here are my own. I have explored practices and doctrines from Catholicism to Pentecostalism. The experiences of various Christian persuasions enrich my faith. If my interpretations of Scripture offend your beliefs or your church's doctrines, please accept my statement that I do not intend to offend. (Please take it to the Lord.) I have worked hard to try to accurately handle God's Word, i.e., to state the truth. I do hope to challenge un-Biblical thinking. So stay open to new ideas.

MY QUEST

Mom's question inspired my own "need to know." You see, I, the one who loved and studied the Bible, the lawyer and veterinarian's daughter, did not have an answer for Mom, either. I did not know what the Bible said on the question of animals going to heaven. I wasn't sure the Bible said anything about that topic! Mom's question started a spark, which kindled a huge fire in me. It burned hot until I found the answer.

However, I had a reputation for finding answers in Scripture. In fact, I love the challenge of hard questions. If the Bible had an answer, I knew the Lord would show me. I would find it.

This quest seeking the truth about Mom's question took a lot of prayer, work, and thought. A fun project to honor Mom became a serious work to honor God and help animal lovers. In the decade or more since the first edition, many have challenged my thesis. I asked several apparently qualified debaters to offer a Biblical rebuttal. I never heard back from them. Either they dropped it or could not produce a viable, credible rebuttal. In fact, I believe the first edition stands as a proven thesis to date. There have been a few changes and additions, but nothing major. No Biblical references have been removed.

Some truths are like gold ore. Johann Wolfgang von Goethe, the great German thinker, aptly said:

It is easier to perceive error than to find the truth, for the former lies on the surface and is easily seen, while the latter lies in the depth, where few are willing to search for it.

This book came about because I prayed and asked the living God, the Creator who inspired the Bible to show me, in His Word, His answer to Mom's question. I asked with fear and trembling, because while God is love, He is also Holy and a consuming fire. I am confident that He has indeed shown me the answer to Mom's question.

There is an answer! The Bible answer is of tremendous import.

What I have learned has been staggering to me. Come, let us dig deep into the Bible. We will also see that other sources support my interpretations of Scriptures. Do animals go to heaven? You betcha! Do all go? The answer is the same as for people.

Join the search for truth that brings freedom! God is and will be with us. I pray your questions will be answered here. If you have questions or comments after reading this book, feel free contact me. I'll make every effort to respond.

May our Creator, the Lord God Almighty, bless you as you join me in examining Bible evidence which answers the question, "Do dogs — and other animals — go to heaven?"

Jean Holmes
P O Box 701252
Tulsa Oklahoma 741252
September 2011

CHAPTER 1

MOM'S QUESTION

I think I could turn and live with animals, they are so
placid and self-contained;
I stand and look at them long and long.
They do not sweat and whine about their condition; ...
Not one is dissatisfied — not one is demented with mania
of owning things;

Walt Whitman, "Song of Myself"

The most predictable thing about my Mom was that you never knew what would come out of her mouth next. My Mom was a master at asking probing questions and making life fun and interesting. Some eight years before her death — when she was in her 70's — Mom asked a series of ministers the question which became the title of this book: *"Do dogs go to heaven?"* She asked it of pastors and priests, all men of the cloth. Each gave a different answer. None gave the same one.

When I witnessed Mom asking this question, I was amused. Only as I heard it repeatedly, did I realize how important Mom's question is. It is a very important question. It deserves a better answer than she got. That's why I have researched and written this book. It's to answer Mom's question. And mine. And yours.

THE DEATH OF MOM'S CHOC

Mom asked her question after Choc died. Choc was the last of Mom's dachshunds. Choc was a rare chocolate point (marked like the black and tan except the black was brown).Choc was the only one I had ever seen. Naturally, "Choc" became her nickname. Choc was born just months before my father (whom we called "Doc") died. After more than twenty-five years of raising pedigreed dachshunds, this pup was from Mom's last litter. Choc was special to Mom.

Choc died a horrible death. Mom and I were living together in Kentucky, and our house had no fenced yard. When we went shopping for the day, we simply tied up the dogs. One day we returned to find Choc had strangled by her own tie. We were devastated. (I hope Choc is with Mom in heaven.)

MOM'S QUESTION

Sometime after Choc died, Mom and I were chatting with the man who delivered our newspaper. He was also a country preacher, and while not well educated, he was a hard-working fellow who appeared to love the Lord with all his heart. Mom and I both liked him. Suddenly Mom asked this preacher:

"Do dogs go to heaven?"

The question took me off guard. Looking back, I wonder if Mom was thinking of Choc. Instantly, I was curious as to how the preacher would answer. He looked surprised. He paused and thought. Then he said, "Well, in the Book of Revelation, it says that Jesus is coming back on a horse. So there are horses in heaven." He paused and thought some more.

From the look on his face, it was obvious the preacher was searching his mind for Bible verses. "It also says, 'without the gates are the dogs.' So, dogs aren't in heaven." He paused again. Then, his face brightened as he stated with confidence, "There are horses in heaven, but there are no dogs in heaven!" He beamed — proud that he'd found a Bible answer. He did not realize how that answer struck a dog lover.

Actually, the man's answer hit my funny bone. I couldn't laugh, however. Mom required us to be polite. Actually his answer seemed logical. The preacher didn't know that the term "dog" in that passage is a slang expression. I knew, but remained quiet. Mom did not show her reaction.

Because I was very active in Christian service, we knew many of the ministers, priests and preachers in our town – from the Roman Catholics to Pentecostals. Some were highly educated. Others were nearly illiterate. Some obviously cared for people. Others seemed to treat pastoring like a mere job.

This project to answer Mom's question has been a journey of faith for me. Faith is still "the substance of things hoped for, the evidence of things not seen." [Hebrews 11:1] Hebrews 11 also points out that without faith you cannot please God. Faith in God empowered me to find answers. It gave me the focus, the calling, and vigor to work until I had answers. Someone said, "Faith builds a bridge from this world to the next." You might say, this book is a bridge for us to take.

DIFFERENT ANSWERS

Within days, we encountered another minister and Mom asked the same question. As I recall, he was pastor of a large church. This second man of the cloth answered stiffly, "I don't know. The Bible doesn't say." It was clear from his tone and body language that Mom's question made him uncomfortable. The subject was quickly changed and he made his exit.

For several weeks, each time we ran into a minister, Mom would ask her question. Most seemed stunned or taken off guard by the question. One said, thoughtfully, "Well, God is love, so surely He **will** let you have your beloved dogs in heaven."

Another said, "No, there's nothing in the Bible that says animals go to heaven." Yet another said, "I don't think so. The Bible is silent about it." And another, "I don't know that the Bible says — but I'm sure God would let you have your pet in heaven if you wanted it."

The answers ran the gamut from negative to positive. One gently replied, his voice full of love, "If you want them to be there, I'm sure they will be."

Of all the pastors, priests and ministers who answered the question, no two answered the same. Most seemed to be voicing an opinion. No one quoted or referred to Scripture, except the country preacher.

The more Mom asked her question, the more my amusement died. I winced inside. It occurred to me that I had never, in all my years of church attendance, ever heard a sermon on animals going to heaven. No seminary or Bible school offers courses on it. Where would ministers look for answers? I began to wonder why the topic is so ignored. And what message does this convey to animal lovers?

Most ministers love God and people. Most ministers love animals, too. Most ministers struggle to please God and do right by people. Such men and women work hard to serve. Many ministers have few resources or little time to seek an answer to such a question. My purpose is not to fault such men and women of the cloth. It is Mom's question that is the focus here.

That question was important to my mother. Hers was no ordinary poll. She loved dogs. Mom had given her heart to Jesus and knew she was going to heaven when she died. She was in her 70's and had no fear of death. But would her dogs be in heaven? She truly wanted to know the answer. It was a very important question to Mom.

I believe it's a very important question for many people.

PIECING TOGETHER THE PUZZLE

"Do dogs go to heaven?" is a question not directly answered in the Bible. It must be searched out. The pieces have to be patiently gathered, carefully laid side-by-side, then prayerfully interpreted. Mom's question requires a look back at the history of Christianity and its diverse theologies. The ministers who gave Mom their answers were uninformed or confused about this question. My research helps us to understand why that is so.

MY APPROACH

I approach the evidence on Mom's question as a lawyer. (Scientific methods[1] obviously don't work well on questions like Mom's.) Attorneys rarely have the luxury of direct, scientific proof. We are accustomed to using circumstantial evidence. A trial attorney's job is to reconstruct past events to prove our case. We also have to reconcile conflicting laws and authorities. Our stock and trade is gathering evidence and authorities, analyzing and presenting them to prove our cases. Whether we need to prove something by "a mere preponderance of the evidence" or "by clear and convincing evidence" or "beyond a reasonable doubt," if lawyers find enough favorable law and evidence, we make our client's case. The legal method is useful in examining spiritual concepts. The Bible is both a law book and is full of circumstantial evidence.

In my search, I have examined theological writings, scholarly dissertations, scientific and popular resources. Even though I am accustomed to the sometimes dry subject of law, most theological works are very arid (and not fun for me). Such works make me wonder about theologians because they seem to believe complicating simple things is a mark of genius! I believe the opposite: true genius makes complicated things simple, not simple things complicated. Jesus makes the Truth very simple. This is what I attempt to do in this book.

You, the reader, must draw your own conclusions. It is your duty and right. May God give you His faith for the task ahead, as He did me.

NO EXTREMES

The polarization in Christianity between animal lovers and animal users is disturbing. At one end of the spectrum, St. Francis of

Assisi called animals "brother" and "sister." Christians, who believe as St. Francis did, are the ones who often sacrifice and work for the humane treatment of all animals. I understand that the SPCA (Society for the Prevention of Cruelty to Animals) and other humane societies have roots in Christian revivals of the past.

At the opposite end of the spectrum are the exploiters of animals. Often, in the name of God, they treat all creation as if it were made for man to do with as man pleases. Such persons interpret the Genesis 1:28 "dominion" to mean that humans may freely use animals — without reservation — for sport and experimentation. They believe it is their right to destroy animals and their habitat with impunity.

I want state up front that I am not an "animal rights" activist. Most extremes make me uneasy. (Only simple Biblical truths are the extremes I strive to adhere to — like loving your enemies, being generous to all, being sober and faithful.) On the other hand, I hold to the belief that good stewardship and kindness to all living things is mandated. Cruelty in any form is a violation of God's law and nature. The Bible tells us how animals are to be treated. Whether or not they have God-given rights is not an issue which this book is meant to address.

The question of animals going to heaven certainly raises ethical and moral dilemmas for the here-and-now. This includes the treatment of animals for work and food, the use of animals for research, the destruction of animal habitats for commercial gain, hunting for sport and the like. While some questions must be addressed, it is not the purpose of this book to join these debates. We address such questions solely for the sake of finding the pieces to our "animals-in-heaven" puzzle.

THE FUN PART
The fun part of writing this book was when I discovered that there are lots of people who also want to know the answer to Mom's question. A lot of folks love their dogs, cats, horses, goats, pot-

bellied pigs, hamsters, parrots, canaries, ferrets, and dozens of other various types and breeds of critters. They too want to know if those departed pets will be waiting for them in heaven. Everyone who has experienced the love of an animal wants to know whether there is a hope of an afterlife for it. Is this life really all there is for that loved creature? What does eternity hold?

YOUR SEARCH

You may have your own personal reason for wanting to know the answer to Mom's question, "Do dogs — and other animals — go to heaven?" Perhaps you've known the attentive love of an animal. Perhaps an animal has been a helper, healer, or rescuer for you or your loved one. You may be upset because someone told you that "this life" is all there is for your pet. You may have a close friend or relative who is grieving over the loss of a pet. You aren't sure what to say to comfort him or her.

On the other hand, your reasons may be none of the above. Instead, you may have a simple childlike curiosity to know the truth, whatever it is.

Whatever your reasons, welcome to these pages. The Lord promises that those willing to do the will of God, shall know if the teaching is truth. [John 7:17] If we abide in His Word, we shall know the truth and the truth will set us free. [John 8:32]

MY QUEST

Mom's question inspired my own "need to know." I, the lawyer and veterinarian's daughter who loved God's Word, didn't have an answer for Mom. I didn't know what the Bible said about animals going to heaven. I wasn't even sure it said anything of substance.

I had acquired a reputation for being able to find answers in the Bible. If the Bible had an answer, I'd find it. It was (and is) a challenge for me to find the answers to the difficult ones. Mom's question caused a spark to be kindled inside me. That spark would smolder and finally burn hot until I found the answer.

The quest for an answer to Mom's question has taken a lot of prayer, work, and thought. What began as a fun project to honor Mom, became a serious project which took years of discipline and careful listening. Johann Wolfgang von Goethe's words on seeking truth are apt:

> *It is easier to perceive error than to find the truth, for the former lies on the surface and is easily seen, while the latter lies in the depth, where few are willing to search for it.*

This book came about because I asked the Lord God to show me, in His Word, the Holy Bible, His answer to my mother's question. I am confident that He has indeed shown me. What I have learned has been staggering. Come with me as we explore the Bible and other sources to find answers to Mom's question. Do dogs go to heaven? There is an answer! A Biblical answer of tremendous import.

ENDNOTES:

1.   The "scientific method" is simply defined as a method which follows these steps: (1) obtain information, facts or data by observation; (2) classify them into categories; (3) form a working hypothesis or theory about the data; (4) conduct experiments, under controlled conditions, to test the hypothesis; (5) if confirmed, the hypothesis becomes a theory or principle of science; (6) other scientists attempt to verify or disprove the results, especially with regard to its value in prediction; and (7) long established theories are accepted as "natural laws" until disproven. M. Winokur & Ruckes *General Biology* (Littlefield, Adams & Co. 1967), p. 2.

CHAPTER 2

IS IT OKAY TO LOVE ANIMALS?

I cannot but have a reverence for all that is called life. I cannot avoid compassion for everything that is called life. That is the beginning and foundation of morality. ... It is our duty to share and maintain life.

* * *

The ethic of the Reverence for Life is the ethic of Love widened into universality. It is the ethic of Jesus, now recognized as a necessity of thought.

Albert Schweitzer

"Then I don't want to go there!" Trish (not her name) responded hotly. This teenager had just asked her minister if her beloved horse would be in heaven. His answer was unequivocal: "No, they won't be." Trish retorted: "Without my horse, heaven won't be heaven to me."

Trish's story came out when I mentioned in a church group that I was writing about animals going to heaven. I noticed this one couple's look of astonishment. Later, cautiously, they approached me. They were Trish's parents.

Trish's parents reminded me of skittish, abused horses themselves! I watched their expressions of anxiety, and heard it reflected in their voices. As we visited, they questioned me. Once they knew I wouldn't condemn them, they opened up to me. These parents then talked freely and identified themselves as animal lovers. They spoke in detail of their pets — each one special. Besides the minister's theology, Trish's family had been accused by some church people of loving animals "too much." Trish's parents solution to the problem was never to speak of their animals at church. They assured me, however, they would never stop loving their animals.

These parents were delightfully surprised when they learned the subject of my book. They had felt alone, outside church doctrine. I was the first Christian they had met who believed animals could go to heaven. They welcomed a kindred spirit. They loved God and were truly concerned about their horse-loving daughter. Trish had been crushed by the minister's harsh answer. Her relationship with the Lord had not been the same since. I prayed this book comes into the hands of Trish and her parents - and all those like them.

LIFE-CHANGING ANSWERS

Never having met Trish's pastor, I have no idea where he got his theology (although I could guess), nor why he believed it. His answer caused no small problem for this couple and their daughter Trish. To bad Trish's minister did not remember the Bible verse which states Jesus is returning to earth on a horse:

Then I saw the heavens opened, and behold, a white horse. And Him who sat on him was called Faithful and True, ... Rev. 19:11

From Mom's experience, I knew there were at least six answers ministers gave when asked if animals go to heaven. What a recipe for confusion! When adults in authority give an answers, especially to a young person, it can be a life-changing moment. A minister stands as God's representative. Thus, his or her words, tone, and deeds have a strong impact and can cause a dramatic change in a person's beliefs. For that reason, the Bible says not many should be "teachers," for teachers will bear a stricter judgment with God. [James 3:1] Jesus emphatically stated a person causing a child to "stumble" would be harshly punished. It isn't a smart thing to do. [Matt. 18:6-7]

IDENTIFYING OBSTACLES TO ANSWERS

The question of animals going to heaven is best begun with identification of obstacles in the way to receiving good answers. Also, true inquiry dispels bad premises, but does not attack people. God sent His Son to die for people, not principles. I am a lawyer skilled in advising people of the law, but I'm not the judge of anyone. We seek to understand the problem, not put down anyone - no matter how silly their beliefs. Understanding the problem is the first step to finding the solution.

Good questions are the key to getting good answers. The first thing I consider is whether I'm asking the right questions. Then, am I asking them in the right way to get a true answer.

HARSH REACTIONS - MY OWN EXPERIENCE

Like Trish, Trish's parents and my mom, I too have experienced harsh reactions to this subject. Since the first edition came out, I have been verbally attacked. I have been told I was not a Christian for saying animals do go to heaven. The attacks were from people who had apparently not dug for answers, not read my book, and were not open to dialog. Their shallow arguments were devoid of love or kindness. It did not appear that any were ordained ministers. But then the most common reaction from ministers appears to be to ignore this topic and book.

Let me give you an example. This incident occurred when I was well along in writing this book. I was invited by an acquaintance to visit her church and was a first-time visitor. After the service, I was introduced to the pastor and several people. When the subject of my book came up, I was speaking to a leader in a church. This leader immediately took issue with me. He seemed compelled to "straighten me out." He interjected emphatically: "Animals cannot go to heaven, because they don't have souls or spirits."

Frankly, his forcefulness took me aback. Because I was a guest and did not wish to offend, I tried to answer gently. Everything I said, he disputed vigorously. My replies seemed only to incite further anger and argument. He was on a crusade, bent on correcting me. He threw Scriptures (out of context or misinterpreted) at me like spears and rocks. He didn't know nor seem to care that I'd spent almost twenty years studying and praying about this subject. He seemed more eager to prove me wrong than to hear truth.

I was shocked and, therefore, taken "off guard." Something inside me wanted to ask him why he didn't love animals, and how much he really knew the GOD WHO IS LOVE! But I refrained. (It was not easy to hold my tongue.) What a stark contrast this was to other conversations I had that very day with people eager to know the answers I'd found in the Bible. Thankfully I've met more like the latter than like this church leader!

As the word has spread among my friends and acquaintances regarding this book project, I received phone calls from Christians grieving over the death of a beloved pet. Many had been devastated by people like Trish's pastor and the church leader described above. Their hope of ever seeing their pet again was shattered or damaged. Some who heard of my project contacted me, desperate for comfort from the Bible.

Such harsh words heap added grief and condemnation on animal lovers. Too many grieving pet owners have been told, in no uncertain terms, that animals don't go to heaven. "Animals are temporal things and you shouldn't love them more than" God, people, etc. The pet lover is told to give up his or her grief and belief that animals go to heaven. The pain this inflicts is appalling. Some say, "Just get another one." A loved companion is not a disposable object, but irreplaceable. Another animal is just that, something other than the one you love and are bonded with.

Is it foolish to love and grieve for a departed pet? Especially when the bond of love was so sweet and strong when the animal was alive? How can the love just stop? There is no faucet one can turn to turn off the love (and pain of loss). Friends who have lost pets they have had for years had been devastated, sobbing over their loss. I have grieved deeply over the animals who have died.

Having your love of animals brought into question by religious leaders and respected church members can be intimidating, very intimidating. Like most of you, I was taught to respect authority – especially religious authority. It requires a good deal of confidence and a strong foundation of Scriptural knowledge and experience to overcome such intimidation. I have not always had either. But I refused to stay that way! How about you?

OTHER QUESTIONS

Before asking *if* animals go to heaven, we need to address some myths about loving animals and wanting them to go to heaven. Can we love an animal "too much"? Is it O.K. to want that animal to be in heaven with you?

A lot of folks think not. Others aren't really sure. Others have been frightened into avoiding the question entirely. Let's look at some of the myths, attitudes and problems which cloud the issues and make it more difficult to look for or to find answers.

MYTH #1: "ONLY A CHILD WOULD ASK SUCH A QUESTION"

Ever hear that one? Many people react to my book topic as if the question were only for children. "It's cute," they might say, "but not a topic for serious Biblical study or scholarship." They see it as trite, not a serious theological issue. Perhaps they have never known the love of a special dog, cat, or horse? If so, maybe we can excuse them.

It is not a question only a child would ask. Mom was not a child. The fact is children ask very important questions. Children have an uncanny way of asking profound questions. I like to be around children for that reason. I love children and challenges! Why are some adults uncomfortable about such questions? Is it because we have no answers? Or because we are lazy? Or too afraid of the truth?

Sometimes a child exposes our beliefs – even long-held ones – as wrong. Sometimes we have been "conned" into believing a lie – even by our leaders. Hans Christian Anderson told a tale about "The Emperor's New Clothes." It is our story, too. Do you know the story? Cheating weavers convinced this emperor they had woven exquisite magical cloth. The weavers said that people unfit for their positions, i.e., the stupid or the incompetent, couldn't see the cloth. The emperor (who couldn't see the non-existent "cloth") commissioned new clothes, so he would not seem stupid or incompetent. The emperor paraded through town naked rather than admit he couldn't see it. All in his kingdom also pretended to see the suit. However, a child, not embarrassed into buying a lie, asked loudly why the emperor had on no clothes. Adults may be afraid to expose a lie, but not a child. Are we afraid of animals going to heaven? Why would anyone come up with the idea that animals don't go to heaven?

I am not sure why Mom's question is treated as one that only children would ask. I do know Mom was no child when she asked her question. It was a very important question to that dog-loving savvy lady. But "why" is not nearly as important as finding the right answers is. I believe adults and children deserve to know the truth. So if you have stumbled over the idea that animals-going-to-heaven is a child's question, pick it up and throw it where it belongs – on the garbage heap. Children ask wonderful questions – and so did my Mom.

MYTH #2: "THE BIBLE DOES NOT SAY"

This is a common reply to Mom's question among evangelicals and Bible believers. While the reply is often given lightly, almost without thinking, this is a serious statement. The Bible is our authority. If the Bible does *not* say, there no basis for a belief that animals will be in heaven.

At first, I too did not think the Bible said much about animals and heaven. In fact, I began my search prepared to accept that where animals were concerned, this life was all there was. Frankly, I have been astonished at how much the Bible *does* say about animals and their roles in God's Kingdom — both in this life and the next. Indeed, the Bible says a lot!

Now there is no Scripture that simply says, "Yes, Mom, dogs do go to heaven!" Like many Bible doctrines, the answer is not spelled out in one clear statement. But when different Scriptures are lined up and put together, a clear picture or answer emerges.

That there are horses in heaven is easy to answer. Elijah and Jesus both travel to and from heaven via horse. [II Kings 2:11; Revelation 19:11-14] So there *are* horses in heaven. (Trish and her parents will be delighted!) The next question is whether these horses ever lived on earth or if they were heaven-born. (Let's save that for later.) Throughout the scriptures, other animals play both large and small roles in God's plan.

In fact, we find very little in Christian literature about God's plans and purposes for animals — and less about their eternity. English translations, from the King James to the more modern English versions, are largely silent on whether animals have souls or spirits. Man's duty of stewardship over the animals is the issue that is most often addressed.

Most Christian theologians believe that since God is Spirit, a soul or spirit must be present in order to live in God's presence. Heaven is a spiritual place ruled by God who is spirit. Some people reason that since their Bible doesn't clearly say, then animals must *not* have a soul or spirit. Most theologians who have addressed this question believe that animals perish when they die. Later we will trace the origins of this idea. Perhaps the concept is rooted in guilt over treatment that animals have received at human hands. If they have no souls or spirits and if they perish at death, the conclusion is, it doesn't matter how they are treated.

Cruel people often cover their cruelty with the cloak of religion — whether it is treatment of enslaved men, women, children or animals. Animals throughout history have been tortured and killed for sport and food, and have been abused as beasts of burden. The Society for the Prevention of Cruelty to Animals, and other humane societies are relatively new in history - although kind people have always been around.[1] Guilt and fear do strange things to people.

MYTH #3: "LOVING ANIMALS TOO MUCH IS PAGAN IDOLATRY"

It should be obvious that loving a person or an animal is not the same as worshiping it as an idol. Perhaps people have not searched the answer due to a fear of violating the Ten Commandments which teach against worshiping other gods and against making idols.[2] [Exodus 20] Fearing sin does not help a search for the truth. (Only hating sin brings real joy and freedom. Sometimes because we fear sinning, we err in the opposite direction.) The Bible makes it abundantly clear that God hates idolatry. Mosaic laws also declared that spirit or soul transfers between men and animals is witchcraft, punishable by death. [Exodus 20:3-5; Deuteronomy 5:7-9] Israel got into a "heap of trouble" when they made a golden calf and worshiped it. [Exodus 32] Idols come in all forms, human, animal and imagined.

Ancient Egyptians and other nations during Bible times worshiped all kinds of creatures from beetles to cats. Idolatry still plagues this earth, even in the Lord's church. [See Col. 3:5.] God is just in His love. His hatred of idolatry is very rational when you understand it. That is why real Christians take pains to avoid non-Christian beliefs — including those regarding animals.

Knowing the truth is complicated by the fact that the Biblical God has not left Himself without a witness in any nation or people. [Acts 14:17] All religions contain some measure of truth. Otherwise, no one would believe them. Sorting out the truth from error is therefore not always easy. In other words, counterfeits can look very much like the real thing. (You have to know the real very well to recognize a good counterfeit.) We must examine what in our Christian theology of animals is true and what is not. That's why we have the Bible.

For example, I know most Native Americans (or Indians) believe or believed humans and animals are "brothers;" and one's human spirit can be intertwined or linked with that of a particular animal or animal species. I used to concerned that this belief was idolatry. I had to lay aside my fear to examine this. It was alien to the Bible teaching I'd received. While there are still elements which make me uncomfortable, I have come to understand that believing an animal is your "brother" is not worshiping the animal. Rather, it is but a statement of respect for another intelligent being with whom we can share a kinship relationship. If my understanding is correct, the Indian belief then is not idolatry but friendship with God's animals.

It is challenging to honestly search Scripture to discover what it said on a subject. To accurately handle or divide the Word of God, as 2 Timothy 2:15 admonishes, we have some work to do.

MYTH #4: "ANIMAL LOVERS ARE IMBALANCED"

We've all heard it. An owner spends several hundred dollars on a sick pet dog, and someone remarks, "Why spend so much? It's just a dumb dog!"

From the facial expression, it's obvious the speaker thinks it's crazy to spend so much money on "a dumb animal." There are some people who regard animals as they would furniture - disposable items with no feelings. Since they believe that animals are to be used and discarded, they view those who love animals as imbalanced.

If you have ever been treated that way, you know. It can mangle your self-image and/or your love for animals. Many of us animal lovers have learned to stifle our exuberance for pets — especially around religious types. Like Trish's parents, we let our love for animals show only if we feel the listeners are of kindred heart. We don't want to appear out-of-balance or ungodly in this love.

There are theologians and ministers who teach that loving an animal "too much" is wrong. Carried to its logical conclusion, it means: "Do not love animals — exploit them." I've heard sermons which condemn spending money on pets because children are starving somewhere. What a guilt trip! Are we supposed to let the animals with us starve, because somewhere someone is hungry? That's as crazy as telling a child to "clean your plate" because somewhere someone is starving.

Do such ministers fear loving animals leads to bestiality (sex with animals) prohibited by Scripture? That's absurd! Anyone who really loves their pet is not interested in sex with an animal — no more than a loving parent is interested in incest or molesting a child.

What is "loving too much?" Is there such a thing as truly loving too much? Did God love us "too much" when He sent Jesus, His Son, to die for you and me? Isn't there enough love to go around?

Jesus identified God's Great Commandment as all-encompassing love! [Mark 12:29-31] I'm talking about the God-kind of love -- not a "co dependent love." A rich, caring, giving-and-receiving love marks a good relationship between two living beings. Can you love God too much? Can you love your spouse too much? Or your child? Or other people? Did Mother Theresa of Calcutta love too much? Absurd! How can anyone really love an animal "too much?"

Unfortunately, this thinking has caused some people to emotionally withdraw from animals. That deprives us of something wondrous. We are expected to ignore animals who have shown us more love and forgiveness, more loyalty and constancy than most humans. If we allow such "religious ideas" to influence us, we tend to withdraw our affections from our animal friends. That must confuse and hurt them, just as we would be hurt if a person we cared about refused to commit in a caring relationship. Both parties suffer.

Hallelujah, some of us "rebel" and continue to love our pets "too much!" But, this can produce feelings of guilt. Such thinking puts the animal lover between a rock and a hard place — with no apparent means of escape.

MYTH #5: "ANIMAL LOVERS ARE A LUNATIC FRINGE"

Have you ever known or heard of a person (usually a woman) withdrawing from society and living with tens, even hundreds, of cats, dogs, or other animals? Usually the home or apartment is in unsanitary squalor with animals everywhere! The type person is sometimes thought to really love animals. Animal lovers are often grouped with these types of people, and called "the lunatic fringe."

In truth, people who withdraw from society, living in squalor – whether with lots of animals or not – are mentally ill. No one who loves animals would cause them to live in squalor. True animal lovers are responsible, caring individuals. They don't lock dozens of animals together in small spaces without adequate hygiene, food or proper exercise. Nor do they purposely avoid healthy human relationships.

If there is a "lunatic fringe" with regard to animals, it is those who treat animal with neglect or cruelty. Some neglect or abuse animals because they have a mental illness. Others, such as serial killers and other violent criminals, enjoy the torture of animals, usually from childhood. These are both kinds of "imbalanced" people who do not or cannot love.

MYTH #6: "ANIMALS ARE NOT IMPORTANT IN GOD'S PLAN"

This myth is based on several assumptions: (1) Man is the only living thing created in God's image, so next to God, we have supreme importance; and/or (2) Animals cease to exist at their death, and are therefore "temporal" not "eternal." [2 Cor. 4:18] Temporal things have no eternal value. Another way of putting it, things with short "lives" have little value. To illustrate the difference, consider that a piece of paper is worth pennies, while gold is valuable. One is "temporal" and easily destroyed; the gold has lasting value.

If animals perish with this life, then what value have they? Even if it's only implied, the message is: "Animals are not important in the great scheme of things." It is like an old fable:

> *A dog, that had been sold by his master, broke his chain, and returned to the house where he had been born. Judge his surprise, when, as a reward for his zeal, he was soundly beaten, and taken back to his new residence. An old cat of his acquaintance, observing his extreme surprise, said to him; "Poor fool! did you imagine that we were prized for our own sakes?"³*

The minister who told Trish that horses would not be in heaven, conveyed to the teenager that animals were not important in God's eyes. The person who is disgusted because someone else spent hundreds of dollars on a veterinary bill for a sick pet, believes this. It is really blasphemy which limits God and His love.

I know many who have closed their hearts to loving an animal because it hurts too much when they die. They never want another pet. To pour your heart into "a temporal thing which is unimportant to God" is foolish. It also hurts when you lose that animal to death, so closing your heart is a protective reaction.

God created and preserves even the smallest sparrow. [Matt. 10:29] How can a person be certain he or she knows the whole plan of God? How can anyone say animals are unimportant to our Creator

God? Animals are important. I'm not sure any of us realize how important.

MYTH #7: "YOU ARE ANTHROPOMORPHIZING"

"Anthropomorphism" is a fancy word which simply means ascribing human characteristics, motivation, or behavior to inanimate objects, animals, or natural happenings. We see this in cartoons, in children's storybooks, and in animated movies. Animals and inanimate objects are portrayed as acting like humans — trees dance, bears hold conversations, dogs drive cars, cats fly spaceships, teacups sing.

The academic world long believed animals lack human abilities, such as thought, reason, motive, and emotion. That is changed. To be accused of anthropomorphizing was an insult (and still appears to be in some circles). You were not a "true intellectual" if you believed animals think, communicate, or are moral. Some Christian theologians and clergy also use the term as an insult.

Nonetheless, animal lovers, including the best trainers, have long observed that animals display distinct personalities. "Personality" includes the ability make choices, to reason, and to feel emotion. Animals have been know to show courage and cowardice, unselfishness and jealousy, love and cruelty, deceit and loyalty.

There is nothing quite like the disdain of a proud academic or theologian. Their confidence in their being right and eruditeness usually overwhelms all but the most confident. I have enough higher education to have experienced those types. (Thank God, all academics and theologians are not like that!) But attitudes about animals are changing or have changed. Time magazine, in 1993, stated anthropomorphism is no longer a sin. Now it's O.K. to say animals think and hope, and are puzzled; that animals have expectations, are disappointed; some make their own little plans in a time scheme of their own.

The term "anthropomorphize" makes man the center – which is the first mistake. As a disciple of Jesus Christ, I believe attributes of personality, motivation, and other characteristics, originate with God Who has all such qualities in perfect goodness and balance. Therefore, I have no trouble with "theo-morphizing" the behavior of animals which God made. (When we study a person's art, we glimpse the artist.) Animals are God's art, masterpieces each one.

Spend time around animals. Observe their behavior with an open mind. You will see character traits, personality traits, language, emotions, the ability to make moral choices — all quite like God, and like man who is made in God's image. Accusing people of anthropomorphizing comes from intellectual pride, not wisdom.

MOM'S QUESTION IS IGNORED

Another obstacle is silence. The question is simply brushed off or ignored. The second preacher Mom asked did that. Few preachers ever touch the subject of animals in heaven, let alone their role on earth. Have you ever heard a sermon devoted to the place of animals in God's kingdom? I have not. God loves all of His creatures. So why is a huge part of this world is simply ignored in the pulpit?

The silence is deafening.

I'm not talking about Biblical animal illustrations to teach us about ourselves. Jonah and the Whale, Daniel in the lions' den, and Balaam and his donkey, as well as the colt Jesus rode on as he entered Jerusalem, are used in lessons for children or to illustrate adult sermons. But the animals themselves are not important. The lessons and sermons are not about the animals themselves.

I'd like to know what God did to have that whale where Jonah was tossed in the sea? Was this a special whale who volunteered or what? And what did the whale think about swallowing a man and keeping him alive inside its belly[4] until the prophet repented? A rebellious man of god had to be troublesome cargo. Talk about indigestion! How did the whale do it? What praise did the Lord have for that "great fish," do you think?

Other than Saint Francis of Assisi (who is thought of as a bit strange because he referred to the animals as his "brothers" and "sisters"), no one else is lifted up by Christian leaders as a lover and advocate of animals.

To be ignored is to be treated as valueless. It's been my experience that the place of animals in God's kingdom has been ignored. Except when children and old women ask about animals going to heaven, the question has been given little or no thought. Only in recent years has that been changing. Many are uncomfortable with the question, which is a message in itself.

GIVEN A GUILT TRIP

Have you ever felt guilty just because you enjoyed something? Maybe you didn't know why you felt guilty — you just did. While any of the things listed here can produce guilt, sometimes a feeling of condemnation creeps in like a fog from nowhere. If there is no truth behind the fog, it may be the condemnation which is not from God. [Romans 8:1, 31-35]

Most of us have experienced feelings of being unworthy, unloved, or falling short. I've struggled with depression a few times. Life is rough sometimes. I suspect all of us have those days, even years. It's a cruel world sometimes. Yet when humans ignore or disdain us, a dog – or cat or horse or other animal — will love us like we're the best! How do we handle that? Guilt? Or acceptance?

Christians have often been taught — directly or indirectly — that every pleasure and joy we experience in this world is "worldly" and "sinful." If you have believe that, then the *joie de vivre*, i.e., the joy of living, which all healthy animals exhibit, probably makes you uncomfortable.[5] Every animal I know enjoys being alive. Most animals are masters at living in the moment to the fullest. If this life is all there is for them, why are they so happy? Mine always try to get me to join in the joy. Enjoying the animals should not make you feel guilty. Animals are so much fun!

Animals can teach us how to enjoy every moment. My German Shepherd made every walk in the park an exuberant adventure. Daily that dog ran the same circuit of trees chasing squirrels, but always with great pleasure. My cats play with the same toys, like they'd never played that game before, and each insect is a new discovery. My horses clowned and teased. Even training is something an animal must enjoy or they are difficult to train.

I know Christians who would never feel right about enjoying themselves as much as my animals do. That's "dead religion" to me, but I sympathize with the guilt trip it produces.

I'm sure I have not covered all the reasons people feel guilty about loving animals. We humans are very creative in how we condemn ourselves. It doesn't help to overcome guilt that we tend to follow Adam's example of rationalizing our behavior. We make excuses and blame others instead of facing the truth in a responsible manner. We are too susceptible to the lies of the devil about God, His nature, and His plans. Please note that I said "we" – for I've done these things as well.

We may feel we aren't worthy of the unconditional love our pets shower on us. It may be true. (If we feel more love from our dog than Christians, our family, friends, or minister or priest, that unworthy feeling can take hold of us.) Dogs treat us like gods, even if we abuse them. Maybe the name "dog" — which in English is "god" spelled backwards — is a message. Dogs do love us "too well." My animals show no guilt about loving me. Why should I hold back from returning their love?

It is so easy to give and receive love from these little friends. Is it Godly to love a pet more than people? Or is it sin? Doesn't the Bible command us to love God and man? It doesn't tell us to love animals, does it? Is loving an animal wrong?

GATHERING PIECES TO A PICTURE PUZZLE
Finding answers to Mom's question has taken me through many steps. In exploring what the Bible says, we will address many

questions. First, we must address the question: Do animals have souls and spirits — believed to be a prerequisite to eternal life or heaven?

We'll look at the roles animals play in God's kingdom throughout history and now. We'll finally line up the evidence of animals in eternity and address the question of whether our particular animals will be in heaven.

Like pieces to a giant puzzle, there are verses of Scripture which, when laid together, present quite a picture.

I look to the Bible for answers in much the same way that I practice law. When a client first presents a problem, I don't know what evidence will turn up. First, evidence must be gathered from all sides. Then I analyze the evidence and legal principles. Only then can we prepare the case and estimate what chance the client has of winning in court.

Gathering evidence is like finding pieces to a puzzle. Until you have the pieces, you don't know how the picture will look. If you cannot find certain key pieces, then you have no case. (If key pieces favor the other side, you will lose.) Only if you find key admissible evidence to prove your client's version of the facts, do you have a chance at winning the case.

The Bible passages about animals are much like pieces of evidence or pieces of a puzzle. Separately, the pieces hold little or no importance. Only when I placed them in order did an image appears. Why others have not done the same, I have no idea. My legal training helps, but that is not critical to good Bible study. Primarily it involves work – albeit a work of faith. All I know is that Mom's question has an answer!

ENDNOTES:

1.   The oldest animal protection society in the world is the Royal Society for the Prevention of Cruelty to Animals (RSPCA), founded in 1824 by Rev. Arthur Broome and Richard Martin. It was founded at a time when brutality to animals was common and therefore they were ridiculed and scorned. See Vida Adamoli, *The Dog That Drove*

Home, The Snake-Eating Mouse, and Other Exotic Tales from the Animal Kingdom,
[St. Martins Press, 1991], (Published in Great Britain under title *Amazing Animals*), p. 183. The U.S. S.P.C.A. was founded in 1866 by philanthropist Henry Bergh.

2.   See chapters 1 & 2 of Rousas John Rushdoony, *The Institutes of Biblical Law* [The Presbyterian & Reformed Publ. Co., 1973] for a scholarly and provocative discussion of the First and Second of the Ten Commandments, for example.

3.   Jean Pierre Claris de Florian, France, *The Great Fables of All Nations* (Tudor Publ. Co. 1928), p. 343

4.   I have been told several times that in the 19th century whalers found at least one man alive in a whale's belly – who'd fallen overboard a couple of days before. The whale's digestive juices made the man's skin "worse for the wear," and he was a bit crazy, but he was alive!

5.   There are worldly pleasures which we shouldn't partake of, but the Kingdom of God has a lot of joy and pleasure. See Ps. 16 & John 10:10.

CHAPTER 3

DOGS AND CATS IN THE BIBILE

In the beginning God created the heavens and the earth, the animals and man. Daily God walked with man in intimate fellowship. When God got very busy, man became downcast. When God asked why, the man said he missed spending all his time with God and was lonely. After pondering this, God made a companion for man. It wagged its tail. Man was happy, but asked God what to name it. God said, "This animal is a reflection, a mirror image, of my love for you; so it will be called "dog." The dog and man became great friends. After a while the man changed under the worshipful love of the dog. The angels came to God and said, "Man has lost his humility due to this dog's worship of him. You must do something." God thought, and then He made another animal. It became another companion of man and taught him humility. Man was happy, the angels were pleased, God was satisfied, the dog wagged his tail, and the cat didn't give a d_ !

Origin unknown

Dogs and cats have long been the most popular domestic pets. Some of us love dogs. Some of us love cats. Some love both. I prefer a home with both species myself. Pets make up a very important part of our lives. However, there is a mystery, a conundrum to be solved if we can: God did not inspire those who wrote the Bible, the Holy Scriptures, to say much about dogs or cats. For those who love dogs and/or cats, that may be disturbing.

Perhaps the answer can be drawn, by analogy, from the Bible account of two trees in the Garden of Eden. There were the tree of life and the tree of the knowledge of good and evil. [Genesis 2 & 3] The second tree receives all the attention, as it was forbidden and Adam and Eve disobeyed, ate the fruit, and got kicked out of Eden. The tree of life is hardly mentioned, but is very important. In this upside-down world, the good often goes unheralded, while the bad makes up the daily news. We don't speak of being "tempted to do good" after all. Nor do people seem to be curious about the good. Think about that a while.

Good dogs and cats are unheralded in God's Word. Maybe it is like pointing out the obvious. The value of a good dog is apparent to all who have experienced a dog's loyalty, loving devotion, and intelligence. A cat's affections, entertaining cleverness and calming effects aren't mentioned either. If you consider the purpose of the Bible, then it makes sense. It has been labeled "The Manufacturer's Handbook" to show "His Story," i.e., the history of God's relationship and troubles with Man, His crowning creation.

The good Lord does not have to instruct humans about the dog's worth or the cat's value. Their merit is apparent to those who spend time with them.

There is only one Bible passage that must be addressed to answer Mom's question. That is the one our country preacher quoted from the Book of Revelation. We need not cover what the Bible does say about cats and dogs in depth, however interesting. Of course as a prelude to that discussing that verse, we must lay a foundation. (The lawyer in me must build a case.)

DOGS IN THE BIBLE

To err is human, To forgive, canine.[1]

Robert Louis Stevenson was remonstrating with a man ... ill-treating a dog. "What business is it of yours?" The man said. "He ain't your dog." "No, but he is God's dog," said Stevenson, "and I'm here to protect him."[2]

The more I see the representatives of the people, the more I admire my dogs[3].

There are about forty references to dogs in the Bible. Two different kinds of dogs are mentioned: (a) feral or half-wild dogs that were ownerless and scavenger, and, (b) working dogs who helped man herd and protect. (These may also have been hunting dogs.) Most of the references do not treat dogs with favor. Of course, there are many wicked *people* mentioned in the Bible as well. Perhaps the bad dogs kept company with wicked people?

The Bible does support a long relationship between man and dog. In the Old Testament we learn that Job kept herd dogs. [Job 30:1] In the New Testament it says that small dogs -- which must have been pets -- ate under their masters' tables. [Mark 7:24-30] Archeology and history provide references to dogs as house pets in the ancient Middle East. Most historians agree that dogs were among the first domesticated animals. Personally, I'm of the opinion that dogs probably became man's friend in Eden.

To those who have taken time to be kind to them, dogs are wonderful companions and heroes. Dogs outnumber the other animals in acts of heroism toward humans.

While writing this book, I happened to catch a TV program called, "Miracles." The show related how a Rottweiler seemed to know her fireman master was having a heart attack, drew him into the house and when the man collapsed, got the portable phone and put it by his hand, so he could call 911. It is one of many remarkable stories I have heard and read about animals.[4] Today, dogs have alerted and warned owners moving into danger from not only heart attacks, but low blood sugar, cancers, seizures, and many medical conditions. Apparently, dogs remarkable sense of smell and perhaps acute hearing allow them to know something is wrong. Dogs are being selected and trained now to alert others to such dangers.

Who knows but what man's best friend may have tried to draw Adam away from the serpent and prevent him from eating the forbidden fruit! It wouldn't be the last time a dog tried to warn its master or mistress of danger! Or the last time an attempt to help was ignored.

O, DESPISED DOG!

Dogs, as we all know, have a dark side. As a lawyer, I know the legal issues dog ownership can bring. Dogs can and do aggressively attack, bark loudly, and carry diseases (such as rabies) -- all real hazards. Dogs sometimes destroy property or injure other animals or children. Barking dogs can be a real and a legal nuisance. Homeowners' insurance generally covers damage or injury by pets, which is a reason people buy the coverage. Last but not least, for city dwellers, there is the problem of dog waste.

Scriptures about dogs indicate the ancient writers had a low esteem for the animal. For example, "Better is a live dog, than a dead lion" (which means it's better to be alive and despised, than dead and respected) [Ecclesiastes 9:4]; "Like a dog that returns to its vomit, is a fool who repeats his folly" [Proverbs 28:11]; "Like one who takes a dog by the ears is he who passes by and meddles with strife not belonging to him." [Proverbs 28:17].

This attitude makes sense when we consider conditions existing when the Bible was written. The ancient world was an unsafe place.

Packs of half-wild, half-famished dogs often roamed towns and villages.[5] [1 Kings. 14:11; 16:4; 2 Kings 9:10] People around the world still despise feral dogs. Wild and half-wild dogs can maim or kill people, pets and livestock. Such dogs often carry communicable diseases.

Ironically, some of these qualities make dogs useful. Then, as now, dogs were useful around the towns and villages as garbage disposals and as guard dogs against strangers, robbers, and wild beasts.[6] Consider this Bible passage:

At evening they return.
They growl like a dog,
and go all around the city.   Ps. 59:6 [NASV]

Much of the world today is the same for dogs and humans as in Bible times. Packs of dogs are extremely dangerous. Untrained dogs are unpredictable. The fear of dogs is understandable. Some dogs were and are vicious. Sometimes dogs get rabies or other diseases. As a child, I saw rabid dogs quarantined by my father. Rabies strikes a healthy fear in anyone who has seen the effects of that fatal disease which destroys the brain.

The fearful, however, never know the love and loyalty which good dogs, dogs which are healthy and well cared for, are capable of giving. The fall of man which brought the curse of sin on the whole world, separated man from animals, too.

The Lord God, in love, warns us about many dangers which occur in this fallen world. It does not mean that the animals, which are subject to the effects of man's sin, are evil. We can enjoy the love of dogs, while acting wisely to protect ourselves from the risk of poorly trained, mean, and diseased animals. Thank God for modern medicine and the wisdom to live better than our ancestors ever dreamed possible. God's kingdom blessings are being tasted here and now. May Jesus' Kingdom ever increase on earth.

WHAT "DOGS" ARE OUTSIDE THE GATES OF HEAVEN?

Let's look at the Bible verse that Mom's Kentucky preacher referred to when he stated that "Dogs are outside the gate. So in heaven, there are will be horses, but no dogs." The passage is Revelation 22:14-15:

> *Blessed are those who wash their robes, so that they may*
> *have the right to the tree of life, and may enter by the gates*
> *into the city. Outside are the **dogs** and the sorcerers and*
> *the immoral persons and the murderers and the idolaters,*
> *and everyone who loves and practices lying. I, Jesus, have*
> *sent My angel to testify to you these things for the churches*
> *I am the root and the descendant of David, the bright*
> *morning star. [NASV]*

When we study Scripture, it's important to study it in the context. What is being talked about in the whole passage? If we don't see the context, we may misinterpret, and distort the true meaning.

It's also important to understand that Scripture contains many metaphors and similes. So we must ask if, in context, what does it mean? Is it a true story or symbolic, i.e., a metaphor or simile?

Another key is to allow Scripture to define Scripture. How are the terms used elsewhere in the Bible? In this technique, we compare as many verses as possible using the same term to shed light on how the Spirit and the Lord inspired its meaning.

Applying these rules of interpretation to this Scripture in Revelation, we can clarify the passage about "dogs being outside the gates."

First of all, in Revelation 22 it says they washed robes. While I'd love to have a clothes-washing dog, our four-legged friends don't wear or wash robes! Dogs don't need clothes (while some humans clothe their dogs, the dogs don't dress themselves). Also, dog paws just were not designed for scrubbing clothes! If they had clothes, dogs would need to operate a washing machine and dryer. (I want that dog!)

Secondly, looking at the context, being a canine is not a "sin." The other things listed, i.e., "sorcerers," "immoral persons," "murderers," "idolaters," and "liars" each describe only sinning humans. The other things cannot apply. I have never seen a dog telling a fortune, casting a spell, or worshiping an idol. A literal dog does not fit in this context. In context, Revelation is not speaking of animals, but humans.

Next, are "dogs" in this passage a metaphor? In the very next verse, the Lord speaks of Himself as a "root" and "morning star." Those certainly appear to be metaphors which describe Jesus, a person. Scriptures have many other metaphors. The book of Revelation, in fact, appears to have a lot of metaphors. Sorting out the metaphor from the real can be a challenge, especially if you do not know the Author and know Him well. After decades of studying God, I am still learning!

Are there other Scriptures in which the word "dog" is used metaphorically to describe people? Yes, there are:

> *Beware of dogs, beware of evil workers, beware of the false circumcision.* Philippians 3:2 [NASV]

> *For dogs have surrounded me; a band of evil doers has encompassed me; They pierced my hands and feet . . . Deliver my soul from the sword, my only life from the paw of the dog.* Psalm 22:16 & 20 [NASV]

> *And the Philistine [the giant Goliath] said to David, "Am I a dog, that you come to me with sticks?" And the Philistine cursed David by his gods.* 1 Samuel 17:43 [NASV]

When the nice country preacher answered Mom's question by referring to this passage in Revelation, he evidently not think about or was unaware the word "dogs" in Revelation 22 is a slang term.

"You dog," is an age-old insult or pejorative term. (It may be so the world over.) It is not to be taken literally in this Bible verse.

How else does the Bible use the term "dog"? In the Bible, "dog" is sometimes a slang term for three kinds of people: (1) malicious or cruel people, e.g., Isa. 56:11 and Psalm 22, quoted above (Psalm 22:16-20 is believed by Christian believers to describe Jesus' torture and death at the hands of Romans; (2) despised, "low class scum," e.g., 1 Sam.17:43 & 24:14; & Prov. 26:11; (3) homosexuals, e.g., Deut. 23:18 which links "dogs" to women prostitutes.[7] The natural behavior of dogs accounts for this Biblical slang.

First, dogs may attack (even without provocation); or take down and tear up other animals in a hunt in a manner which looks very cruel. Heinrich Friedrich Wilhelm Gesenius (1786–1842), author of the Hebrew lexicon, said:"Fierce and cruel men are sometimes called dogs." The term "dogs" in Psalm 22:16, is obviously a metaphor for cruel, fierce people.

Secondly, dogs are often smelly, unclean animals. Dogs will eat their own vomit, other animals' excrement and garbage. Therefore, dogs often carry diseases. The non-Alpha dogs grovel and crawl on their bellies when shown force. Dog are too easily abused. These behaviors are despised in men and by humans.

Thirdly, dogs "mount and rut" each other indiscriminately, males on males, and females on females. This looks like aberrant sexual behavior which we call homosexuality. So the Biblical slang terms where humans are called "dogs" have their origin in common doggy behavior.

From the above analysis, we must conclude the Bible is referring to people, not animals. The terms in Revelation 22:14-15 describe human behavior. If the term "dogs" is taken literally, the Revelation passage makes no sense.

THE TEST OF GOD'S LOVE

Last (but not least), it is best to measure one's interpretation of Scripture against what we know of the character of God. If the interpretation agrees with His holiness, His purity, His very nature as love, wisdom, truth, and righteousness, then it is likely correct. If it violates any part of God's nature, then it is questionable or even erroneous. Mom taught me that, "God is love, and if it isn't love, it isn't God." That great test has served me well, so I pass it on to you!

The term "dog" in Revelation 22 must refer to a type of human behavior which is being condemned. Our loving God would not condemn an entire species of animals unless all members were rotten to the core! There are too many good dogs for that conclusion to be correct.

Without this understanding, one can make the mistake our Kentucky preacher made in interpreting Revelation 22:15. That mistake produced the incongruous conclusion that "there are horses in heaven, but no dogs." When we use Scripture to interpret Scripture, the results are far more accurate. While it is work, you don't find gold, without digging in the dirt.

Don't you think this is a piece of the puzzle – the answer to Mom's question? If there are horses in heaven, why not our canine friends? Why not a lot of animals? So let's see what other puzzle pieces there are. A picture of some sort will emerge, if there are enough pieces.

Back to the subject of dogs, Mom would have heartily agreed with Missouri Senator George Vest's description of the dog, when he was a lawyer defending a dog in a lawsuit in 1870. Mom and Vest would have argued that a dog's goodness alone might be its ticket to heaven:

> *The one absolute, unselfish friend that a man can have in this selfish world — the one that never deserts him, the one that never proves ungrateful or treacherous — is his dog.*

> *Gentlemen of the jury, a man's dog stands by him in prosperity and in poverty, in health and in sickness. He*

*will sleep on the cold ground, ... if only he can be near his
master's side. He will kiss the hand that has no food to offer,
he will lick the wounds and sores that come in encounter
with the roughness of the world. He guards the sleep of his
pauper master as if he were a prince. When all other friends
desert, he remains. When riches take wings and reputation
falls to pieces he is as constant in his love as the sun in its
journey through the heavens. ... And when the last scene of
all comes, and death takes the master in its embrace, and
his body is laid away in the cold ground, no matter if all
other friends pursue their way, there by his grave side will
the noble dog be found, his head between his paws, his eyes
sad but open in alert watchfulness, faithful and true even to
death.[8]*

Many of us totally agree with Senator Vest. My dogs have been
some of my most faithful friends.

Other authors have extolled the virtues of the dog. For example,
see:

To err is human, To forgive, canine.

*The more I see the representatives of the people, the
more I admire my dogs.*[9]

WHAT ABOUT CATS?

*When God made the world, He chose give each animal
whatever it wanted. All the animals formed a line before
His throne. The cat went quietly to the end. To the elephant
and the bear God gave strength; to the rabbit and the deer,
swiftness; to the owl, the ability to see at night; to the birds
and the butterflies, great beauty; to the fox, cunning; to the
monkey and chimpanzee, intelligence; to the dog, loyalty;
to the lion, courage; to the otter, playfulness. These were
things which the animals begged of God. At last He came*

to the end of the line, and there sat the little cat, waiting patiently.

"What will you have?" God asked the cat. The cat shrugged modestly, "Oh, whatever scraps you have left over. I don't mind."

"But, I'm God. I have everything left over."

"Then I'll have a little of everything, please."

And God gave a great shout of laughter at the cleverness of this small animal. He then gave the cat everything she asked for, adding grace and elegance and, only for her, a gentle purr that would always attract humans and assure her a warm and comfortable home. But He took away her false modesty. [10]   Author unknown

Cats make me laugh, too. Mine are such monkey-like clowns! At this writing, my house is the playground of three Siamese. I love all animals, but cats have been among my special friends. Albert Schweitzer said: "There are two means of refuge from the miseries of life: music and cats." I tend to agree.

I searched the Bible for references to cats. Except for lions, the Bible makes no mention of cats. There is nothing about the domestic cat. Lions are mentioned with some frequency in the Bible. I counted over 150 references to lions.

All of God's creatures are fascinating, but cats have special magnetism. People tend to be polarized about them, loving or hating them. Few creatures beat a cat for graceful movement, an air of elegant mystery, or the intelligence to infinitely irritate. Someone said that God created the cat and keeps to Himself the reason for it.

Perhaps the reason is that God likens Himself to the lion. The Bible says that the Lord God acts like a lion at times of judgment. [Hosea 5:14] His Cherubim, which are in His presence constantly and represent the Almighty, have four faces. One is the face of a lion. [Ezekiel 1:10; 10:14; Rev. 4:7] One of the descriptions of Jesus of

Nazareth, the Messiah, is He is the "Lion of the tribe of Judah." [Rev. 5:5] Ponder what "the Lion of the tribe of Judah" means. If we are imitators of Christ, we must consider the lion -- which is a big cat.

The Lord God's people also are likened to lions. Both Judah, one of the strongest tribes of the Hebrew people, and the tribe of Dan were called "a lion's whelp." [Gen. 49:9 & Deut. 33:22] Some princes or rulers of Israel were described metaphorically as lions who learned to tear their prey and devour men. [Ezek. 19:1-9] The description is not always good, describing a wild, carnivorous, rebellious people. [Jeremiah 2:30]

ATTRIBUTES OF CATS

All I know is that cats are marvelous creatures. Although cats are often frustrating to those who don't know them, cats have proven to be intelligent[10] and even heroic animals. Some animal behaviorists put cats just below Chimpanzees in problem solving abilities and memory capacity. In my observation cats get bored just like humans -- which means fun or trouble.

Ordinary house cats have jumped would-be burglars and rapists, and sent them packing with claw and bite marks the men will never forget. Cats have awakened family members when lethal fumes or fire would overcome them. A family cat warned a mother of a baby choking to death. Cats have attacked or held at bay poisonous snakes traveling toward the children's rooms or ready to bite their owners. Cats have demonstrated numerous other acts of genuine affection. There are documented cases of cats finding their way home, even as far as some 1,400 miles from California to Oklahoma, or to a new location of their family.[11]

In the opinion of many experts, all cats, both large and small, have much in common. Apparently the main difference between the cat families is one of scale, i.e., size. Perhaps in studying lions in Scripture, we can include all cats. Like dogs, the big cats get good press, as well as bad, in Scripture.

Those of us who attended Sunday School as children heard the stories of Samson and Daniel. Samson killed a lion with his bare hands because the spirit of the Lord came upon him –showing miraculous strength. [Judges 14:5-6] Daniel was thrown in a den of lions and lived; while his accusers were eaten. [Daniel 6:22] Bible accounts about lions have lessons and insights into God's purposes for cats, as well as people.

MIRACULOUS BEHAVIOR CHANGE

In 1 Kings 13, we find the story of a disobedient and deceived prophet who was killed by a lion. The Hebrew people were, at the time, divided into two kingdoms. Israel, with ten tribes, on the north; Judah and Benjamin lay to the south. Israel had turned to idol worship in a big way. (Judah had its idols, too.) The Lord sent a man from Judah to Bethel in Israel, to pronounce judgment on the idolatry and sin.

This unnamed prophet had strict instructions to prophesy, then return directly to Judah without eating or drinking in Israel. His mission was high drama. The prophet confronted King Jeroboam and Israel, alone. After he issued God's warning, Jeroboam became angry. When the king stretched out his hand to harm the prophet, the Lord withered his hand and split the altar in two! Humbled, Jeroboam asked the prophet to pray for him. Also, the king invited the prophet to eat. The man refused. So far, so good.

On the way out of Israel, an old prophet went after the man, entreating him to eat and drink. When the man refused, the old prophet lied to him. He told the man that an angel told him to bring the man back and feed him. The young prophet turned aside, ate and drank with the old prophet. The Lord then spoke through the old prophet, and said the man of Judah would "not come to the grave of his fathers." Probably terrified, the young man left and headed home. (I bet he took the back roads.) On the young prophet's way, a lion met him on the road and killed him. (Makes you wonder if the lion knew where the prophet would pass by.)

*And there, men passed by and saw the corpse thrown
on the road, and the lion standing by the corpse. Then they
went and told it in the city where the old prophet dwelt. So
when the prophet ... heard it, he said, "It is the man of God
who was disobedient to the word of the Lord. Therefore the
Lord has delivered him to the lion, which has torn him and
killed him, according to the word of the Lord which He spoke
to him." ...**Then he went and found his corpse ... and
the donkey and the lion standing by the corpse. The
lion has not eaten the corpse nor torn the donkey**.*

*And the prophet took up the corpse of the man of God,
laid it on the donkey, and brought it back... Then he laid the
corpse in his own tomb.*

1 Kings 13:24-30a [NASV] (Emphasis by author)

Look at the unusual behavior of the lion and the donkey. The
lion did not eat the corpse, but stood guard over it. Also, the lion
and donkey, natural enemies, stood by the dead prophet, next to
each other! The lion did not harm the donkey! The donkey did not
run away! That's several miracles! It must have taken hours until the
body was discovered and removed. The old prophet was notified and
he came and took the corpse. Those animals stayed there a long time.

I have never heard of any person walking up to a lion and taking
its kill away from it. This old prophet had the Spirit of God operating
in him, even though he was a deceitful old cuss. He knew the lion and
the donkey were obeying the Almighty. I dare say, he knew something
about animals and about God. God intended for the man from Judah
to have a proper burial, since he had obeyed in confronting the King
and Israel.

This is quite a series of miracles involving a big cat.

DOMESTIC CATS

Domestic cats are mentioned in the non-canonical Apocrypha.[12]
For instance, in Baruch, the writer speaks of Jeremiah's prophetic

teaching that the Israelites will endure slavery or captivity in Babylon; and that these people of God will encounter sin and idolatry there. While the heathen and foreigners fear such gods, the Lord's people should not fear idols. Reasons are given, like the fact that the idolatrous priests must lock the temple doors from thieves; they light lamps to see, but the images of their sightless gods are black with smoke and *"Bats, swallows, and birds light on their bodies and heads; and so do cats. From this you will know that they are not gods; so do not fear them."* Baruch 6:22-23. Animals seem to know what is God and what is from the devil. I usually trust the "instincts" of my animals when they don't like someone. So the lesson of Baruch is good.

The domestic cat was certainly known in the Holy land. Cats were domesticated at least 4,000 years ago. In rabbinic literature, there are a few references to the cat.[13] The rabbis did permit the breeding of cats in Israel, as well as other animals which rid the house of rodents and snakes. The cat apparently was not bred to any great extent. Other animals were apparently preferred for catching mice and snakes. Mosaics with figures of cats have been uncovered at Nirim in the Negev. This is evidence of cats being bred in Israel in Byzantine times. In Babylonia, the cat was highly regarded as a remedy to rid a house of poisonous snakes. It was considered dangerous to enter a house after dark where there was no cat.

Rabbis praised the cat for its extreme cleanliness: "If the Law (Torah) had not been given, we could have learned modesty from the cat," one said. Even after the time of Christ, rabbis or Jewish leaders have recommended that cats or some domestic pet be kept in the home to teach children to fulfill the duty or *mitzvah* of feeding animals before partaking of food oneself. Perhaps it was to teach modesty also? (I wonder if rabbis believed dogs teach humbleness and forgiveness, by example?)

CAT LEGENDS

There are legends or myths about cats from Bible times. Several are about Noah's ark and the cats are amusing. An Arab legend has it that the mice on the Ark so multiplied that life was rendered unbearable; so Noah passed his hand three times over the lioness' head and she obligingly sneezed the cat. (What an image of the fastidious cat!) Another story has it that the monkey and lioness forgot their vows of fidelity and the cat was the result — together the spirit of such coquetry.[14]

CAT HEROES

Like their lion cousins, the small domestic cat can be fierce and aggressive in the face of any enemy. Even nowadays, domestic cats have been known to deal with snakes as well as rodents. My friend Jana was picking up a sack of grain in her barn, when her cat leaped between her and the sack. Under the sack was a copperhead, a very poisonous snake. That cat saved Jana from a nasty experience.

In their book on *The Mysteries of Animal Intelligence, supra*, the Steigers describe a cat in California which prevented a rattlesnake from entering the nursery while the baby was in the room. House cats have also attacked would-be rapists and robbers.[15] Like those lions, some cats serve the Lord by serving us. They do good, while executing judgment on the disobedient.

My Siamese, Kitty, however, had the snake and mouse thing backwards. Kitty was my faithful friend of 17 years. I was still in law school when my father died. I left Kitty with Mom a few months at her hillside home in California and returned to school. Boy, did Kitty prove to be some companion for Mom. Kitty would go hunting out through the "doggie door." Mom wrote me that every evening Kitty brought in live mice and dropped these gifts at Mom's feet. One night Mom went to bed before Kitty came back in the house. A quote from Mom's letter describes what happened next:

> *About 12:30 a.m., I awoke with Kitty on my chest releasing a live mouse! From there on, there can be no clear cut story. I leaped from the bed, throwing the covers over*

the cat and mouse. I spent the next hour looking for the mouse, mad at Kitty. She went about flicking her tail, mad that I'd rejected her mouse!

Kitty switched to live lizards and snakes. Fortunately Kitty never dropped **them** in Mom's bed. Mom was concerned that Kitty would "gift" guests with these live treats, however. Kitty never did – but maybe it was the closed doors. A couple of years later, Kitty gifted me, first with a dead mouse in my bed, and then with a huge live cricket in my lap! We have laughed a lot at her gifts and manner of delivering them.

As a lawyer, I was delighted to find that my profession has a patron saint, who loved cats:

In passing it is interesting to observe that St. Ives, the patron saint of lawyers, is represented as accompanied by a cat. ...holy men as well as devils found the cat the most attractive of animals. The profound wisdom, the concealed claws, the stealthy approach, and the final spring, all seem to typify the superior attorney. We should not be astonished, therefore, that Cardinal Wolsey placed his cat by his side while acting in his judicial capacity as Lord Chancellor.[16]

In closing this part about cats, it seems fitting to quote a Christian pastor. More than one clergy person has written on cats, and other pets. Carl Van Vechten explored the history, manners, and habits of the cat, including folklore or religious references, music, painting, law, poetry and fiction. Dr. Carl Van Vechten wrote:

The Orientals are more astute about cats than we are. They ascribe to them a language, a knowledge of the future, and extreme sensitiveness which allows them to perceive objects and beings invisible to man. ...It may be said here that an occidental clergyman has written a book to prove that animals have souls and will share our future existence. A heaven without cats would, of course, be deserted for a hell with them.[17]

We understand. If God had not peopled the earth with our animal friends, we would not know how poor life would be without them. Death has taught most of us how barren life is without the love of a dog, or cat, or other pet. The fact is that a heaven without our dogs, cats, parrots, horses, and other loved animals would not be heaven for most of us. The wonderful thing is that the God who is Love, has a plan, a heavenly plan, for all His creation.

ENDNOTES:

1.   Origin unknown

2.   Source: *Electronic Dictionary of Quotations*

3.   Alphonse de Lamartine (1790-1869) in a letter to John Forster (1850)

4.   See Paul Drew Stevens, *Real Animal Heroes; True Stories of Courage, Devotion and Sacrifice*, [Signet Books, 1988]; Stephanie Leland Animal Angels [1998 Conaci Press Books]; *Reader's Digest Animals You Will Never Forget* [1969, Reader's Digest]; *Listening to the Animals*; Best Friends [1999, Guideposts]

5.   See *GESENIUS, HEBREW-CHALDEE LEXICON*, #3611, the Hebrew word for "dog".

6.   See also, Ps. 68:23, I Kings 14:11, 16:4, and 23:38 which speak of dogs kept in cities who cleaned up after battle.

7.   I wish it was not necessary to say that it is not my intention to condemn any person experiencing the temptation of homosexual lusts, as I don't. I have deep compassion for anyone caught in any kind of sin. The Bible treats all sexual sins (all sex practices outside a marriage between one man and one woman) as "sins against our bodies"; and therefore worse than other sins.   Unfortunately, many have been taught that homosexuality is "natural" or "normal." The Bible treats it as an aberration and the practice of sex with members of the same sex as sin. Statistically, the Bible is right. All healthy humans have sexual desires. None have to be gratified outside the marriage bed. We have choices in that department. I know. I am single and heterosexual. I live celibate – not because I have little or no desire or "sex drive," but out of choice -- by the Lord's grace. (So don't tell me it cannot be done!) Those failing to control their sexual desires need compassionate help. There is no condemnation from the Lord Jesus for

the person trapped in homosexuality -- or any other pattern of sin. God sent His own Son to redeem all humans from all sin, but one. Sexual sins are all in the redeemable category. While some sins appear harder to get loose from than others, our God is able to do what is impossible for man. But we must hate the sin and want His help.

8.   From a speech given by Former Senator George Graham Vest of Missouri. Delivered in 1870 when he was acting as a lawyer in a suit against a man who had killed the dog of his client. -- He won the case.

9.   Alphose de Lamartine (1790-1869), letter to John Forster (1850)

10.   *Your Incredible Cat*, by David Greene [Ivy Books, 1984] Chapter on "Your Brilliant Cat" p. 24

11.   See, *Mysteries of Animal Intelligence* by Sherry Hansen Steiger and Brad Steiger [Tom Doherty Assoc. Inc. 1995) and *Cat Scan* by Robert Byren and Teressa Skelton [Atheneum, 1983]; and *Your Incredible Cat* by David Greene [Ivy Books, 1984].

12.   A group of early writings of disputed authority, not included in the Protestant Bibles or Hebrew canon.

13.   See *Encyclopedia Judaica,* "Cat"

14.   *The Tiger in the House*, by Dr. Carl Van Vechten, Ph.B. (Afred A. Knopf, 1920, 1936), p. 84.

15.   Paul Drew Stevens, *Real Animal Heroes; True stories of courage devotion and sacrifice*, [Signet Books, 1988].

16.   *Tiger in the House*, by Carl Van Vechten, p. 161

17.   *Tiger in the House*, p. 93, referring to Rev. J. G. Wood, Man and Beast: Here and Hereafter.

CHAPTER 4

DO ANIMALS HAVE SOULS ANDSPIRITS?

Soul. *1. The animating and vital principle in man credited with the faculties of thought, action, and emotion and
conceived as forming an immaterial entity distinguished
from but temporally coexistent with his body. 2. Theology.
The spiritual nature of man considered in relation to God,
regarded as immortal, separable from the body at death,
and susceptible to happiness or misery in a future state.
3.The disembodied spirit of a dead human being; a ghost;
shade. . . . 6. A central or integral part of something; vital
core. ... 9. The emotional nature in man as distinguished
from his mind or intellect.*
Spirit. *1. That which is traditionally believe to be the
vital principle or animating force within living beings.
2.Capital S. The Holy Ghost. ... 4. Any supernatural being,
such as a ghost. 5. a. That which constitutes one's unseen,
intangible being. b. The essential and activating principle
of a person; the being.* [1]

L ike many of you, I have watched a beloved pet die. I've held the
still-warm corpse when the life-force left and breathing ceased.
Their death appeared to be no different from that of humans. When

death took my friends and relatives, their corpses looked, felt, and smelled the same. Death looked and felt no different whether it was man or beast. Suddenly they were gone. Their body was an empty shell. What left? Was it the animal's "spirit" or "soul?" Does the Bible say?

Tulsa, Oklahoma, where I currently live, has earned the nickname, "Buckle of the Bible Belt." We have a number of mega-churches, a Christian university, seminaries and Bible schools. This provides me with ample opportunity to observe the reactions to Mom's question from Christians of diverse backgrounds, both laity and clergy. Over the years it has taken to write this book, I've witnessed a number of reactions.

"Dogs are not rational beings, so they cannot have souls," has been a common response to Mom's question from a number of Bible-believing Christians. Sometimes the speaker inserts "spirit" instead of "soul."

For centuries, the prevailing Christian theology has denied that animals have soul or spirit. Roman Catholics and others hold the doctrine that animals do not have souls. Even today, well-known Christian leaders teach that animals do not have souls or spirits. It appears a majority of Christian leaders believe animals do not go to heaven – although that has been changing. It would be interesting to know what they imagine heaven is like. Picturing a cat and mouse playing at the feet of God is very upsetting to some folks — even if only in spirit form!

Why is having a soul or body important to animals' going to heaven, you might ask? "Souls" and "spirits" are the stuff of eternity – the metaphysical "stuff" it takes to live with God in heaven. At death the mortal body returns to dust — the elements from which it came. "For you are dust and to dust you shall return." [Genesis 3:19] If you and I are nothing more than flesh and bone, then there is no afterlife. The same is true of animals. "You gotta have soul!"

If an animal has only a mortal body, then when it dies it is gone forever. If the animal lacks a soul or a spirit, there can be no heaven (or hell) for that animal. However, if animals have a soul and a spirit then, theologically, a hereafter for animals becomes a real possibility.

Christians are often double-minded about animals. Strangely, some who believe animals don't have souls or spirits, still believe their pets will be in heaven. This is the same reason others give for animals not making it past this life. Isn't that confusing?!

We say that animals have no soul or spirit, and yet we recognize their ability to make choices, to show emotion, to problem-solve. Such abilities are attributes of intelligence and personality, so the two conclusions do not mesh well. (I, too, tended to be double-minded as well before this study.) We do this without realizing how odd and illogical it is.

Another problem is that if we believe an animal has no life beyond this brief span on earth, then we tend to hold back from loving any animal. Such behavior, in turn, confuses the animals. Certainly, animals don't hold back love as humans do.

POLARIZED VIEWPOINTS

People are polarized in their attitudes toward animals. On the one extreme are those who treat animals as unfeeling machines (like Pavlov's dog experiments). B. F. Skinner,[2] an atheistic animal behaviorist, carried Pavlov's thinking to its logical conclusion. With his famous "Skinner box.," he studied learning processes in pigeons and other animals.[3] A major problem with Skinner's box is that humans and animals confined in small spaces go crazy, i.e., exhibit aberrant behavior. Skinner and his followers ignore or are ignorant of Aristotle's admonition to study specimens which retain their nature and not those which have been corrupted.[4] Today behaviorist say animals must be studied in natural habitant to get good data. A prison box does not produce natural behavior.

On the other extreme are those convinced animals do have souls and spirits. The best animal trainers and pet owners tend to fall in the latter class. Trainers know that animals communicate and reason, and that animals make moral choices. Most pet owners observe the same. The gulf is obviously very wide between the two camps.

Where did these ideas come from? Does the Bible vindicate one side or the other?

We need never be afraid to ask God to show us His truth and give understanding. [James 1:5] If we don't ask, we'll never know God's truth. [Mat. 15:2-6; Mark 7:8-13] We need never be afraid to question our "leaders in the faith." Jesus did it as a twelve-year-old boy in the Temple. [Luke 2:42 & 46] Checking out a teaching to see if it agrees with God's truth, does not dishonor a good teacher. The answers found in my study do contradict long-held beliefs – which can be disturbing. If we want to really know who God is, as well as who we are and why we were created, we must ask about our companions and fellow inhabitants of this creation. I suggest, if you haven't already done so, that you pray for God's grace to know and understand the truth. That requires an open heart and mind — not easy commodities to come by.

This chapter particularly will challenge some long held beliefs. It challenged some of mine. While I do not compare myself with those who penned the Holy Bible, God still inspires people to write and speak His truth. Otherwise, I would not be presenting these answers to Mom's question.

A LOOK AT HISTORY

In philosophy past and present, the prevailing attitude has been that any questions having to do with nonhuman animals are of decidedly secondary importance . . . Animals may be studied scientifically as part of the natural world, but their philosophical importance lies in what they lack. They are not just nonhuman, but less than human.[5]

The theories that animals lack souls and spirit have their roots in early church history. Some of it is confusing. For example, according to one source, St. Augustine (354-430 A.D.) believed that animals had souls. However, another source said the theory that animals cannot reason or feel — and therefore are not eternal — came from Augustine.

By the end of the first millennium, Christianity had spread the Good News across Europe, but had not made the same inroads on other continents. Christianity was gradually transforming primitive, barbaric groups of people. However, the humane treatment of slaves, women, children, and animals was slow in coming. Possibly was that the written Bible was only available to a few. Primarily church leaders in Europe, such as monks and priests, could read and write, and books were few (being hand-copied).

As we will discuss further in the coming chapters on heaven, by the 1200s or 1300s, European Christian theologians believed the hereafter was a place of pure light and pure spirit, and that Heaven was devoid of animals.

The Gutenberg printing press, invented in the 14th century, revolutionized the world — much like the Internet did in the 1990's. Among the first things printed were Bibles.

A copy of the 1611 King James Version is instructive about the attitude at that time about animals. Consider the translators' introduction:

> *A man would think that Civilities, whole-some Laws, learning and eloquence, Synods, and Church-mainte-nance,... should be as safe as a Sanctuary, and out of shot, as they say, that no man would lift up the heel, no, nor dog move his tongue against the motioners of them. For by the first, we are distinguished from **bruit-beasts led with sensualities**;* ... (Emphasis supplied)

The common view was that animals were "brute-beasts," i.e., ruled by base cravings or instinct. Many still hold to this view today.

We tend to be products of our times. Personally I think both Bible translators and readers are products of their time. Medieval and Enlightenment Bible readers either had the Latin Vulgate or a translation based on the Vulgate. They did not use the original Hebrew or Aramaic texts, and only a few Greek texts were available. Medieval church leaders did not fellowship with Jews and, therefore, did not consult rabbinical sources to interpret Scripture. Their interpretations were colored by their world view or experience.

While I don't profess to be a scholar, it appears to me that the early Bible translations set the tone for all translations since then — even though modern translators have many more ancient manuscripts available in the original Hebrew and Greek. Challenging long held interpretations can get you labeled a heretic or the like.

As near as I can tell, in early translations, the treatment of "soul" and "spirit" were the same. This treatment is still followed today in most translations. A translator's theology will influence him to continue interpreting Scripture one way, even when other choices are as good or better. A reader's world view also influences his or her interpretations. We all have preconceptions, preconditioned responses. I know. Many of mine have been challenged while writing this book.

The Medieval Church believed that man, who was created in the image of God (Gen. 1:28), is different from and superior to all animals. If animals are truly only "bruit beasts led with sensualities" then man has little to learn from them. Man also has nothing to lose by exploiting them. Even today, this "human superiority" colors our behavior toward every living creature.

The consequences of this thinking seems to have come into full fruit with Charles Darwin(1809-1882), an English minister and naturalist. Darwin is the "father" of evolution as a theory of the origin of life. The "flower," which preceded this "fruit," seemed to have blossomed in the Age of Enlightenment (16th-17th centuries). By this time the first Bible translations were available to the "masses" in England and Europe.[6]

A key figure in this "flowering" of the idea that animals lack souls and spirits was the French philosopher, scientist, and mathematician, Renee Descartes (1596-1650). Descartes is famous for his philosophy or theology expressed in the Latin phrase: "Cogito, ergo sum" ("I think, therefore I am"). Descartes viewed the material world as mechanistic and entirely divorced from the mind. He believed the only connection between the mind and the physical world was by intervention of God. Therefore Descartes believed that rationalization and logic replaced experience, and, experience could be illusion. You might say the sum of Descartes' philosophy was "mind over matter." Logically, if the material world was mindless, then animals were like machines, totally preprogrammed, moved solely by instinct. Descartes' influence on philosophy and religion was incalculable.[7]

Important for our study is also a protégée of Descartes, Nicolas Malebranche(1638-1715). Malebranche carried Descartes' argument to its logical conclusion, i.e., animals are "beast-machines" which cannot feel or suffer. For example, Malebranche was said to have kicked a pregnant dog at his feet. When the dog cried out, an acquaintance rebuked him. Malebranche replied, "Well! Don't you know that it does not feel?" However, Descartes reportedly owned a dog which he treated with great kindness. Malebranche, denied animals have any conscious experience, thinking he was following Descartes' teaching, i.e., Cartesian philosophy.[8] How ironic!

The Cartesian (Descartes) argument goes like this: (a) Since God is just, and (b) many innocent animals suffer, especially at the hand of man, then (c) there must be recompense to the animals. If there is a recompense, (d) it is obvious that there is often no relief or reparation in this life for many suffering animals. Therefore, (e) God must reward animals in the hereafter and (f) justice would require that God takes suffering animals to heaven. Therefore, (g) we must avoid the distressing consequences of attributing a rational soul to beasts. The reason for animals lacking sould given by Cartesian thinkers was that: Surely heaven could not hold all these beasts and humans, too! So Descartes' disciples argued that: (1) Animals do not have true intelligence, souls or spirits; therefore (2) animals lack the ability to sin, and, hence (3) are incapable of salvation or redemption; so (4) animals cannot go to heaven.

In short, Enlightenment thinkers justified cruelty to animals by rationalization. They refused to believe heaven could handle an infinite number of souls in time and infinity. They limited God.

They also got hung up on the issue of whether animals have free will and can therefore commit sin. If the animals are innocent, then likewise it follows there must be a recompense for animal suffering. So the rationalists, including Darwinists, avoid the issue of animals having souls or spirits. Most of us know that avoiding issues can make worse messes.

Enlightenment thinkers argued that three things in the Bible support this Cartesian philosophy: (1) only man is created in "the image of God" — Gen. 1:26-27; (2) the mandate to man to "subdue the earth and have dominion" over fish, birds and every living creature — Gen. 1:28; and (3) that "sin" or "salvation" is apparently not mentioned in relation to any animal. These verses are still used today when arguing animals lack souls and spirit, and don't go to heaven.

> *Debates about animal consciousness fall into two periods: before and after Darwin. Cartesian metaphysics cast its shadow over both periods. ... The animal without consciousness — the beast-machine — was then preeminently a Cartesian creature . . . The Cartesian beast-machine breaks down under the weight of analysis within Descartes' own framework. The behavioral and theoretical*

case for it fails, and it fails for Cartesian reasons. Even the theological arguments for it are weak.[9]

WHAT IS WRONG WITH CARTESIAN ARGUMENTS?

Is the Bible discredited by the Cartesian use of Scripture? Or is something else wrong? Daisie and Michael Radner state the thinking of many who oppose Cartesian theology:

> . . . *it does not say anywhere in the Bible that animals receive compensation for their suffering. There is no reason why Scripture should provide an answer one way or the other on this matter, since nothing hinges on it as far as human salvation is concerned. It is strictly between God and the brutes.*
>
> **The notion that God should take on some sort of obligation with respect to animals is not without precedent in Scriptures.** *After the flood, God establishes a covenant not only with Noah and his descendants, but also "with every living creature that is with you, of the fowl, of the cattle, and of every beast of the earth with you; from all that go out of the ark, to every beast of the earth" (Gen. 9:10). . . .* **It is revealing that when Malebranche discusses the covenant of the rainbow in connection with natural laws, he refers to it simply as God's covenant with man (OC 10:80). Most clergy do the same.** *** *The choice is between two prejudices, one against animals in heaven, the other about animal suffering.*[10]   (Emphasis supplied)

The Radners' observation matches my experience and research. I found nothing like Cartesian philosophy in Jewish or early Christian writings which I examined. Nor is the idea prevalent in other cultures. As we have seen, the issue of whether animals have intelligence, souls, or spirits appears to be European and relatively modern in origin.

A LICENSE FOR CRUELTY TO ANIMALS

Using these Scriptures, many ministers and theologians concluded that Descartes and his followers were right. The unfortunate natural result is that humans have abused animals with impunity. Unspeakable cruelty to animals was excused in "Christian" society — whether killing baby seals with clubs or dissecting animals alive.

Vivisection was practiced here and abroad. (Vivisection is the cutting open and examination of an animal's organs while it is still alive — without anesthesia.) Students used live cats and dogs in biology classes until recent years – to examine the animals' insides. This was done in the name of Christianity — because man has dominion over animals, and animals are not rational beings!

I believe it is blasphemy to think that God of the Bible has anything to do with such cruelties. The Jews have always interpreted Scripture to condemn brutality to animals. Christians have led the drive to abolish vivisection. Humane societies were started by British and American Christians to combat animal cruelty.

Dr. Albert Schweitzer, an exemplary Christian missionary physician, said:

> ... thoughtless injury to life is incompatible with ethics. ... I cannot but have reverence for all that is called life. I cannot avoid compassion.

C. S. Lewis, scholar and Christian author, was a staunch anti-vivisectionist. (Lewis did, however, struggle with whether or not animals have individual souls.)[11] The success of this anti-cruelty movement is felt today and undoubtedly influences animal-rights and ecology activists, whether they understand the spiritual roots or not.

No honest observer of animals believes animals neither think or feel:

> I have noticed that my companion animals' nerve endings react instantly to the gentlest caress, and that if I should

accidentally step on the tail they react as I would if a giant stepped on my foot. Dr. Louis J. Camuti states, "Never believe that animals suffer less than humans. Pain is the same for them that it is for us. Even worse, because they cannot help themselves." [12]

DO ANIMALS HAVE "TRUE" INTELLIGENCE?

If a being must have "true intelligence," as well as other abilities, to have a "soul" or "spirit" does the Bible have any support for this idea about animals? In fact, Holy Scripture **does not** support the Cartesian theology or Darwinist thinking about animals. Let's look at stories or lessons relating to animals in the Bible which treat them as having intelligence and skill.

Many passages tell us to learn from animals. For example, Proverbs 6:6-8 tells the lazy person to learn about work habits from the ant. We are instructed to learn wisdom from rock badgers (building safe homes in rocks); from locusts who advance in ranks; and from spiders (or lizards) due to their survival skills in kings' palaces. [Prov. 30:24-28] Majesty can be learned from the lion, greyhound,[13] and the male goat. [Prov. 30:29-31] The bloodsucking leech is a lesson in selfishness. [Prov. 30:15] The eagle and serpent are used to teach us about wonder and awe:

There are three things which are too wonderful for me, Four which I do not understand: The way of an eagle in the sky, The way of a serpent on a rock, The way of a ship in the middle of the sea, And the way of a man with a maid. Prov. 30:18-20

Scripture uses animal metaphors to instruct, also. In Numbers 24:8-9, likens Israel to a wild ox and to a lion— fierce, protective and untamable. Ezekiel 19:2-3 compares Israel to a lioness who loses her young lion to captivity — an image of grief and rage.

Several Bible accounts illustrate that animals have a heart of compassion in addition to intelligence. "Compassion" and "intelligence" are components of "moral choice." Those who argue that animals lack souls because they cannot make moral choices, have never looked closely at the animals in the Bible.

BALAAM'S DONKEY

In the delightful story of Balaam's donkey (or ass) in Numbers 22, intelligence, bravery, compassion and loyalty are demonstrated. Balaam's donkey was anything but a "dumb beast!"

Balaam was a prophet, a respected position in ancient times. The king of Moab sent for Balaam to curse the nation of Israel. God had a covenant with Israel to give them land. The Lord had just brought Israel out of slavery in Egypt. Having been offered money and honor, Balaam saddled his donkey and along with two servants went to meet the Moabite leaders. God was not pleased, since He told Balaam not to go. God sent His executioner, an angel.

Balaam's donkey saw the Angel of the Lord with a drawn sword ahead of them. Realizing the Angel meant harm to her master, she turned off the path into a field. The prophet, blind to the Angel's presence, beat the donkey. Next, the Angel took a stand in a narrow roadway, walled on each side. The donkey seeing the Angel, pressed against the side of the wall to avoid him. Balaam, having his foot crushed against the wall, beat the donkey again. The third time, the Angel picked a place where there was no way to turn. So the little donkey lay down. This again provoked Balaam's anger.

Furious, Balaam beat the little donkey with his stick — probably a walking stick of some size. At that point, the Lord gave the donkey the power of speech. The animal asked Balaam what she had done to deserve three beatings. In anger, Balaam replied that she was "making a mockery of him" and if he had a sword, he would kill her.

It appears the donkey didn't realize Balaam could not see the angel. But we know that animals see things in the natural realm which the human eye cannot see — just as they smell things, hear sounds and feel vibrations that we cannot. My dogs and cats have looked at me as though I were deficient when trying to get me to realize something was happening that they could hear or see. The account of Balaam's donkey shows that animals see things in the spirit which we humans do not see. Do you wonder, as I do, how often this happens?

Consider the loyalty and love of this little donkey. That donkey had a deep affection for her master to take what she did! On three occasions, that "dumb" animal faced the Lord's angel. This huge angel had an assignment to execute Balaam for disobeying God. The angel of the Lord stood in Balaam's path with sword drawn ready to do his business. Unseeing, the prophet beat his rescuer unmercifully.

Ponder her next question, "Am I not your donkey on which you have ridden all your life to this day. Have I ever been accustomed to do so to you?" Balaam had to answer, "No." She was a good donkey. She made good choices, heroic choices, to endure pain for the sake of her master's life. Even under Cartesian theology, that is clear evidence of a "soul" and of a "spirit."

Even more remarkable is the favor the Lord gave to the donkey's intercessions. Due to the donkey's efforts, the angel sent to destroy Balaam did not or could not touch the man! How could a small donkey stop a warring angel of God Almighty? Such is the power of love to a God who is love, don't you know? We learn from other Bible passages that the Lord's angels possess awesome power. Some have single-handedly destroyed cities and armies. God permitted that not-so-dumb animal to intercede for her master. Perhaps God appointed her for that task.

Isn't it interesting that Balaam believed this donkey had the ability to mock him? If animals lack intelligence, souls, or personalities, how could they make mockery of anyone? Why would Balaam react to the donkey as though she were a person? Balaam clearly believed the animal had a will, and therefore she possessed choice of action.

Balaam clearly felt that the two servants who witnessed the donkey's behavior would think the donkey was mocking him, or else he would not have become angry.

Before granting Balaam the ability to see the angel waiting to kill him, God honored the donkey by giving her voice. I've heard sermons about this donkey, most of which make the point: "If God used a dumb donkey, He can use anyone." Such a sermon overlooks the point that this was by no means a dumb donkey. Nor was Balaam's donkey just any animal. She was very special to have such loyalty and devotion.

Any animal who challenges God's avenging angel to spare its master's life and wins, has both soul and spirit! If a human did that we'd call him or her a saint! Are you willing to take a beating for a disobedient preacher? How many humans do you know who would serve a greedy man for a lifetime, then take a series of beatings to save his life? Do we love those in authority over us as this donkey loved Balaam? Balaam's donkey showed intelligence, love, vision, loyalty, and perseverance. Those comprise the definition of "soul," don't they?

OTHER BIBLE EXAMPLES

Other Biblical accounts of intelligent animal behavior offer more proof of "soul" or "spirit." Most of us are familiar with the account of the ravens which brought food to the prophet Elijah for weeks, months, or possibly a year or two — "until the brook dried up." [1 Kings 17:1-7] During a severe drought, birds and animals suffer just as the humans do. If you were those ravens, would you have brought meat across drought-stricken land to a man? Only the Lord knows what those intelligent, independent birds went through to feed that prophet day in and day out. Tell me why those ravens lack souls?

Consider the unusual bovine behavior described in 1 Samuel 6. Two cows were commandeered to pull the cart holding the Ark of the Covenant from ancient Philistia back into Israelite territory. Not a difficult task? Well consider that these cows had never before pulled a wagon. No human trained nor drove them. Both cows bawled loudly as they went. Why? Because they left nursing calves behind. Now that's a whole series of miracles!

Then there is that lion who killed a disobedient prophet, and the prophet's donkey. Remember the story? The lion stood next to the corpse with the man's donkey until another prophet came, loaded the body on the donkey, and then buried the dead man. [1 Kings 13] "The lion has not eaten the corpse nor torn the donkey." [1 Kings 13:28b] Sounds like the lion would have even helped load the body, if given the chance.

OTHER ANCIENT SOURCES

The Greek philosopher, Aristotle, wrote a *History of Animals.* Aristotle illustrated animal intelligence with several examples. Aristotle reported when swallows have no more mud to use to make their nests, the birds get wet, roll about in the dust, and make their own mud.

The ancient historian, Plutarch, in *The Cleverness of Animals,* used stories from others ancients. These included such great minds as Aristotle, Aeolian, and Pliny. For example, someone observed foxes in Thrace refused to cross a frozen river upon hearing running water underneath. The ancients felt this illustrated wisdom or intelligence: (a) what makes noise is in motion; (b) what is in motion is not frozen; (c) what is not frozen is liquid; (d) liquid gives away under weight; therefore (e) what makes noise gives away under weight. Thus the ancients knew that foxes demonstrated the ability to reason or problem solve. Ancients also recorded seeing a dog on a ship putting pebbles into a half-full jar of oil until the oil rose high enough for the dog to lick the oil. Who can argue the dog lacked intelligence? (Of course, I know some people who'd argue that grass is orange if someone else stated it is green.)

One of my favorites is the story of Thales' mule. Crossing a river with a heavy load of salt, the mule fell. The sacks of salt, upon getting wet, dissolved. Thereafter the mule, upon coming to a river or stream, lay down to lighten its load. The wise owner loaded the mule with sponges and wool. So that smart mule stopped lying down and was careful to keep its cargo out of water!

MODERN DAY EXAMPLES

Just in case ancient wisdom and powers of observation are in question, modern animal observers confirm these incidents of animal intelligence. Television, movies, books, and magazines present a variety of fictional animals or animal-like beings which match or surpass humans in intelligence and wisdom. From *Winnie the Pooh* books to the *Star Wars* trilogy, we find examples of various intelligent life-forms — some attractive, some repulsive. *E.T.* and *Teenage Ninja Turtles* are reptilian personalities of high intelligence and abilities. *Lady and the Tramp* feature special talking dogs and cats. New ones are invented daily. Why this inclination to ascribe intelligence and personalities to such "animals"?

Good animal trainers have long related to animals anthropomorphically, i.e., as "persons" possessing intelligence with abilities to lie or be honest, to love or to hate, to be cowardly or brave. This is in spite of the academic world's disdain for such a view of animals.

Trainers, for example, have no hesitation in talking about how much a mare loves or worries about her foal, a cat her kittens or a dog or a horse their work. But for phi-losophers and psychologists to speak of love was to invoke abilities that are, for reasons I am still not clear about, as rigidly restricted to Homo sapiens as some religious doc-trines have restricted the possession of a soul to members of certain races, cultures and sometimes genders.[14]

Animal behaviorists are challenging the Enlightenment doctrines about animals lacking souls or intelligence. Scientists in recent years are disputing traditional conclusions that animals live by instinct and reflex alone. For example, Dorothy Hinshaw Patent, in *How Smart Are Animals?*,[15] explores the science of animal intelligence and the difficulties of examining totally different species. As we study animals in the wild, not in artificial laboratory settings, animals are proving to be far more "mentally talented" than lab scientists ever thought possible.[16] Just browse through the animal section of a modern library or in any university and look at animal intelligence studies which have come out in the last few decades. It is awesome what they are observing and chronicling about animal intelligence and behavior.

CLEVER BIRDS

Another example – a favorite of mine – is the story of little English birds which outfoxed milkmen for years. Starting about 1921, a little bird, the blue tit or titmouse, discovered it could break the foil tops of milk bottles after the milkman delivered them to people's doorsteps in the predawn cool. (Decades ago in the U.S., milk came in glass bottles with paper or foil stoppers or lids, and in urban areas were left on people's doorstep. I assume this was true in England, as well.) The birds sipped the cream at the top of the milk. (This was not homogenized milk.) It took the humans a while to figure out what was causing the loss of cream. A war of cleverness ensued between man and bird. The birds learned to follow milkmen and hammer off lids. Milkmen put rocks or other objects on the milk jars. The birds shoved them off, sometimes with several birds acting together. Finally, the milkman put the jugs in a box, turned on its side so the box top just covered the milk jug top, only to turn and see the birds in the milk wagon sipping their cream! This behavior was first seen in southern England about 1921. By 1947 the sightings had spread all over England as well as to neighboring Scotland and Ireland. Apparently this art passed, by imitation, from bird to bird, and generation to generation. Those who enjoy home delivery still have some thievery.[17]

So much for the validity of the statement "dumb bird" and "bird brain" as demeaning terms. Recent studies reveal that "bird brained" may be a high compliment, not an insult.

> ... *Parrots can deal with abstract concepts, communicate with people, understand questions, and make reasoned replies. This is amazing information. Saying that the parrot can deal with abstract concepts, listen carefully to questions, and give an answer that has been "thought out" changes entirely our whole concept of the animal kingdom.*
>
> *Linking this with the new research coming out on dolphins, whales and chimpanzees indicated that we* **may have to rethink our position of what separates the animals from humans.**
>
> *The ability to rationalize and reason used to be one of the central and main differences that distinguished man from beast.* **Philosophically, it was even thought that the aptitude for reasoning meant the presence of a soul** *and was what separated higher from lower intelligence.*[18] (Emphasis supplied)

MORAL CAPACITY IN ANIMALS

Another doctrine from the medieval church was that animals lacked moral capacity — the capacity to know right and wrong and make choices. We have already addressed Balaam's donkey and other animals in the Bible which belie that Cartesian theology. Observation of animals also puts that doctrine to the test. Consider the growing use of animals, dogs, monkey's, cats, horses, and birds, as service or therapy animals, i.e., as healers. Also, there are numerous anecdotes of animals which have acted as heroes or rescuers.

People magazine featured an article about heroic animals who had saved peoples lives. Cows, like dogs and horses, can do strangely compassionate things. Daisy, a 25-year-old "bell" cow, daily led the other cows to a Welsh farmer each day for milking. When a 3,300 lb. bull, on loan for breeding, knocked the man to the ground and was stomping him, he thought he would die. The farmer lost consciousness. When he came to, he found himself in a circle of his cows. Daisy was directing them. The cows kept the circle around him, keeping the bull at bay until the farmer crawled home. This farmer recovered in spite of the injuries. When asked about the "bovine intervention," the farmer replied:

I have treated the animals reasonably, and they have looked after me in return. People say I am too soft, but I believe you reap what you sow. [19]

An issue of *Angels* magazine told about a large family dog who refused to get in the vehicle with the family as they left to escape a flood. The dog chose to go ahead of the vehicle down the middle of the flooded roadway. He guided the way so they would not go into either ditch — ditches which were impossible to see due to the swirling water. This family was convinced that their dog was on a mission from God. The dog certainly acted like an furry, four-footed angel of God.

The truth is, animals of various species have been observed making similar choices. A dog was observed giving the first bone he received from a butcher to a lame "dog friend," then returning for a second bone for himself. And cats have been known to act as guides for blind dogs. [20]

Aiding each other is not so uncommon, as observers note with regularity. Even wild animals show an ability to make "moral choices." Consider the accounts of a lion pulling out an antelope stuck in a mud hole and letting it go,[21] and an elephant stopping to carefully cover a sleeping infant with palm leaves which kept the flies off. Why didn't the lion kill the antelope and eat it? Why would elephants care about a human child? Is this not an act of mercy – a moral judgment?

Anyone who says animals lack intelligence or the ability to make moral decisions is ignorant or blind — just as Balaam was. They are also ill-informed of the Bible and a poor observer of animals — God's creation.

Game-playing is a form of problem solving and many games involve a high degree of shrewdness, judgment, perspicacity and acumen. Would you agree that the ability to play games is a sign of intelligence and the ability to make choices?

Many of us have observed our cats, dogs, and horses playing games. The wild otter's play is well documented. A most unusual scene was a small herd of buffalo which ran and slid, spinning, across a frozen lake one after the other. When it slowed, the slider would make a sound. Each would then carefully make its way across the ice and back up the slope to repeat the action.[22]

Sounds like fun to me!

While Cartesian theology attempts to tell us that animals lack souls and spirits — even lacking the ability to feel — this has no basis in truth or Scripture. Only by twisting a few verses can you believe this doctrine is Bible-based. Yet this heresy has excused unspeakable arrogance and cruelty toward animals. Such nonsense must be stopped! That is where we who have the Bible - with modern sources to better understand it, and who are believers in the Lord Jesus Christ, have an advantage.

We have much to learn from animals and about them. Since the theologians conclude that the soul is the seat of intelligence, wisdom, will, and emotions, then if animals evidence these attributes, how can we say that they have no souls? Love is an attribute of God, and God is spirit. Is it not logical that if a creature can love, it is a spiritual being? Animals evidence "spirit" because they love.

And for those who would argue that animals don't love, but are "acting instinctively," they need to get educated in the ways of animals (or go have their heads examined). "Instinct" does not explain the well documented complexities of animal behavior. Besides, there is even more Bible proof of animals having "souls" and "spirits."

SOUL AND SPIRIT DEFINED

What is a "soul" or a "spirit?" The dictionary definitions (quoted at the beginning of this chapter) provide a good starting point. In the English language, "soul" and "spirit" are defined as the "animating force" of a person, the "seat of the mind, will, and emotions." We must go to the Bible to see if there is any Scripture which states that animals have either a "soul" or "spirit," i.e., that invisible "animating force."

In case you didn't know, our English Bibles are all translations. The King James Version is a translation of a translation, since the Latin Vulgate was a translation. (It is still a masterpiece of English literature.) "Even at its best, the art of translation is an inexact science," says Dr. Brad Young, (Ph.D. Hebrew University).[23]

Most translations into other languages are translations from English. The miracle is that God's inspiration comes through the translations — often with remarkable clarity.

While revolutionary in its time, the 1611 King James Version is now understood to contain many errors in translation. The translators did not have the manuscripts or archeological evidence which modern translators now possess to aid in more accurate translations. The wonderful research tools available today enables anyone who is willing to study, to find answers — without being literate in Hebrew or Greek. Mom's question has required a bit of work, but I thank God for the scholars who have made it possible for me to do so.

SOUL — NEPHESH

In the English translations of the Old Testament of the Bible or Hebrew Scriptures, the term "soul" is the Hebrew word "nephesh" [Strong's #5315]. It means literally, "a breathing creature." In the King James Version, "nephesh" was invariably translated "soul" in reference to man. However, when nephesh refers to animals, it was never translated "soul" but only "beast" or "living creature" or "life." Are you surprised?

This matches Cartesian philosophy. Those who know Hebrew probably never question whether animals have souls, unless their thinking is contaminated by this theology.

The first few chapters of Genesis establish this pattern. Let's look at the King James version on a series of verses:

And God said, Let the waters bring forth abundantly the moving creature that hath life [nephesh], and fowl that may fly above the earth in the open firmament of heaven. And God created great whales, and every living creature [nephesh] *that moveth, which the waters brought forth abundantly, after their kind, and every winged fowl after his kind; and God saw that it was good.*

*   * * **

And God said, Let the earth bring forth the living creature [nephesh] *after his kind, cattle, and creeping thing, and beast of the earth after his kind: and it was so.*

*   * * **

And God blessed [humans], and God said unto them, Be fruitful and multiply, and replenish the earth, and subdue it: and have dominion over the fish of the sea and over the fowl of the air, and over every living thing [nephesh] *that moveth upon the earth.*   Genesis 1:20-21, 24, & 28

Compare those verses with Gen. 2:7 [KJV]:

And the Lord God formed man of the dust of the ground, and breathed into his nostrils the breath of life; and man became a living soul [nephesh].

Thus animals are referred to as living "things," and man as a living "soul," yet are translated from the same word.

Next we move from creation to God's speaking to Noah and the animals following the Great Flood:

Every moving thing that liveth shall be meat for you; even as the green herb have I given you all things. But the flesh with the life [nephesh], which is the blood thereof, shall ye not eat. And surely your blood of your lives [nephesh] will I require; at the hand of every beast will I require it, and at the hand of man; at the hand of every man's brother will I require the life [nephesh] of man. Gen. 9:3-7 [KJV]

The King James translators carried this distinction between man and beast throughout the Old Testament. A few examples are: Genesis 8:17 says every "living thing" was to be brought into Noah's Ark; and in Leviticus 11:46 the law was regarding every "living thing."

So the great distinction between man and animals is a translator's philosophical construction!

More recent translations correct this error somewhat but not completely. The *Open Bible* version of the King James, for example, adds "soul" as a footnote to "life" in Genesis 1:20. The *Amplified Bible* stopped using "soul" altogether, and replaced it with the term "living creatures" (animal) or "living being" (man) or "life" (as in Gen. 9:4). A similar change is seen in the *New King James, New American Standard, New Revised Standard, New International, Jerusalem, New Century Version*, to name a few.

The distinction is still there to the uninformed reader. How could you tell that "living creature" or "living thing" (used for animals) is the same as "living being" — the term used for humans? Humans are "beings" but animals are still "creatures" and "things." No modern translation uses "soul" for both man and animal. It has to be a translation problem to find a suitable term and still give a "nod" to Cartesian philosophy.

Some modern references are correcting this Cartesian error. For example, different editors of two Bible Dictionaries use the same

definition of "soul" stating it includes animals.[24] Some Christian
writers are doing the same.

> *The Hebrew word for "soul," nephesh, is used 393 times.*
> *Properly it means "a breathing creature" — i.e., any "ani-*
> *mal." In the abstract it means "vitality." Nephesh is used*
> *widely in a literal, accommodated or figurative (bodily or*
> *mental) sense. It has many meanings, including appetite,*
> *beast, body, breath and creature. Biblically, then, the soul*
> *is simply the life of a breathing creature, which departs*
> *when that living creature dies.*

* * *

> *The words "living soul" (nephesh chayah) were used in*
> *Genesis 2:7 when God originally gave life to man. You can*
> *read the same phrase in twelve more passages in Hebrew*
> *where, surprisingly they all refer to animals! The first five*
> *appear in the first two chapters of Genesis.[25]*

I was surprised by these definitions. Aren't you?

Why would "*nephesh*" be translated "soul" only in reference to
humans by English translators? The distinction is not in the Hebrew
Scriptures. Why are animals only referred to as "beast," "living
creature," "living things" when the Hebrew "nephesh" appears? It
must be that the Cartesian theology was already deeply entrenched
in the minds of church leaders and translators.

"SOUL" IN THE NEW TESTAMENT

What about the New Testament? In the New Testament
Greek manuscripts, the Greek word "psyche" is the one commonly
translated into English as "soul." "*Psyche*" [Strong's # 5590] means
"breath," "life," and "soul, mind, or self." The Greek word is a root
word for many English terms, like psychology and psychedelic (mind-
altering).

The same patterns used in translating "*nephesh*" are followed in
translating "psyche" and its relatives. For example, see Luke 6:9 and

9:24. In Acts 20:10 regarding the death of Eutychus, Paul embraced the boy's body and said, "His psyche is still in him." Revelation 18:13 refers to the wicked selling of human psyche along with slaves, animals and other merchandise. Contrast that with Revelation 8:9, the only passage which used *psyche* in reference to animals:

...a third of the creatures, which were in the sea and had life [psyche], *died.*

This passage has a familiar ring to it. Doesn't it remind you of Genesis 1:20-28? John, who wrote Revelation, would have known Genesis in Hebrew. That may be why John, when writing Revelation 8:9, used *psyche*. He could have used the Greek word "zoe" (as in "zoology") which means all living things, from amoeba, to dandelions, to whales — not just breathing "souls." Perhaps it was put there for us — those of us who want to know the answer to Mom's question.

Looking again at definitions of "soul" based on Bible sources, it becomes clear animals fit the definition. If you have an "ego" or "self" then you have a soul:

Soul ... [T]he word [is] commonly used in the Bible to designate the nonmaterial ego of man in its ordinary relationships with earthly and physical things. It is one of a number of psychological nouns, all designating the same non-material self, but each with a different functional relationship.[26]

Animals have *psyche* or *nephesh*. Observers note that dogs, cats, horses and other mammals clearly have a sense they are separate "selves" from others of their species, other animals, and humans. They hoard things showing a sense of ownership, act possessive or jealous, are territorial, act heroic and kind to others, including other species. They problem-solve and also use tools. Animals show every indicia of "ego" or "self."

All you have to do is observe animals to know what the Bible means. I have cats who look alike physically, but have strikingly different personalities. The same is true of other animals. Shepherds know their sheep by name. Farmers working with milk cows daily, can tell them apart both by looks and personalities. And the list goes on. Animals do have personalities or personhood, or "non-material egos" — just as man does. Therefore, it cannot be the soul that distinguishes man and beast.

"Soul" is a hard word to define clearly. What is a soul, anyway? *The Pictorial Bible Dictionary* definition of "soul" has this commentary:

> *The above remarks assume dichotomy, that is, that there are only two substantive entities which make up the whole man (1) the body, which at death returns to dust, await-ing the resurrection, and (2) the nonmaterial self which, if regenerate, goes to paradise or heaven; if not, to the abode of the wicked dead. There are many, however, who hold to a trichotomous view, arguing that "soul" and "spirit" are two distinct substantive entities, and the body, a third. They cite I Thessalonians 5:23; I Corinthians 15:44 and Hebrews 4:12 for evidence.*[27]

What about animals? According to Scripture, are they two-part or three-part beings? We see they are two parts, having *nephesh* and their physical bodies. In the minds of some, possessing a soul is enough for animals to be candidates for heaven or hell.

However, I suspect some will hold out: "If animals lack spirits, they cannot go to heaven, since God is spirit, and it takes 'spirit' to worship Him." [John 4:24]   Are animals three-part beings, like humans? Do animals have spirits?

DO ANIMALS HAVE SPIITS, TOO?
Would you agree that if animals have spirits, the case becomes stronger than animals are candidates for heaven? If so, we might answer Mom's question in the affirmative.

I was taught the Bible does not say that animals have spirits. Many Christians have repeated this lesson to me. Is it correct? What does the Bible say?

Again, we must return to the original languages to find the answer. In the Old Testament Hebrew, *"ruwach"* [Strong's #7307] is the Hebrew word translated as "spirit." Ruwach is Hebrew word used for the human "spirit."

Ruwach literally means "breath." It has figurative meanings, such as: "life," "anger," "unsubstantiality" and, of course, "spirit." When you think about it, the connection between "breath" and "spirit" is no great intellectual leap. Both describe the intangible. Both describe something essential to life. When the breath leaves the body, the spirit has departed. The spirit is the core of a living being, the vital principle.

According to *Strong's Dictionary of the Hebrew Bible*, published in 1890 and part of the Strong's Exhaustive Concordance (1894), when *"ruwach"* is translated as "spirit," it denotes only "a rational being." (Do I hear echoes of Descartes?)

Gesenius' Hebrew-Chaldee Lexicon To The Old Testament, published in 1847, defines *ruwach*, similarly, adding that it is also used to describe the "wind." When describing humans Gesenius said *ruwach* means *"animus"* or "seat of the senses, affections and emotions of various kinds," as well as "the mode of thinking and acting," "will and counsel" and "intellect."

This term is used to identify the Holy Spirit of God, "ruwach ha kadosh" [Ps. 51:13; Isa. 63:11-12]. It is also used to identify demons, i.e. evil "spirits," which torment humans [1 Sam. 16:15-16]. That is intriguing, given our question.

"THE EXCLUSIVE RATIONAL-BEING CLUB"

This "Rational-Being Club" has been exclusively human and supernatural for centuries. Animals need not apply! *Ruwach*, the word used for "spirit" has received the same treatment as "n*ephesh*" or "soul" in English translations. This is not surprising. It is consistent with the Cartesian viewpoint.

The first passage where ruwach is used in connection with animals in Genesis 7. This passage illustrates a Cartesian bias affecting translation:

> ... *they [Noah, his sons and their wives] and every beast after its kind, all cattle after their kind, every creeping thing that creeps on the earth after its kind, and every bird after its kind, every bird of every sort. And they went into the ark to Noah, two by two, of all flesh in which is the breath [ruwach] of life. [vs. 14-15]*

Only in one place do translators use "spirit" when connected to an animal: Ecclesiastes 3:21. In any well-known English translation, you cannot find ruwach translated as "spirit" where it refers to an animal in any other verse. The only reason it is translated "spirit" in Eccl. 3:21 is there is no other way it would make sense. Consider the passage, using the New American Standard Version, one I like for its reputation of being very literal:

> *I said in my heart regarding the subject of the sons of men that God is ... trying them that they may see that by themselves ... they are but as beasts. For that which befalls the sons of men befalls beasts, even one thing befalls them; as the one dies, so dies the other. Yes, they all have one* **breath (ruwach),** *so that a man has no preeminence over a beast; for all is vanity . . .*
> *All go to one place; all are of the dust, and all turn to dust again.*
> *Who knows that the* **spirit (ruwach)** *of man whether is goes upward and the* **spirit (ruwach)** *of the beast whether it goes downward to the earth?*
> Ecclesiastes 3:18-21 (NASV)

When he wrote Ecclesiastes, King Solomon, was considered both the wisest man who ever lived and the Playboy of his world. He was learned, a prodigy. Solomon wrote Ecclesiastes under the inspiration of the Spirit of the Lord, according to both Jewish and Christian canons. Solomon's final question is a rhetorical one; it is answered in the statements preceding it: all have the same *ruwach*; all die the same. Who can say one goes up and one goes down? Can you?

Solomon observed that humans and animals die similar deaths. Whether they are killed, die of disease, disaster, or old age, there is little difference in how the physical body dies. All flesh goes the same way. No one who has witnessed the death of a human or animal can honestly question that observation. When the *ruwach* — the animating force — leaves the body of man or animal, what remains is an empty shell of clay. I've seen a number of dead bodies and I am still shocked how different a body is when empty of life.

Animals have spirits just as humans do. This is the word from the Holy Bible. This is from the inspired Word of God. Twice in this passage the word *ruwach* refers to animals. Solomon repeatedly states man and animals are no different: we both have spirits and we die the same!

Theologians, like Descartes, sidestepped the issue of animals having "spirits." They used learned sophistry and kept readers in the dark. I submit they were less than intellectually honest. Isn't it time to dismantle this cruel philosophy?

Solomon was meditating on the vanity, the futility, of humans in thinking we are so superior. He stated that as we die just like animals. We go to the same place. He never questioned that animals have spirits, *ruwach*.

MORE REFERENCES

There are more references, more "witnesses." The psalmist described the provision which God makes for animals and then says:

You open Your hand, They are filled with good. You hide Your face, they are troubled; You take away their breath [ruwach], They die and return to their dust. You send forth

Your Spirit [ruwach], They are created; And You renew
the face of the earth. May the glory of the Lord endure
forever; May the Lord rejoice in His works.

Psalm 104:28b-31

Note the play on words which is missed in the English. The psalmist juxtaposed the spirits of animals to the Spirit of God. Animals die when their spirits leave their bodies. The Holy *Ruwach* sustains and creates animal *ruwachs!* The Holy Spirit is a Person, a part of the Godhead, the *Elohim*. God actively cares for animals! (I think the psalmist was also saying man is no different from animals — we all need God's Spirit to sustain our spirits.) The psalmist knew. Wow!

Another interesting phrase appears in Numbers 16:22 and again in Numbers 27:16:

...the God of the spirits [ruwach] *of all flesh...*

In both of these Scriptures, the context is addressing human need. However, there is no dispute that in the Bible, "flesh" and "all flesh" are used in reference to animal as well as human flesh. The writer of Numbers also uses "all flesh" as it is used in Genesis 2:21, 23; 6:12-13; 7:15, 16, 21; & 9:15-16. The Hebrew term refers to animals as well as humans.

ANOTHER PIECE TO THE PUZZLE

Another piece of the puzzle is in the familiar phrase from Psalms:

Let everything that has breath praise the Lord.

Ps. 150:6

This is a different Hebrew word for "breath" or "spirit." This word is *"neshamah"* [Strong's #5397]. It means "puff" as "wind." Figuratively, it has come to mean angry or vital "breath," divine "inspiration," and "intellect." You might say it is activated spirit.

Neshamah is translated into English as the "breath" or "spirit" of life. Neshamah is used in Genesis 2:7 regarding Adam, and in

Genesis 7:22, Deuteronomy 20:16, and Joshua 10:40 regarding all life, i.e., including animals. Let's look at Genesis 7:22:

> *All in whose nostrils was the breath [**neshamah**] of the spirit [**ruwach**] of life, all that was on the dry land, died. So He destroyed all living things which were on the face of the ground: both man and cattle, creeping thing and bird of the air. ... Only Noah and those who were with him in the ark remained alive.* Gen. 7:22-23a [NKJV]

This passage is interesting because "spirit," ruwach, is in ancient Hebrew texts, but is left out of the Greek Septuagint, and the Latin Vulgate translations. The Septuagint is a translation of the 39 Hebrew books of the Old Testament, prepared in the 3rd century before Christ for Greek-speaking Jews in Egypt. The Latin Vulgate translation was prepared for the early Roman Christians by Jerome, using Hebrew and several Greek translations including the Septuagint. One of the questions I have for the Lord when I reach heaven is, why would these translators leave out *ruwach*? Was it because they did not believe animals had "spirits"?

"Neshamah" is also translated as "soul," as well as "spirit" — whether human, animal or divine. See, for example, its use for God's breath or Spirit in Job 32:8 and 33:4. It seems to be linked with the term for life or living. "Let everything that has breath praise the Lord," is commonly understood to mean humans and animals. But the information that "breath" also means "spirit" is hidden to uninformed English readers.

When you understand that the word "breath" — whether "ruwach" or "neshamah" — can also be translated "spirit," then you see there are multiple references in the Bible which show animals have "spirits." What was hidden, is now revealed. The Bible does say! And it says animals have spirits, too!

SPIRIT IN THE NEW TESTAMENT

The New Testament is very skimpy in speaking of animals and their natures. Perhaps this is because it is well covered in the Old Testament or Jewish Scriptures. Jesus came to fulfill the Hebrew Law, not abolish it. [Matt. 5:17]

The Greek word commonly translated "spirit" is *"pneuma"* [Strong's 4151], from *"pneu"* "to breathe or blow." This is a familiar term to English-speaking folks. We use pneumatic pumps and tires and we contract pneumonia, a disease of the "air pumps" we call lungs. It is therefore basically identical to the Hebrew *"ruwach." "Pneuma"* likewise means "breath" or "wind." By extension it also means "spirit," "rational soul," "vital principle," or "mental disposition."

"Pneuma" is used by New Testament writers to identify divine, human, angelic and demonic beings. The Holy Spirit, or Holy Ghost, is the "Hagia Pneuma." "Pneuma" is not used in the New Testament to refer to any animal's breath or spirit. But a relative of pneuma is.

The God who made the world and all things that are in it, since He is Lord of heaven and earth, does not dwell in temples made with hands; neither is He served by human hands, as though He needed anything, since He Himself gives to all life and breath [pnoe] and all things; and He made from one, every nation of mankind to live on all the face of the earth, having determined their appointed times, and the boundaries of their habitation, ...

[Acts 17:24-25 NASV]

The term *"pnoe"* [Strong's # 4157], means "respiration." It is closely related to "pneuma" [#4151]. They share the same root word. The distinction seems to be in the activity described: "Pneuma" describes a current of air, i.e., breath or breeze. *"Pnoe"* describes "respiration" or breathing. Both are translated "spirit" or "wind." That makes sense in English – we are all living breathing creatures, sometimes full of wind!

The only other place this word "pnoe" is used is Acts 2:2 to describe the sound of the coming of the Holy Spirit on the day of Pentecost, when Jesus' disciples were filled and changed. It can be read: "And there came suddenly out of heaven a sound as a rush of violent wind" or " ... of a mighty Spirit." It is not hard to picture the Almighty — excited about the wonderful gift He was sending to believers — expelling His breath in a violent rush. It must have sounded like a tornado! Atomic breath! God's Mighty Spirit came rushing to fill His disciples with power!

BOTH THE OLD TESTAMENT AND THE NEW AGREE

So we have authority in both Old and New Testaments, Hebrew and Greek, that animals have "spirits." They are tripartite beings just like humans. As we discussed above, modern scholarship agrees.

> *The time is long overdue for abandoning the anthropocen-*
> *tric approach to philosophy . . . So long as animals are ig-*
> *nored, either as objects in the world or as perceivers, they*
> *will continue to make messes. ... When the chickens come*
> *home to roost, [a contrary philosophy] silently wrings*
> *their necks at the entrance to the coop, before they can get*
> *in and cackle." ...*
>
> *Here we let the chickens cackle loud and clear. . . Certain*
> *issues in philosophy of science, philosophy of mind, even*
> *history of philosophy, take on new light when animals are*
> *given center stage.*[28]

The intent of this book is not to "give" any creature, including man, "center stage." Rather it is to find the Author's placement of animals – the place He intended and intends them to have — on His "stage" in His Kingdom. No more. No less.

The consequences of the Cartesian philosophy are heavy. Christian theologians passed this nonsense to ministers, who taught ordinary worshipers. For a long time scientists excused animal pain in experiments under this dark belief. It still goes on. The results have been a license to those who chose to be cruel on the one hand, and a guilt trip for animal lovers on the other. It's past time to turn these tables, don't you agree?

It may not be easy. If one cannot face judgment for his or her unpaid debts to God and man, one certainly won't want to bear account for injury to animals! Those who follow the Cartesian model, must be tempted to bury their heads in the proverbial sand of "reason," while reality bites them in the rear! If you have been caught in that philosophy, please reconsider!

Why would anyone believe the heartless Cartesian philosophy? One might ask, "Why do people become abusers or neglect their children?" In all societies where the life of man or beast is not valued, insane cruelty reigns.

Throughout history, animals have been treated badly. There are exceptions, but this has been the general rule. Ignorance of animals, and their needs, as well as blatant cruelty, results in animals being ill-fed, poorly doctored, cruelly worked, tortured or beaten — as though they were disposable machines. Wild animals also suffer.

But then human history shows we are no less unkind to our fellow man. Experts today know, from studies of violent criminals, there is a link between animal cruelty and deranged, vicious crimes.[29]

Beware the child who enjoys hurting little animals!

HANDLING BIBLE ERRORS

As you read this brief assessment of Christian history and the Bible, I hope you see where, if not why, we went astray. For those deeply troubled that "the Bible has errors in translation," the Almighty is able to handle all kinds of human error. He has done so since Adam's fall, and he has a plan to help.

The Bible is still divinely inspired — even most translations can't escape God's anointing. The Bible cautions that no one should to add to and take away from God's Word. [Deut. 4:2; 12:32; Rev. 22:18-19]

We humans have a tendency to continue to do so, however. Eve added to and took away from the first commandment to not eat the forbidden fruit. [Compare Gen. 1:16-17 with Gen. 3:2-3] Bad translations which imply animals don't have souls and spirits violated this command.

Because of preconceived ideas and cultural bias, translators may not have realized their errors. I hope that their errors were unintentional. We must all bear account to the Lord for how we handle His Truth. There is abundant mercy for unintentional transgressions.

You don't have to learn ancient Hebrew and Greek to read the Bible. Modern translations get the major points very well. Just because some translators did not everything right, we can believe that they tried. They had a very difficult task. Translation is not easy.

Anyone who has learned more than one language, knows the difficulty in accurately translating anything. Words with multiple meanings are very difficult to translate. Additionally, since the Lord confused men's words and language at the Tower of Babel [Gen. 11], we've all had trouble communicating clearly. We daily need the Lord's help to understand each other! Sometimes only He can un-confuse us. (Maybe He intended it that way!)

Allow the Holy Spirit to be your teacher, as I have striven to do here. The Lord has promised that His disciples will know the truth. Even if God has to move heaven and earth, He will show us His way. He certainly has done that to give me these answers — the details of which would fill another book!

IT'S IRREFUTABLE!

The Bible is clear. Animals have souls and spirits, just as man does. In that regard, we are no different. We can celebrate our similarities! We humans are all part of the animal kingdom. God intends for all His creation to be part of His kingdom, it appears.

Now you know what the Bible says. It is irrefutable. The difference between man and beast is not that man has a soul or spirit (Gen. 1:20; 7:15; Eccl. 3:21). We are both tripartite beings: Spirit, soul and body.

The difference between man and beast is not that man has a soul or spirit (Gen. 1:20; 7:15; Eccl. 3:21), but that man is created in the image of God, whereas the beast is not[30]

While I am not sure what being "created in the image of God" truly means, I am not ashamed to be compared to animals. Most are of the highest character and very good company. We have much to learn about and from animals. Now we will have a groundwork laid to explore more about animals in eternity. Let's see what else the Bible has to say!

ENDNOTES

1. *The American Heritage Dictionary*, [1969] p. 1245

2. Frederic Skinner, [1904-1990], is known for his contributions to behaviorism. Skinner founded radical behaviorism and experimental analysis of behavior. Other behaviorists, like Sigmund Freud, explained behavior by referring to nonconscious, purely mental states. Skinner instead adopted the view that "mind" is mythical. For Skinner, behavior was controlled by the environment (including the private environment of consciousness), not by internal forces. Skinner and his followers studied simple animal and human behaviors under carefully controlled experimental conditions, hoping eventually to build a complete psychology.

3. *Grolier Multimedia Encyclopedia*, 1998

4. Politics, I, v. 5

5. Daisie and Michael Radner, *ANIMAL CONSCIOUSNESS* (Prometheus Books, 1989) p. 7-8

6. "Masses" had to be literate to read, but even the illiterate were hearing Scripture from pulpits and literate laity who were talking about or quoting Scripture.

7. *The Columbia Encyclopedia, Second Ed.*, (Columbia Univ. Press, 1935, 1950), p. 531

8. Daisie and Michael Radner, ANIMAL CONSCIOUSNESS (Prometheus Books, 1989) p. 8-9

9. *Animal Consciousness* (Prometheus Books, 1989) p. 8-9

10. *Animal Consciousness,* supra, p. 90-91

11. See, C. S. Lewis, *THE PROBLEM OF PAIN*, chp. 9 "Animal Pain" [MacMillan Pub. Co., 1962, 1986]

12. Stephanie Laland, *Animal Angels,* [Conari Press 1998], p. 188

13. The Hebrew is difficult here. Some translations substitute "a strutting cock" for "greyhound".

14. Vicki Hearne, *Adam's Task; Calling Animals by Name,* [HarperPerenial, 1982, 1983, 1985, 1986, 1994] p. 6

15. Harcourt Brace Jovanovich, Pub. 1990

16. Id. P. 159

17. Id, and see *Amazing Animals* [Time-Life Books] p. 130; & Felicity Brooks, *Usborne Science and Nature: Animal Behavior* [Usborned Publ. 1992] p. 11.

18. *Mysteries of Animal Intelligence,* p. 128-129

19. *"Brave Hearts" People,* 7/14/97, p. 106 at 108-109

20. Stephanie Laland, *Animal Angels,* supra, p. 42 & 63

21. Winkey Pratney, *Healing the Land,* supra

22. Jack Canfield, et al, *Chicken Soup for the Pet Lover's Soul* [Health Communications 1998], pp. 225-226

23. *Jesus the Jewish Theologian,* [Hendrickson Pub. 1995], p. 280

24. *Pictorial Bible Dictionary,* edited by M. Tenney & S. Barabas, (Zondervan, 1963, 1974), [at p. 807] and *The New Compact Bible Dictionary,* edited by T. Alton Bryant, (Zondervan Pub. 1967) at p. 563-64]

25. Winkey Pratney, *Healing the Land,* p. 109-110

26. *Pictorial Bible Dictionary,* edited by M. Tenney & S. Barabas, (Zondervan, 1963, 1974), p. 807

27. Id.

28. Daisie and Michael Radner, *ANIMAL CONSCIOUSNESS* (Prometheus Books, 1989) p. 7-8

29. See for example, Article "Talk Set on Violence, Animal Cruelty Link", *The Daily Oklahoman,* 2/2/98, p. 3

30. *Pictorial Bible Dictionary,* edited by M. Tenney & S. Barabas, (Zondervan, 1963, 1974), [at p. 807] and The New Compact Bible Dictionary, edited by T. Alton Bryant, (Zondervan Pub. 1967) at p. 563-64]

CHAPTER 5

IN AWESOME WONDER OR ANIMALS AT CREATION

O Lord my God, when I in awesome wonder, consider all the worlds Thy hands have made, I see the stars, I hear the rolling thunder, Thy power throughout the universe displayed, Then sings my soul, . . . How great Thou art!¹

Fair songsters, come; beneath the sacred grove We'll sit and teach the woods our Maker's name. Men have forgot His works, His power, His love, Forgot the mighty arm that reared their wondrous frame.²

All things bright and beautiful, All creatures great and small, All things wise and wonderful, The Lord God made them all.³

A n ancient fable tells about a mouse born in a chest, who lived all her days on food stored in the chest by the housewife. One day the mouse dropped out the side. As she searched to get back in the chest, she stumbled on a very delicious morsel. As soon as it was in her mouth, she exclaimed what a fool she had been to believe that there was no happiness in the world but in that box.[4]

When I study Scripture and this vast world around us, I am often confronted with new things. There are lots of "delicious morsels" outside my chest or box. It's overwhelming at times to think how much! Do you, like me, feel a bit like that mouse?

Another thought is that: True genius makes complex things simple. The Bible, starting with Genesis, is a record of astonishing genius. In a few hundred words, Genesis' first chapter describes the creation of stars, planets, moon, earth, plants, birds, fish, insects and mammals in a few simple words.

Whether you takes Genesis account as literal or metaphorical, is between you and the Lord. There are other authors who address these issues on both sides of the debate between creation and evolution. Here we will assume the Bible is true and operate from that assumption. How that truth is interpreted is again a matter of faith. But then so is the whole subject of this book.

Knowledge is exploding, and has been for decades.[5]   In the 1980s, a microbiologist friend, a specialist in genetics of viruses, told me she could not keep up in her own "small" field. The information collected to date on the origins of life is gargantuan. There is a lot more to discover!

Consider how the Bible begins: [6]

"In the beginning, God created . . . "   Gen. 1:1a

This brief statement tells profound things. Before there was a beginning, God was there! Think about that. This Creator is un-created and outside time as we know it. This earth was created, not "evolved out of chaos." An Infinite Mind and Heart conceived and executed a plan for earth and its inhabitants. You are the product of a Divine Plan. Earth's complex beauty testifies: A consummate Artist created this universe. And that was only the beginning! The

Artist still works. The plan, the picture, is not complete. This leaves me awestruck. How about you?

The Bible begins and ends with animals in an important role. In the first book, first chapter, we find God and His creation of animals. God made animals before humans. In the last book of the Bible, Revelation, Jesus returns to earth on a horse, with a huge cavalry. Genesis sets a pattern. Could these things be a foretaste of heaven, a piece of the answer to Mom's question?

GOD CREATES

Let's be honest. It is a journey of faith to "look" before recorded history. As a lawyer I deal with legal proof, meaning eye witnesses and hard evidence. We have no human witnesses to creation and the early days of earth. There's no way to reproduce it in a laboratory. All we really know is that the earth, and all in and on it, exist. Only God Himself knows the truth about the beginning, the *genesis*. What you believe is by faith. Whether you take the creation story literally, figuratively, or not at all, is ultimately based on your belief, not provable facts.

No one has proven conclusively that this world, and all that is in it, was not created just as the Bible states. In fact, the Bible contains remarkable insights into scientific and historical facts.[7] It is impossible for man to duplicate the creation of earth, so there is no hard proof of any theory man thinks up. No one was there at the beginning except God, and He does not fit into any laboratory test tube.

Another problem is how would we know if someone did prove it? The Bible gives only a skeletal sketch of most things: Sometimes in clear simple terms; sometimes in illustrations and parables. The Creation story is like that. It's very difficult to know what really occurred without direct proof. The only One there was God.

Debates among scientists about our origins will likely continue as long as this earth remains. Scientists cannot agree how to interpret what they have now. New things are discovered daily – so that adds to the problem. The Bible settles the matter for people of faith. The Bible needs no defense. Its Author is alive and well able to defend it.[8]

Because the Lord Jesus Christ is real to me, and I have chosen to obey Him, the Bible is my primary authority — my constitution and law, if you like. If I cannot find Scriptures — and that is plural — to back up my beliefs, they are mere theories and not a basis for faith. I choose to take the Bible literally unless it is obvious a passage is not meant that way. I always ask God to show me the truth and whether I'm wrong.

Every time I ask my Lord for wisdom and understanding, He gives it to me. That promise is in James 1:5. Sometimes the answer has been years in coming -- because I have a habit of asking "Ph.D." questions when my grasp is kindergarten level – but God gets it to me! The answers to Mom's question took years to collect and comprehend.

MY BELIEFS

When God made Himself known to me and I made a total commitment to Him, I realized my intellectual and spiritual heritage conflicted with the Bible a great deal. It was a bit confusing.[9] I read: God is not the author of confusion. [1 Cor. 14:33] "My thoughts are not your thoughts, Nor are your ways My ways," says the Lord. [Isa. 55:8]

I am not a scientist, however, I can claim to know the Creator. I determined to let Him be my source of knowledge, wisdom, and understanding. [See Prov. chp. 1-3; Isa. 11:1-2; 1 Cor. 1:18-31] As a result, my thinking seems to be amazingly clearer (and life more fun). I no longer worry about the answers, while I looking for them. I have no problem believing Almighty God *could* make everything in six literal days if He desired. He is God and nothing is too difficult for Him.

The Bible implies God made a mature world. It is not logical and practical that the Lord would make a mature world? As a veterinarian's daughter who grew up with farm animals, it seems rational that a quick creation was necessary. Have you considered the old debate on which came first, the chicken or the egg?[10] Eggs need chickens. Babies need mothers. Change in fragile ecosystems kills the highest animal forms first. To me, a creation of a mature world throws a monkey wrench in dating the Beginning. Adam himself couldn't verify if the first cow was five minutes old, or five years old, since he was created last. (Nothing has changed really.) The Bible answers this. Think about it, wouldn't the world appear much older than it is, if God made a mature world?

Whether the creation account is literal or metaphorical is not a stumbling block to my faith.[11] I pray it is not to yours. The omnipotent omniscient God can do anything He pleases. [Eccl. 8:3] I'm thankful He is also all good and always acts in character!

THEORY OR FACT

The purpose of this book is not to debate evolution and creation science. Or whether Biblical creation account means the earth was created and populated in six days or some number of years. I'm a lawyer, not a scientist. Still, even a non-scientist can observe and read. Many things have not been explained by any theory. Physical evidence, biological complexities and anomalies belie "evolutionary" development outside of a species - which by definition is comprised of living creatures which can genetically crossbreed (like dogs, cats, cows, etc.).[12]

Think about the woodpecker's long tongue which is attached and stored uniquely in its brain cavity; this tongue is too unique to have "evolved." Complex human-like eyes are found only in squids, octopuses, and humans. Yet it's believed these species "evolved" from different roots.[13] As a veterinarian's daughter, I learned mutants seldom live or are healthy. Those which do live are sterile, like mules and jennies.

Too often the theories are taught as proven fact, when many evidentiary and logical holes are found in it. This is why there is a debate about evolution and creation science. Science advocates don't have it altogether in any camp. Somehow, as verifiable evidence accumulates, my gut feeling is the Bible is a decent record of scientific truths (as far as it goes). Just as the Bible has been shown by archeology to be a good historical record. Nonetheless, the debates rage on about methodology and evidence. (Egos and politics are fueling the debates, as well as religious faith.)

No science can reconstruct the Beginning. Men can only guess. An "educated guess" is still a guess. Sorting through the name-calling and rancor is difficult. It is not easy to separate theory from fact. We all bring biases into our formulae, biases which we hang onto like bulldogs. In this writer's observation, the jury is still out. No theory of earth's origin appears to have earned the right to be elevated to the status of "proven fact."

It is very unsettling to learn that: what we believed to be truth is in fact not truth at all. My college professor, Dr. R. Wik, introduced us to college, saying that: "new ideas" are very difficult and disturbing, especially when they uproot old ones; and "change is painful." I know he was right. I also know to be truly alive is to be forever changing.

The following quote by Bosworth regarding faith in God puts things in clearer perspective:

Because of God, His faithfulness, and His promises, faith is the surest ground that it is possible to stand on. To the man who is not enlightened or who does not see the promise of God, it is stepping out into space; but to those who have faith in God's Word, it is walking on the foundations of the universe.[14]

BIBLE EVIDENCE

Let's go walking on the foundations of the universe! With childlike faith, let's examine the Bible. Science can help us, but this is not a science debate. Whether your faith is in science or other methods, we can look at the Bible together. It doesn't matter whether we believe the Bible creation account literally or metaphorically to discuss the issues in Mom's question. Mom's question doesn't hang on whether God made the world in six days. Like that proverbial mouse-in-a-box, let us find the goodies awaiting outside our comfort zone.

A useful method of Bible study is to collect everything about a topic, and then prayerfully analyze it. Also, I believe God plans each lesson, each topic-encounter with care. I pay attention to the first mention of a topic in the Bible, for in it are clues to God's plans or meaning for the topic. To the observant, first impressions are usually reliable. Succeeding images should also confirm and expand on the first interpretation.

ORDER FROM CHAOS

The Bible begins with a description of God creating this universe, this green earth, and all life upon it — and doing so by design. Creation is remarkably orderly and beautiful, demonstrating careful planning and skilled craftsmanship. From this we gain our first impression of the Creator's attitude about His animals.

Consider the miraculous construction of this blue-green jewel, our home, the earth. Christian astronomer, Hugh Ross, identified more than forty different criteria which are essential in order for life to exist.[15] Some seem to be at variance with "natural laws," but without these variations life would not be possible. For example, consider the unique way water behaves among liquids, the way H_2O behaves among gases, and the way our Sun behaves.[16] Many scientists today say current evidence points irrefutably to an "anthropic principle," i.e., this earth did not happen by chance.

The mathematical probability of this creation, with all its life forms, happening by chance is so low as to be essentially impossible. Life on earth seems designed especially and uniquely for humans and other living things; it is "an exquisite harmony of critical factors."[17]

ORDERLY PROGRESSION

Read the first two chapters of Genesis. Note the progression. Only after making the heavens and earth, the waters, the sun, moon and stars, and plant life, did our Creator make animals. First, the "stage" (Earth) was constructed. The "sets" were placed (the sun, moon, stars, planets and plant life). Then, He filled it with "actors" in this drama of life. Animals needed this stage to live and procreate. What would have happened it the animals or man were created too early? They would have perished, surely.

The number and variety of actors is incredible. Depending on who's counting, millions of species have been identified, some extinct. Science has not even identified all the species and subspecies of animal life. Consider, too, the variations within each species. The dog family alone consists of a large variety — from African wild dogs and Australian dingoes to domestic Great Danes and Chihuahuas. Huge varieties and numbers exist. That's awesome!

GOD FILLED THE SEAS AND AIR WITH LIFE
In making animal life, first God filled the seas and air:

Then God said, "Let the waters abound with an abundance of living creatures, and let birds fly above the earth across the face of the firmament of the heavens." And God created the great sea creatures and every living thing that moves, with which the waters abounded, according to their kind, and every winged bird according to its kind; and God saw that it was good. And God blessed them, saying, "Be fruitful and multiply, and fill the waters in the seas, and let birds multiply on the earth." So the evening and the morning were the fifth day.   Gen. 1:21-23 (NASV)

BIRDS IN THE AIR
The Lord must love birds. He made such a variety, and endowed them with so many talents! They range from tiny hummingbirds to great condors. Coloration goes from drab sparrows to brilliant-hued parrots and peacocks. From the screech of the owl to the song of the nightingale, bird sounds fill the earth. Watch a swallow's graceful

whirl through the air, or the soaring eagle riding the wind with grace and ease! Birds scatter seeds, fertilize the fields, eat insects, and do other useful things. Birds have served us as companions and couriers. Birds are also are food for other birds and species. Remarkable creatures, birds are.

As we learned in a previous chapter, birds are not as dumb as we once thought. Birds communicate, use tools, take care of others, and exhibit complex social structure. Consider the monogamy among species of geese and ducks. Henry Thoreau, in *Walden*, described the intelligence of a partridge hen and her chicks avoiding being discovered.

In their migratory flights, geese fly in "V" formation to conserve the energy of those which ride the wake of the lead birds.

God's feathered friends are fascinating. Helicopters are but a poor imitation of the mobility of a miniature hummingbird. Airplanes have nothing on the swooping agility of hawks, falcons and eagles. On the jet stream, eagles have been observed asleep, wings locked, coasting on the wind current. This makes even more meaningful God's promise that a man who trusts Him shall "mount up with wings as eagles." [Isa. 40:31] Birds, the first of the animal kingdom to be created, are wondrous!

LIFE IN THE WATER

Consider the animal life in the waters, both fresh and ocean waters. In the Amazon River alone, are more than one thousand varieties of catfish! Mom and I watched a television program that told this fact. One type of catfish after another was shown. Some were humorously strange; all were distinctly "catfish," whiskers and all. More types of catfish could yet be discovered.

This was only one species of fish in one river! Mom and I were awed. We talked about what fun God had making those catfish. That's proof of a Divine sense of humor. A thousand kinds of catfish? Why? Why not!

We weren't alone in thinking the Lord had fun:

In any case, God has done unusual things. I think He did much of creation just for fun, while His sense of design humor gives the materialist and skeptics some sleepless nights.[18]

It boggles the mind to consider all varieties of fish, fowl and furry friends the Lord made — not to mention the insect world. Counting the balanced life in each ecosystem, "awesome" seems a very weak term to describe our Creator.

This could not be accidental. The beauty and harmony in the seas, ponds, creeks and rivers are a wonder indeed. From the phosphorescent waves lapping a shore at night, to the colorful tropical fish, to the songs of whales, the sea is a wondrous place. Recently, at the Long Beach California Aquarium, we heard how sea lions are necessary to control the ecosystem along the coast.[19] The way species help each other and need each other is also mute testimony to the genius of their Creator.

Man is just beginning to explore secrets of the waters. The ocean and outer space are the last great frontiers. We've been gaining knowledge of depths formerly unknown. Mapping the ocean floors by satellite has opened a view that man has never before seen. Studies of porpoises and whales are revealing that these large-brained mammals have great intelligence and complex languages. They have sonar abilities inspiring our present science and mechanical inventions, and a social structure showing a high degree of cooperation. Whales "midwife" the birth of each other's babies. Watch whales or porpoises sporting in the ocean or a sea horse caring for its young. Researchers are finding unusual life forms in the depths, too. Be prepared to stand in awe when exposed to ocean life.

They that go down to the sea in ships, Who do business on the great waters;

They have seen the works of the Lord, And His wonders in
the deep.   Psalm 107:23-24

The way things work together demonstrates a presence behind it
of a caring, patient, infinitely creative Person of unlimited intelligence,
wit, and wisdom. It leaves me almost speechless. (As woman and a
lawyer, I am rarely at a loss for words.)

LIFE ON THE LAND

Coming to the land, the Bible succinctly describes God's sixth
day of the Creation, when the Lord made the land animals and
mankind:[20]

Then God said, "Let the earth bring forth the living crea-
ture according to its kind: cattle and creeping things and
beasts of the earth, each according to their kind"; and it
was so. And God made the beast of the earth according to
its kind, cattle according to its kind, and everything that
creeps on the earth according to its kind. And God saw that
it was good.   Gen. 1:24-25 (NKJV)

God made myriads of animals, from amoeba to elephants. Insects
are the most varied, numerous, and fascinating. I enjoy butterflies
and praying mantises. Many are useful, although I have not found a
liking for cockroaches.

I recall hearing that engineers who studied the bumblebee said
it was impossible for that bug to fly. Its large yellow and black body
was too large for its small fly-like wings to lift and sustain its flight.
Nobody told the bee.

Where I lived in Kentucky, the timbers of my old garage had deep
holes about 1/3-inch wide. The holes were made by a wood-boring
bee which looks like a bumblebee. My garage was made of oak. Oak
gets harder with age. I could not hammer a nail into the timbers! Yet
this bee could drill that large hole!

The Lord thoroughly enjoys making wonders. The insect world is full of marvels. The bumblebee and the wood borer give lessons in faith. The impossible is possible for our Lord, and to those who believe Him! [Jer. 29:17, 27; Luke 1:37]. If you really know the Lord, you know He loves do to the impossible.

ANIMALS AS TEACHERS

As Proverbs 6:6 and 30:25 says, we can learn from the ants. Humans make careers of studying plant and animal life. Our universities and libraries are full of human research. Yet we still have much to learn, don't we? Our earth-home is a marvelous ecosystem. From ants to zebras, there are complex communities of animals.

Go study the animals. Even in this fallen world, animals can teach us much about our Creator. Ponder what He has made. If not in person, then perhaps through videos and books about animal intelligence, animal wonders, animal antics. Meditate on nature's harmony and interrelated diversity. The reading and observation I've done have been eye-opening, instructive and fun!

Consider the evidence of harmony in diversity, love between animal, even of different species and humans. Animals are full of humor and playfulness! My pets have always interrupted me when I'm too serious for too long to make me play and laugh.

God is the God of Isaac ("Isaac" means "laughter" in Hebrew). That's reflected in His creation. Possums play dead. Certain caterpillars defend themselves by looking like vomit or bird droppings. Birds fake broken wings to draw predators from their nests. Some fresh water mussels have a body part which fools fish, so the fish unwittingly carry off mussel larvae. Otters, ferrets, cats and buffalo play regularly. I've never owned a horse who did not tease in horse-play! In my research I learned that mice sing; bears and birds get intoxicated (intentionally by all appearances) by imbibing fermented berries; other animals intentionally slide on the snow and ice in winter games. God is joy and made this world to be fun -- as well as interesting! Life is meant to be hilarious!

ANIMAL BEHAVIOR

Consider personalities of different animals. Behaviorists have discerned affection and emotion in the interaction among and between species. Terms such as loyalty, kindness, honesty, and unselfishness (as well as negative terms) are used to describe animal behavior in their natural habitats.

Animals show attributes which humans share: Intelligence, language, problem-solving, social structure, play, food-storage, tools-usage, and artistic ability. Animals display emotions ranging from fear and anger to love, from grief and depression to mercy and compassion, both to their own and to other species. Animals also show other "human traits," like cruelty. This includes slavery and warlike behavior.[21]

If animals are "beast-machines" which cannot feel, then the U.S. Federal Drug Administration should be notified, as should pharmaceutical companies. On January 5, 1999, the Wall Street Journal reported the FDA approved the first antidepressant for dogs who suffer from "separation anxiety"![22]   A number of drugs have been developed to "treat behavioral problems" in pets. There are now therapists as well as treatments for animals' emotional disorders. Animals *are* emotional beings. It is incontrovertible.

GOD'S ATTENTION TO THE ANIMALS

In the fifth and sixth days, the Bible says God created the sea and land animals, including birds and insects. If you take those "days" at face value, what percent of the time was spent creating living things versus creating inanimate creation? One third of those "six days" was put into making the animal kingdom vs. two-thirds getting the "habitat" of heaven and earth ready for life. If time is valuable, then the animals are surely important. The Personality of the Universe loves His animals!

ICING ON THE CAKE

Then God said, "Let us make man in Our image, accord-
ing to Our likeness; let them have dominion over the fish of
the sea, over the birds of the air, and over the cattle, over
all the earth and over every creeping thing that creeps on
the earth." So God created man in His own image; in the
image of God He created him; male and female He cre-
ated them. Then God blessed them, and God said to them,
"Be fruitful and multiply; fill the earth and subdue it; have
dominion over the fish of the sea, over the birds of the air,
and over every living thing that moves on the earth." ...
Then God saw everything that He had made, and indeed it
was very good. So the evening and the morning were the
sixth day.   Gen. 1:26-28, 31 (NKJV)

At the end of the sixth day, God took a few minutes and made the human race. Humans are the crown of God's creation, made in His image, to be His family, His sons (and daughters). Like newborn infants, we have little idea what He wants from us and a dim idea of who He is. We humans may be a five-minute special, but special we are to God.

But let us not get an inflated idea of our value. Our value has more to do with the Creator than anything we do. For example, time and size can reflect value. If God charged by the hour, what would be the relative value of fish, birds, beasts compared to man? A humbling thought, isn't it? We are more like animals than some philosophers and theologians will admit. Humans share characteristics of insects, fish, birds, and mammals, physically, intellectually and emotionally. Observing the animals can be life-changing. Animals tell us something about the Artist who made us all.

God took obvious care in making His animals. The proof is in creation itself: the huge variety of species totally suited to and integrated into their habitats, living in incredible harmony in delightful diversity. Because this earth is marred by sin, trying to picture it when God first made it is like trying to picture an exquisite banquet when it's already half-eaten. Yet, the evidence is there of consummate artistry. The signs point to a caring, witty, intelligent Creator.

As the grand finale, He made us — the human race. Humans may be the icing on the cake of creation. But what is icing without a cake? We need the cake more than the cake needs the icing.

ENDNOTES:

1.   Carl Boberg (1859-1940 translated Stuart K. Hine, [copyr. 1955, Manna Music, Inc.]

2.   Isaac Watts, *The Works of Isaac Watts: Psalms Paraphrased* [London: 1813], p. 328

3.   Cecil Frances Alexander

4.   Luarentius Abstemius, *The Great Fables of All Nations* (Tudor Publ. Co. 1928), p. 207 — Italy 16th century

5.   The Bible says knowledge would explode. Dan. 12:4: "many shall run to and fro, and knowledge shall increase."

6.   Consider   http://www.eternal-productions.org/101science.html,   which states in Fact #16: "The first three verses of Genesis accurately express all known aspects of the creation (Genesis 1:1-3). Science expresses the universe in terms of: time, space, matter, and energy. In Genesis chapter one we read: "In the beginning (time) God created the heavens (space) and the earth (matter)... Then God said, "Let there be light (energy)." No other creation account agrees with the observable evidence." Note: this site provides links to other authorities, which is good.

7.   See for example, http://www.eternal-productions.org/101science.html or do an Internet search for scientific facts in the Bible.

8.   G. Richard Bozarth, *"The Meaning of Evolution,"* American Atheist, Feb. 1978, pp. 19, 30, is quoted by John D. Morris, Ph.D. in *The Young Earth* as saying: *Christianity has fought, still fights, and will fight science to the desperate end over evolution, because evolution destroys utterly and finally the very reason Jesus' earthly life was supposedly made necessary. Destroy Adam and Eve and the original sin, and in the rubble you will find the sorry remains of the son of god. Take away the meaning of his death. If Jesus was not the redeemer who died for our sins, and this is what evolution means, then Christianity is nothing!* It is true that evolution

is contrary to the Bible. Pure science, however, is supposed to be neutral, like justice in a perfect court. Separating "real science" from science contaminated by political, religious, or other human agenda, is a challenge. People use science to help or hurt others. Likewise, people use religion, including the Gospel of Jesus Christ, for mixed purposes. It can be very demanding to find the truth.

9.   My intellectual heritage was challenged when I became a committed Christian. I chose to believe the Bible, whether I understood it or not. I've let the Lord be my source of knowledge, wisdom and understanding. [Proverbs 1-8]. That has served me well for about 40 years.

10.   See http://www.eternal-productions.org/101science.html #12.

11.   I've learned that many scientists challenge the facts and logic of the evolution theories and evidence which used to support them. See, John David Morris, Ph.D., The Young Earth; Henry M. Morris and Gary E. Parker, *What is Creation Science?* There is a vigorous debate : See Alan Hayward, Ph.D. *Creation and Evolution* and, Hugh Ross, *A Matter of Days: Resolving a Creation Controversy* (2004)

12.   See   http://en.wikipedia.org/wiki/Species,   or   http://www.answers. com/topic/species. "Species" is the fundamental or lowest "category of taxonomic classification."

13.   Bartleby Nash and Ptolemy Tompkins *Mother nature's Greatest Hits; The Top Forty Wonders of the Animal World*, (Living Planet Press, 1991) pp. 30-32

14.   F. F. Bosworth, *Christ the Healer*, p. 115

15.   Hugh Ross, *Fingerprints of God: Reasons to Believe*, cited in Winkey Pratney's *Healing the Land*, p. 60.

16.   Winkey Pratney, *Healing the Land*, Chapter 6, "Three Life Exceptions to the Natural Law"

17.   *Healing the Land*; p. 60

18.   *Healing the Land*, p. 72

19.   "...sea otters play a critical role in maintaining the kelp forest ecosystem... [as] the main predators of kelp-eating species such as sea urchins and abalone. Without sea otters, kelp forests are greatly reduced, resulting in the loss of habitat for many fish species. The coastline would also lose its buffer against storms." Long Beach Aquarium website (2/2011).

20.   The Bible states that God created life according to *kinds* (Genesis 1:24). The fact that God distinguishes *kinds*, agrees with what scientists observe – namely that there are horizontal genetic boundaries beyond which life cannot vary. Life produces

after its own kind. Dogs produce dogs, cats produce cats, roses produce roses. Never have we witnessed one kind changing into another kind as evolution supposes. There are truly natural *limits* to biological change. http://www.eternal-productions. org/101science.html #10.

21. See *Mother Nature's Greatest Hits*; A.B.C. Whipple *Critters*; *Adventures in Wildest Suburbs*, [1994]; Karen Gravelee, *Animal Societies* [1993]; David Attenborough, *The Trials of Life*, [1990]; Dorothy Hinsaw Patent, *How Smart are Animals?supra*; and *Amazing Animals*, [1990], for a few titles on animal behavior and intelligence which shows the remarkable variety and complexity of the fish, bird and land animal world.

22. The drug is the old human antidepressant, Anafranil. *Wall Street Journal*, 1/5/99, p. A1 & B5

CHAPTER 6

THE NAMING OF
THE ANIMALS

And the Lord God said, "It is not good that man should be alone; I will make him a helper comparable to him." Out of the ground the Lord God formed every beast of the field and every bird of the air, and brought them to Adam to see what he would call them. And whatever Adam called each living creature, that was its name. So Adam gave names to all cattle, to the birds of the air, and to every beast of the field. But for Adam there was not found a helper comparable to him.

Genesis 2:18-20 (NKJ) (Emphasis supplied)

"Naming something gives it worth," my priest, Vic, once said in a sermon. That resonated in me. This concept is not new. Naming something establishes character and importance as well as worth.[1]

A light came in me regarding Mom's question. Why did God have Adam name the animals? Adam was not around when God made the animals. By naming them, Adam became acquainted with every animal. Did God have Adam name the animals so each animal would have worth to Adam?

NAMING PETS

Children often make a big deal out of naming pets. I did. So do adults. Most pet breeders do not name kittens or puppies in order to give the new owner that privilege. Naming a pet is a big deal! The names we give our pets often reflect our own values, as well as the value we place on the animal.

When our 90-pound, 9-month old German Shepherd came to our home, her AKC registration had her name as "T-Bone." Mom and I were unwilling to call that beautiful dog T-Bone, so we quickly renamed her Gretchen.

Mom's toy poodle came to us as "Chico." Chico was a nickname of Mom's recently deceased nephew, whom we loved. We renamed the poodle as well. We had Gretchen. So we decided the 6 lb. poodle needed a *big* name. Killer and Goliath were quickly eliminated. We finally agreed on Samson, a Biblical strong man and lion-killer. I later discovered Samson means "sunlight" in Hebrew. Mom's happy poodle was always a ray of sunlight. The proverb, "A good name is more to be desired than riches," works for dogs, too. [Proverbs 22:1]

UNINHIBITED NAMES

Why people pick certain names for animals is another question! In *St. John In Exile* (a favorite video of mine), the Apostle John (played by Dean Jones) is an old man living on the Isle of Patmos. John's cell is a cave. John names the rats in the cave — "Caiaphas," "Annas," and "Pontius Pilate" — after the Jewish and Roman leaders who sent Jesus to die. I laughed with the rest of the audience at these rat names. Creativity in naming animals is not uncommon. I've heard of "Edgar Allen Poo" for a dog and "Zorro" for, I assume, a black cat. Anyone remember the 1960s song that went: "Walking my cat named Dog"? Our pets have included Tabuk, Ruckus and Hey-U.

If we develop a relationship with an animal, we usually name it. In her book, *Naming the Animals*, Adrian Room says,

So because animals play such an important role in our

lives, we give them names, just as we give names to the children who are born into our families. Well, not in quite the same way, since we are often less inhibited, more adventurous, when it comes to the naming of animals.

The only animals we avoid naming are those we intend to eat. It's difficult to kill anything which you've come to know by name. (Military trainers know that killing an enemy is difficult when that enemy ceases to be a nameless, faceless entity.) Farmers may name their milk cows, but not steers meant for the butcher. Few people have "the stomach" to eat an animal they have raised and named. "Boy, doesn't Sweetpea taste good," just isn't palatable to people with any conscience!

Isn't that interesting? We are all descendants of Adam.

HUMANS AND ANIMALS RESPOND TO NAMES

To be nameless and ignored is to be a non-person or valueless. Animals, like people, react to this, too. Animals know when they are not valued and behave accordingly. Animals who are called by name, who are spoken to and listened to, behave differently. The more attention you give them, the more personality animals show us.

This is demonstrated in humans as well. Some homeless people go for years without being touched or called by name — with attendant depression. According to letters to Ann Landers, women whose husbands never use their given names feel neglected and unimportant. Lovers enjoy hearing their name called by their beloved. A teenager grows giddy when the "first love" calls him or her by name! If the object of his or her affection doesn't know his or her name, it is crushing.

When someone remembers our name, we usually feel special. Politicians, salespersons, and teachers know this. We are all given names, nicknames, bad names, and good names. "Names" can include titles, like lawyer or doctor, mother or father, friend or enemy. Our self-worth and identity is often tied up in our name.

Animals learn the names we give them. My Gretchen knew both her own and Samson's names. Gretchen would go find Sampson on command. This tells us animals perceive themselves as persons.

"Naming" cements a relationship with the animal. Naming becomes the vital communication which connects you with the animal. Animal trainers and experts agree, the more you "call an animal by name," the more you discover the animal's intelligence and worth. Here we find more keys to the answer to Mom's question.

The first work God gave Adam was to keep God's garden. [Genesis 2:15] The first task in keeping the garden was to name the animals. In this slim verse, much is said. In her book, *Adam's Task; Calling the Animals by Name*, animal trainer Vicki Hearne discusses what it means philosophically to "name" an animal. I found her statements profound:

> ... *when God first created the Earth He gave Adam and Eve "dominion over the fish of the sea, ... the fowl of the air, and over every living thing ..." Adam gave names to the creatures, and they all responded ... without objection, since in this dominion to command and to recognize were one action. There was no gap between the ability to command and the full of knowledge of the personhood of the being so commanded. Nature came when called, and came the first time, too, without coaxing, nagging or tugging.*[2]

The Lord had Adam call His animals by name. Adam became cemented in relationship with those first animals, because of naming them, don't you think?

THAT FIRST "NAMING PARTY" IN EDEN

Imagine, if you will, the scene in the Garden of Eden as Adam named the animals. Adam looked with new eyes, literally, upon God's fresh creation. Adam was not there when the animals were created. Creation must have sparkled with newness. The very air must have felt charged with God's fragrant presence. The energy of creation must have hung in the atmosphere like the aftermath of a lightning storm. Imagine the intoxicating perfumes of the flowers and fruit. The beauty of the new earth and sky must have been incredible.

Adam had a veritable feast for all his senses. No discord, evil, or death existed in the Garden of Eden. Harmony reigned in all the diversity of pristine creation. Life was green and strong! Perfect creation reflected the pure unadulterated image of the Creator — the God who is love, light, peace, wisdom, joy, and life! This is the setting in which the Lord brought the first animals for Adam to name. It was party time!

Young animals are full of curiosity and play. Having watched my own animals lovingly groom each other and also tease one another into play activities, makes me think this naming party was joyous. I imagine it filled also with the melodious sounds. The calls, cries, and music of every creature from the crickets to that mastodons trying out their new voices, was surely glorious. Eden must have been a huge romp of animals frolicking in the sheer joy of living! Birds, bats, and insects may have cavorted in the air on new wings. Animals have good noses, so each had their own aromatic feast. Imagine each one exploring the Garden, enjoying new smells, tastes, sights and sounds for themselves. Fun sport — a real party!

A puppy, kitten, pony or other young animal is so full of trust, curiosity, and play. Imagine Adam being both amazed and entertained by those first animals. What an adventure of discovery! Think of it! Remember the first time you touched the velvet soft nose of a horse or looked in the beautiful brown eyes of a deer? Touching the lizard's strangely cool and smooth skin is very different from burying your hands in the lanolin-rich wool of a sheep! Adam's eyes must have "popped" at the splendid colors of the tiny hummingbird in contrast to the huge dark condor or black bear. The grass-sweet smell of a cow's breath can be pleasant, but I wonder what the skunk smelled like before man's fall?

Humans and animals became acquainted with their new selves, with one another, and with Eden. Their sense of discovery, coupled with good will, must have been wondrous to see. Wouldn't you love to go back in time to join them? I would! God found it very good indeed. (Gen. 1:31) And so did Adam.

NAMING ESTABLISHES RELATIONSHIP

Did God wish Adam to develop a relationship with each animal? What a brilliant way to introduce newly-created Adam to the whole animal creation. What a clever way to begin the relationship between man and animals.

In Bible times, naming a person or thing was an important event. Look in any Bible dictionary or history of the Hebrew people and the Near East; there you will find a section on names. Much thought and prayer went into the naming of Hebrew babies.[3] The belief was that names reveal the character and nature of the one being named or his or her calling. Names were often picked by a person in authority. God gave Adam authority, remember.

Names usually had meaning. Many times the name signified position, function, or relationships. Sometimes it was chosen prophetically. For example, Jesus or Yeshua means "The Lord Saves." [Matt. 1:21; Luke 1:31] Or the name may have related to a circumstance of birth. For example, Jacob means "heel catcher" or "supplanter," since he came out of his mother's womb holding the heel of his twin, Esau. [Gen. 25:26]

Naming is still important in most cultures. Americans tend to pick names for sound or association, more than for meaning. Most parents everywhere carefully choose their child's name. A person's name may influence his or her character, calling, and destiny because of the power of words. ("Jean" means "gift of God" — which I strive to be.) Johnny Cash sang a song about a man named "Sue" which made him tough from the ridicule. Being called nicknames, like "stupid" or "smart," influences children strongly, too.

In the Bible, the Lord sometimes gives a person a new name when that person enters a covenant relationship with Him. A covenant signals a major life change or a change in the character of that person. Abram (exalted father) became Abraham (father of a multitude). Abram's wife, Sarai (contentious) became Sarah (princess). Jacob was renamed Israel (he who strives with God). Jesus gave Simon (hearing) the additional name of Peter (rock). A friend of mine told me about a cabdriver, who after becoming a Christian, legally changed his name from "Sin" to "Christianson."

Walking my dogs some years ago, I met a boy. Mike (not his real name) lived in a rundown house in a neighborhood not far from the path I walked. Mike joined me on my daily walks with the dogs. Mike and I became friends. During one of our walks, Mike said their dog's name was Satan. The name disturbed me. Such an evil name! The name "Satan" demeaned the dog, and revealed something about the namer. Satan lived with them and their lives were hell. I began praying for Mike and his family. Thank God, Mike was making an effort to escape the poverty of mind and body. He attended a good church and sought out friends like Mom and me.

Mike told me his father was an abusive alcoholic. (Mike was rightly afraid of the brutal man.) Not long after we met, Mike's father shot himself, in front of his family. We lost track of Mike. His family moved and so did we. I've often wondered what became of Mike (and his dog). What a contrast Mike's life was to the peace and love that Mom and I knew with our animals. Samson brought sunlight into our home and hearts. There's something significant about names we bear and choose.

There is some God-given inclination within us that prompts us to name our animals good names. We are all sons and daughters of Adam. God wished the animals to be named. God's wishes are programmed into our consciousness. Like Adam, the names we choose reflect the value we place on each animal. It also reflects the value we place on ourselves and things around us.

What sort of meanings did those first names hold? How and why did Adam pick the names? Did Adam name the animals to identify species and families of animals, or did he give them individual names? Or both? In picking a name, did Adam focus on a character quality or other trait, or a circumstance which reminded him of the animal? I wish we knew. The Lord knew that naming something gives it worth. It's a piece of the puzzle to answer Mom's question.

ADAM AND THE FIRST ANIMALS

What were those first animals like? What relationship did Adam form with those animals? What happened at that "naming party?" Lacking eyewitnesses, we must rely on other evidence. All we have is the Bible and traditions. We can glean enough to reconstruct a bit of the scene. (This is where my legal training becomes useful.) Bear with me as we make a case.

The few things we glean from Genesis include: all were vegetarian; communication between species, including man, was uninhibited; harmony and love prevailed or ruled; and the God of the Universes walked among them daily.

Eat your vegetables!

"Eat your vegetables," was the admonition from the beginning. (Maybe even "eat your broccoli"!) From Scripture, we learn man and beast began as vegetarians. God told Adam that plants were for food for man and animals. [Gen. 1:29-30] Flesh-eating may not have occurred until after the Great Flood of Noah. [Gen. 9] That would have made Noah's task for feeding the tigers and lions easier! There is a promise that carnivorous behavior will end in the new creation, or Heaven. [Isaiah 11] From tiny plankton to trees which provide fruit, nuts, leaves, bark and wood, plants of all kinds still provide the "staff of life" for the animal kingdom, directly or indirectly.

What were those first animals like? Without the ability to time-travel, it remains a guess. Science may look at prehistoric bones but cannot truly prove the past. Bones cannot tell us about intelligence, character traits, or social structures of the animals. Studying living animals may not give an accurate portrait of how their ancestors were in Eden. Reconstructing the past is as difficult as predicting the future. By analogy, different juries hearing the same case might or might not reach the same verdict.

LEFTOVERS

It is difficult to imagine what the pre-Fall earth was like. Eden, the Garden of God, must have been heaven on earth. In Hebrew, Eden means *delight* or *pleasure*. What most of us have known in this life as delight or pleasure would fall far short of Eden. The image that comes to me is arriving very late for a lavish banquet. The master chef's artistry is demolished. Only leftovers are strewn about the table in disarray. The freshness and beauty are gone. Decay has entered the banquet room. It doesn't even smell as good. That's what the earth is like now. Our view of Eden is skewed.

Patterned after heaven, the first Eden knew no decay, pain or death. Everything was beautiful. [Rev. 21:4] No cruelty or corruption marred Eden. God, man and animal were in harmony. Every living thing was perfect and healthy, and of good temperament. Total peace and harmony ruled.

Even now, in its fallen state, some of earth's wilderness areas reveal harmony and incredible peace. The premise of "survival of the fittest" is a lie. I have experienced that peace and harmony in wilderness areas where humans had not been in years. Entering a deep forest or gazing upon glaciated mountains garlanded with ice and dancing streams, I have felt the same quiet awe that I feel in a church where God is worshiped. A calm peace exists there, seldom felt in areas filled with humans. Such harmony is not available anywhere among men, except where the Lord God is worshipped. Perhaps it is because creation – except humans — willingly worships our Creator.

Untouched by human cruelty, wilderness animals are usually unafraid and often exhibit sensibilities unlike those dulled by cruelty and other vices of man. Consider Charles Darwin's words:

*No man can stand in the tropic forests without feeling that
they are temples filled with the various productions of
the God of nature, and that there is more in man than the
breath of his body.[4]*

The Bible says in the beginning, the new earth was watered in the
morning by a mist. A cool breeze blew in the evenings. God and man
walked together. [Gen. 2:6 & 8] Don't you know the animals trailed
along? Dogs, cats, horses, birds, elephants, kangaroos, monkeys and
meerkats joined God and man in fellowship. Mine treat me that way
when I go for a walk. I recall not just dogs and cats, but our horses
and cows following us around. One horse liked blackberry picking –
we picked; he ate from our hands.

What beauty Eden's occupants shared! Eden must have been
a feast for the eyes, a symphony for the ears, a delight to the nose
and palette, and a sensory tapestry to touch. But the king and queen
of pleasures must have been the sweet fellowship between God and
Adam, and between Adam and the animals.

TALKING ANIMALS?

From ancient times, people have believed the first animals could
talk, think, feel and make moral choices. Have you ever spoken to an
animal and swore it understood you? Or had it understand without
a word from you! Most animal lovers have. All animals evidence
communication skills, even if primarily nonverbal.

That's not crazy. Why would books, movies and television with
talking animals be so popular -- from *Babe* and *The Horse Whisperer*
to the old "Francis the talking mule" movies, and the old TV program
Mr. Ed? Parables, myths, and fables dating back thousands of years
have animals talking among themselves and to humans. Whether
Adam spoke the language of the animals, or the animals spoke like
men, there may be something to this legend.

From the growl of bears to the dance of the honeybees, all living
creatures appear to communicate. In fact, animal behaviorists are

discovering they not only communicate, but have complex social structures. For examples, see *Amazing Animals*,[5] Felicity Brooks, *Usborne Science and Nature: Animal Behavior*,[6] and *Mysteries of Animal Intelligence* by Sherry Hansen Steiger and Brad Steiger. Google "animal intelligence" or search Amazon.com and a number of titles will come up. Looking at the table of contents of *The Smartest Animals on the Planet* by Sally Boysen & Deborah Custance, reveals that: animals from birds to sea otters, to rats to elephants, use tools; animals, from honeybees to whales, communicate – apes have learned human sign language; animals learn by imitation and "social learning;" animals evidence self-recognition and numerical abilities; and animals show cooperation with and altruism to others.

It's it obvious that "complex social structures" require communication skills? The "language" may be primarily "body language" -- a mix of sounds or gestures, but that can be very effective. This is no surprise to most animal owners. All of my animals, from cats to dogs to horses to cows to geese, have understood me when I spoke to them. They clearly read body language – both mine and that of other animals. That is the common experience of all animal observers. The fact is, animals are remarkably good at understanding humans.

Brad and Sherrie Steiger instigated an experiment using human language with their Labrador Retriever, Moses. Moses developed a remarkable understanding of human language.[7] The Steigers learned that silent-movie producer, J. Allen Boone, read daily to the famed German Shepherd, Strongheart (first major dog movie star), who showed remarkable intelligence. The Steigers read the Bible to Moses daily and said a prayer with him. The Steigers spoke to Moses as though he were a child rather than a "dumb animal." Soon Moses did exactly as he was told even when the owners gave no voice inflection or physical motion with the words. The Steigers kept records. The Steigers concluded the dog understood not just words but conversations; and Moses also could problem-solve.

The Steigers collected animal intelligence and communication stories. A favorite of mine is the account of a small girl who climbed into the pen of a supposedly dangerous rhino. The child and rhino achieved instant communication — something no other human had ever done. The huge rhino became "a love rag" in the little girls' hands.[8] This child had "dominion" over this beast, in the send of Genesis 1, I believe.

HORSE TALK

From his youth, Monty Roberts observed wild horses in Nevada and learned the language of horses.[9] Becoming a master at it, Roberts used horse language to effectively and gently train roping, gaming, and race horses, as well as other animals. Roberts calls himself a horse *gentler*, not a horse *breaker*. Roberts' philosophy and life experience in "joining up" with horses, deer, and other animals excites me. It matches my own amateur experience.

Through gentleness, humans can become a productive team with animals. If asked to do so, such animals will injure or kill themselves to please their human masters. Cruelty, on the other hand, breaks an animal's spirit, resulting in a poor slave rather than a working companion. Or worse, creates a man-hating beast. But, man working in partnership with an animal is one of the most beautiful things in the world.

Monty Roberts and those like him, prove beyond a doubt that animals have a language and will work willingly with humans when humans understand and treat them properly. Roberts (who was endorsed by the Queen of England) and Buck Brannaman[10] have both influenced modern horse training for the better. Brannaman, another "horse gentler," was a consultant for the movie, *The Horse Whisperer*. Their work provides insights into how horses communicate. Roberts holds seminars to instruct in the language of horses.

LOVE IN THE GARDEN OF EDEN

I can see Adam developing a personal relationship with each animal. Adam must have learned each animal's likes and dislikes, character traits, strengths and talents. Each personality became dear to Adam, don't you think? The first animals, fresh from the Creator's hand, would have been full of love. Can't you see Adam, caretaker of the earth, spending time with each animal? Adam would be petting heads and scratching behind ears, and the animals licking and nuzzling Adam. How they must have loved one another, this first man and these first animals.

This is not so strange. Many of you have bonds with domestic animals. Trainers and naturalists have bonded with lions, gorillas, and other animals (in captivity and in the wild). There are well publicized accounts, like Elsie the lion, Koko the gorilla, Dian Fossey's wild gorillas, as well as Namu the killer whale. In recent years a video has circulated the Internet about "Christian" the lion, who was raised in captivity and released to the wild, but still knew and loved his human "parents" -- even after one and two years. These human observers knew these animals as sentient beings — as personalities who gave and received affection. The shadow of Adam and the Garden falls long!

ST. FRANCIS OF ASSISSI

In the person of St. Francis of Assisi, church history perhaps provides the closest example to what Adam had with animals. Born in Italy in 1182 A.D., Francis converted to Christianity as a young man. Francis was faithful in his spiritual journey until his passing in 1226. Founder of the Franciscan order in the Roman Catholic church, Francis is one of the most loved and pivotal figures in Christian history. Francis' prayer, "Make me an instrument of Thy peace," is still repeated today in word and song.

Of importance here was Francis' relationship with animals. Francis developed his relationship with animals when he spent time in woods and fields, sleeping on the ground. To Francis, both animals and man belonged to God and were loved by their Creator. Francis called animals "brother" and "sister." Francis had a democratic catholic faith which treated man and beast universally alike.

Legend has it that Francis' first congregation consisted of a flock of birds. Seeing a gathering of a large number of birds of different varieties, Francis began to preach. More birds came. The birds remained motionless, even as Francis moved among them and touched them. Francis told the birds they owed much to God, since they had the freedom to fly, wonderful and colorful clothing, food without work, and the ability to sing. Francis discussed birds preservation in Noah's ark and the environment which was theirs to enjoy. His sermon allegedly ended with:

> *So the Creator loves you very much, since He gives you so many good things. Therefore, my little bird sisters, be careful not to be ungrateful, but strive always to praise God." [The birds began to] spread their wings, and reverently bow their heads to the ground, showing by their movements and their songs that the words St. Francis was saying gave them great pleasure. ... Finally, when he had finished preaching to them and urging them to praise God, St. Francis . . . gave them permission to leave. Then all the birds rose up into the air simultaneously, and in the air they sang a wonderful song.*[11]

While there is no way to confirm or deny Francis' story, there is evidence of similar experiences today. Entertainer Pat Boone wrote in one of his books that crickets joined him one evening as he sang praises on his parents' porch in Tennessee. As a professional musician, Mr. Boone would know when the random cricket "songs" changed to harmonize with his vocalization.

I have seen my own pets respond to the Gospel. During prayer meetings, my late Siamese "Kitty," acted as though she were in catnip when we sang praises to God. Kitty did the same thing when I sang in the Spirit alone. (Kitty came to me for prayer when injured or ill, and received healing.) Others have told me of their animals behaving in similar ways. "Let everything that has breath praise the Lord!" is a Scripture which says more than most folks realize. [Ps. 150:6]

Another favorite story of Francis concerns a large wolf which was terrorizing an Italian town, eating both humans and animals. Unafraid, Francis went to find the wolf.[12] Upon finding the animal, Francis admonished the wolf about terrorizing this town, whereupon the wolf cowed at his feet in sorrow. After they reached an agreement, the wolf walked back into town with Francis. The frightened townspeople were introduced to the wolf by Francis. The people agreed to feed the wolf and the wolf never hurt anyone again. Due to Francis' intervention, the wolf lived as friend to the townsmen until it died several years later. To this day, there are images of a wolf connected to the town of Gubbio, Italy. The Scripture, "Blessed are the peacemakers for they shall be called sons of God" [Matt. 5:9] takes on a new meaning, doesn't it?

Another report involves St. Anthony of Padua (ca. 1195-1231), an associate of St. Francis.[13] Unsuccessful in trying to convince persons in the town of Rimini of the true faith, Anthony went to the mouth of the nearby river. There he called to the fishes in God's name since the faithless Rimini heretics refused to listen to the word of God.

And as soon as he said that, all of a sudden such a great throng of large and small fishes gathered before him as had never before been seen in that sea or river.[14]

The idea of these fish with their heads out of the water looking at Anthony — big fish beside the small fish — seems unreal. Once the fish gathered, Anthony preached to them in a fashion similar to Francis with his birds. Anthony reminded the fish of the greatness of their freedom, provision, and privileges from God their Creator. Anthony referred to the Bible, which states that a great fish rescued Jonah the prophet; another fish offered tribute money for our Lord Jesus; and still others became food for Jesus, the Eternal King. At these words, the fish opened their mouths and nodded their heads, giving signs of their reverence. When the townspeople of Rimini came and saw the fish, they were shamed into listening to Anthony and repented. Anthony dismissed the fishes with a blessing. The fish swam away, "expressing their joy and applause in amazing games and gambols."[15]

REAL AND COUNTERFEIT COMMUNICATION

Some claim to have the ability to communicate with animals nonverbally or telepathically today. See for example, Beatrice Lydecker, *What The Animals Tell Me*; Lydecker writes of her experiences of being able to share or experience animals' "feelings, thoughts, direct factual information, memories, and past experiences." She wrote that she is a practicing Christian and denied that her "gift" of talking to animals was occult or supernatural. (p. xi) Her anecdotes are remarkable, but not incredible.

In reading various accounts and knowing the gifts of the Holy Spirit [1 Cor. 14], I know God could give people the ability to know an animal's mind or memory. The Lord does that in gifts of healing for people. I am not alone in "knowing" things about animals which appear to be beyond normal observation.

At the same time, I am skeptical when such abilities appear to be based in occult or ESP practices. These are often counterfeits of the Lord's spiritual gifts which are taboo or warned against in Scripture. (It can be challenging to verify which are God's gifts and which are not.)

I have no doubt that we have some like St. Francis and St. Anthony among us today — gifted in understanding animals' own languages and communicating with animals. Not all of that "gifting" is supernatural. Most animal-human communication just requires intelligent observation to learn how the animals communicate, and to teach the animals what we are saying, too.

Was Adam able to commune with the animals more than Francis, Anthony or Monty Roberts? It's very probable. Adam's God-given job was to care for the Garden, including the animals. God surely gave Adam natural and supernatural abilities to understand and care for each different species. It makes sense to me!

JOHN WESLEY'S THEOLOGY

John Wesley was an Anglican priest and forefather of Methodism. Wesley believed God endued animals with innate principles of self-motion, understanding, will, and liberty (freedom of choice) -- just the same as man, although perhaps in different degrees. Wesley believed animals possess moral goodness and are beautiful, and that animals were created immortal.[16] That matches my observations. Don't you agree?

Wesley further believed that only man is "capable of God," that is, of knowing, loving and obeying God; and that animals obey and love God through knowing, obeying and loving man. That was his explanation of why, when Adam sinned, all creation was subject to the penalty.[17] Scripture and human experience do *not* bear out Wesley's idea that God and animals communicate only through man.

For example, the Lord told Elijah that He, God, was commanding the ravens to bring Elijah food during the time Elijah was hiding from King Ahab during the drought. 1 Kings 17:4-6. The Ravens who fed Elijah surely got their orders directly from the Lord. [1 Kings 17] There are other examples of the Lord communicating directly with animals, but this is enough to disprove that particular point.

Nonetheless, most of Wesley's ideas are sound in my opinion. Men and animals communicated in the Garden, as Adam and Eve conversed with a serpent. [Gen. 3]. God made Man steward over all creation. Therefore, God's garden and the animals will only thrive if man is a good steward. The best stewardship requires understanding of what the creation is "saying." Man is the primary channel of blessing to the whole creation, as well as a major channel of neglect and destruction. Man's fall from grace affected the whole earth. Wesley is not alone in his beliefs. That is pretty much universally believed.

PURPOSE ACCOMPLISHED

In short, Adam came into a vital relationship with every animal at the first naming party. The Lord wisely accomplished His purpose.

Man was established as a steward over all living things, plants and animals.

To communicate is to establish a relationship. The more you communicate with someone, the more intimately you know them and they with you. The same is true of animals. That is why when you have a pet for many years, its death or loss is a very painful thing. Relationship is the foundation for love.

God saw to it that man and animals had relationship. Adam's relationship with those first animals must have been awesome. Sin had not yet entered the world. Nothing was "wild" in the sense of being an enemy to humans or to other animals. There was no disorder, no confusion. Nothing killed nor ate each other. The lion lay down with the lamb, and the ox and bear ate grass together. When God walked the earth in the cool of the evening, can't you see the animals gathering around, too. I'll bet Adam was not the only one who sought out the company of the Creator. Those loving animals would likely not be left out! Mine sure get pushy to be with me. What a frolic! What a delightful pleasure!

Everything that had breath praised the Lord and rejoiced in God's goodness and His gifts. Wonderful peace and harmony existed in all creation. It was the Garden of Eden — the Paradise we lost.

ENDNOTES:

1.   See, R. J. Rushdoony, *The Institutes of Biblical Law*, supra, p. 124-126.

2.   *Adam's Task*, pp. 47-48

3.   R. J. Rushdoony, in *The Institutes of Biblical Law*, [The Craig Press, 1973], (p. 124-126) discusses naming. He also, as part of his interpretation of the Sixth Commandment (You shall not murder) speaks of God's laws relating to animals, including insects, and our relationship to them and the earth at pp. 255-262. He covers hybridization, bestiality, and man's attempts at being god over creation. See also, W. Pratney's *Healing the Land*, supra, for an enlightening discussion of animals, plants and insects in God's order and plan.

4.   Charles Darwin, quoted from *Evolution in Science and Religion* by R. A. Millikan, [New Haven: Yale University Press, 1927], at p. 60. I was told before he died, Charles Darwin repented of his advocacy of a Godless world and his theory of evolution. His writings belie a true atheism..

5.   *Time-Life Books*

6.   Usborned Publ. 1992

7.   *Mysteries of Animal Intelligence*, [Tor Book, 1995]

8.   Id., pp. 1-7, 122-124

9.   *The Man Who Listens to Horses*, by Monty Roberts [Random House, 1996, 1997]

10.   See Paul Tarchtman's article in *The Smithsonian*, "The Horse Whisperer; Legendary Trainer Buck Brannaman.." Buck Brannaman is a Wyoming cowboy who taught Robert Redford to handle horses with "Brannaman's touch" for "The Horse Whisperer." The two men's techniques are both are based on communication, i.e., horse language. The article also references J. Allen Boone, *A Kinship With All Life*, which speaks of communication and consciousness in living things.

11.   Raphael Brown, trans. *The Little Flowers of St. Francis*, [Image Books; Doubleday, 1958], p. 76-77

12.   Id., pp. 88-91; 320-322

13.   Id., pp. 131-133

14.   Id.

15.   Id.

16.   *Sermons of John Wesley*, Sermon 60, p. 440

17.   Id.

CHAPTER 7

THE FALL OF MAN AND THE ANIMALS

And the Lord God took the man and put him in the garden of Eden to tend and keep it. And the Lord God commanded the man, saying, "Of every tree of the garden you may freely eat; but of the tree of the knowledge of good and evil you shall not eat, for in the day that you eat of it you shall surely die." Gen. 2:15-17 [NKJ]

So when the woman saw that the tree was good for food, that is was pleasant to the eyes, and a tree desirable to make one wise, she took of its fruit and ate. She also gave to her husband with her, and he ate. Gen. 3:6 [NKJ]

"Cursed is the ground for your sake; In toil you shall eat of it all the days of your life. ... In the sweat of your face you shall eat bread till you return to the ground, For out of the ground you were taken; for dust you are, and to dust you shall return." ... Also for Adam and his wife [Eve] the Lord God made tunics of skin, and clothed them. ... the Lord God sent him out of the garden of Eden to till the ground from which he was taken.
Gen. 3:17, 19, 21, 22[NKJ]

THE BIBLE IS BLOODY

S ome people avoid the Bible because of the bloodshed. From cover to cover the Bible is bloody with slain animals. The bleeding starts immediately after the fall when God clothes Adam and Eve[1] with animal skins. The Bible records events, such as the dedication of Solomon's temple, when hundreds and even thousands of animals were ritually killed.[2] Thousands of bulls, goats, and sheep were sacrificed and their blood poured on the temple altar. The priests and Levites, at such sacrifices, likely stood deep in blood and gore within the Lord's temple. It must have been a nauseous experience to anyone not hardened to blood and death – or given grace to handle the carnage.

Animal sacrifice seems very cruel. Why would a loving God require the lives of innocent, sweet-natured animals? To answer Mom's question, we must address this difficult question. In the next two chapters, we will attempt to do so.

A LICENSE FOR CRUELTY?

Too often such cruelty is justified by using Scripture. God's command for animal sacrifices has been misconstrued as a license for cruelty to animals. This, in turn, has offended many animal lovers, and caused them to turn away from the Bible and its God.

What sort of God requires the lives of countless animals? What kind of God allows human cruelties to animals? As I prayed about this, this thought occurred to me. If a person, who knew nothing of modern medicine, watched a surgeon performing open heart surgery, what would he or she think? Wouldn't that uninformed person wrongly conclude the doctor was brutally cruel?

Our ignorance of God and His ways clouds our judgment in the same way. Some people never get beyond the slaughter to know the truth. What good reason would the God -- who is Love -- have to require the bloodshed of guiltless animals? Keeping an open mind, let's explore what the Bible says.

ADAM'S DISOBEDIENCE

What does this have to do with Mom's question, you may ask? "How relevant is this to whether my dog or cat will be in heaven?"

In the seeds of Genesis are the hidden images of the heaven and earth to come. Key pieces of the puzzle which answers Mom's question are in these first short chapters of the Bible.

We must know where we came from to understand where we are heading. We don't get to heaven by accident. We must learn how to get to heaven. Besides, we appreciate most those things we had to take action to obtain.

To understand God and the role of animals, we must examine Adam's disobedience. Everything on earth changed with Adam's disobedience. We need to understand what was lost to know what may be regained in heaven. Read this in Genesis Chapters 2 and 3.

DON'T EAT - DON'T DIE

Let's look closely at this first problem in paradise. God had given Adam – male and female — one job: Care for the garden. Also, God gave one command, the first law: Don't eat from one tree, or you will die that very day. A simple command. Adam (male and female) could eat anything they wanted from any plant except one — the tree of the knowledge of good and evil.

Would you find that hard to obey? (I'm not sure about me. I like to think I'm a good, basically obedient type person, but I've done too many ornery or stupid things.) We already know the variety offered was and is endless. Why are the forbidden things so attractive?

THE WILEY SERPENT

Now the serpent was more subtle and crafty than any liv-
ing creature of the field which the Lord God had made. And
he [Satan] said to the woman, Can it really be that God has
said, You shall not eat of every tree of the garden?

Gen. 3:1[Ampl.]

Among the animals in Eden, there lived a certain snake — a very wise and crafty beast. We will talk more about him later on. This serpent is mentioned in Revelation 12:9-13, 15-17; Isa. 27:1; Ps. 74:14; 104:26; & Job 41. Job says this serpent was created to be "king over all the sons of pride." [Job 41:34] Legend says this Serpent had legs on which he walked about; and he was very beautiful. Legend also has it this Serpent was a real fast talker.

This snake questioned Eve about the forbidden fruit. Eve listened. There was no reason not to trust this intelligent animal — unless "crafty" is a clue. Newly created, this woman had no experience of deceit.

And the woman said to the serpent, "... from the fruit of
the tree which is in the middle of the garden, God has said,
'You shall not eat from it or touch it, lest you die.'" Gen. 3:3

Because of that con-artist snake's subtle questions, the woman's understanding of God's simple command became twisted. It still happens today. Eve made several mistakes. Eve added to and took away from God's command. She added "touch it" and took away the "surely," the certainty of death. [Compare Gen. 2:17 with Gen. 3:3.]

That paved the way for what followed – a fatal mistake. Eve began to examine the forbidden fruit. (There's a difference between healthy and unhealthy curiosity.) Eve found the forbidden fruit attractive. It was gourmet food, delightful to look at, and desirable to make one wise. Three wonderful things, right? Can't you hear her brain work: "What could it hurt to take one little bite?"

That lying serpent persuaded the First Couple that the forbidden Tree of the Knowledge of Good and Evil was a good thing. The Tree would make them like God! [Gen. 3:1-5]

Neither human rejected the snake's distortion of the truth. The man knew God's command. He stood by and did nothing. Rather than dealing with the snake and confronting the woman, he joined his woman in eating the fruit. Perhaps it seemed easier. Perhaps both were seduced by the promise of power. Knowledge is power after all.

So did God not want man to have the knowledge of good and evil? Did God not want man to be like Him? "No" is the correct answer to both. The Bible is clear that God made man in His own image and created humans to become His sons and daughters. The issue of obtaining any power is that we obtain it safely and use it wisely. God loves us, therefore He is the only safe source from which to obtain power. God wants us to gain knowledge, especially of good and evil, from Himself, not man's enemy, Satan.

Our ancestors rejected their Creator and attempted to be his and her own god. How foolish to think we can become "like God." In one sense, we already are, since we are made in His image. But, we are created beings. God is the uncreated Creator. God has all power, all wisdom, all understanding; and He is the source of all knowledge. As neither my dog nor my child can become me, I cannot become God.

Adam and Eve fell for it. They disobeyed God's first law. Adam chose to eat the forbidden fruit.

FALL OF MAN

Theologians refer to Adam's disobedience, his sin, as the "Fall of Man." This Fall resulted in immediate changes.

First, Adam and his wife became ashamed and confused. Anyone who covers their private parts with tree leaves is clearly mortified and confused.

Second, major foolish fear flooded Adam and Eve. They hid from God, the only Being Who both loved them and Who could help them.

Third, Adam lied to God. God knows everything we think, do, and say, even before we do or say it — and loves us anyway. How dumb it is to lie to God!

Fourth, Adam, man and woman, rationalized their mistakes by passing the blame. The man blamed God for giving him the woman

AND blamed the woman for giving him the fruit. Blaming God takes either a lot of guts or little sense. (Adam had no "temporary insanity" defense.) The woman had no one else to blame, so she blamed the snake. Neither owned up to their own responsibility. Imagine that!

A CHANGED WORLD

The day Adam and Eve took a bite of the forbidden fruit, the world changed. We still live with the consequences. Because God assigned Adam (male and female) dominion over all the earth, everything under Adam's authority went down with them. When man sinned, all of creation was subjected to "futility." (Rom. 8:20) It does not take a theologian to see a proverbial Pandora's Box of good and evil was opened.

All creation is connected. Ask any biologist. Adam's Fall set off a chain reaction felt to this day. Adam's sin affected the land and all living creatures. Kill the trees, insects die; kill the insects, birds die; kill the birds, carnivores die. Everything we do affects others. It's the ripple or "butterfly" effect. As a stone thrown in a pond sends ripples to the shore, so good words and deeds benefit others, who do the same, on and on. Evil words and deeds ripple also, effecting grief, pain and death.

For instance, when someone commits a crime, or when married couples break their marriage vows, or people abuse each other, that person affects all around them. His or her families (adults, children, and animals), health, finances and employment suffer. All are altered, even shattered. Ultimately, lawless deeds and divorce affect the community, state, and nation negatively. When people live righteously, that likewise affects society for good, as stable families, healthy people, and prosperity are produced by good behavior. Studies have proven this (if you need studies). Adam's sin infected all human offspring and the whole earth. In a "butterfly effect,"[3] that one "little" sin produced a tremendous tidal wave of death and destruction only God could stop.

DEATH CAME THROUGH ADAM'S DISOBEDIENCE

In the day Adam ate the forbidden fruit, death came – as God promised. God saw it arrive, riding Adam's disobedience. Like a parent watching his child fall into a fire, it had to be a terrible thing to behold. Like a fire in a wind storm, sin and death spread to all creation — to all the things God referred to as "very good." Death's effect would impact all under Adam's authority. [Romans 8:20-21.] This sin entered Adam's essence; all Adam's offspring have this fatal tendency to sin. [Romans 6]

Imagine what happened to the Garden. The darkness of disobedience and death flooded the Garden. This darkness permeated everything. Like an evil fog, such darkness continues to cover this earth. Because we were born in that fog, we cannot know what was lost. We truly see, as through darkened glass, only a shadow of what was, and what will be. [1 Cor. 13:12]

While the animals were innocent — except for that crafty serpent — the Fall brought death to them, too. Animals were affected by Adam's sin. But we all experience the effects of our own and other's sins, don't we!

GOD'S LAW AND ORDER

Adam's disobedience to God's commandment or law brought the forewarned consequences — *death*. God is holy and just. God is the source of all law, of all that is good. God's law is holy and good. [Rom. 7:12, 16; 1 Tim. 1:8] Without God-based law, there are anarchy, chaos, and death. This principle is illustrated in history and science. (God's Word is His law.)

To understand the Fall we need to look at the nature of God's laws. I see two types of laws operating in nature. The first type is immutable or unchangeable. The second is variable. I believe both operate from God's being.

UNCHACHANGEABLE LAWS

The Bible says God does not change. [Malachi 3:6] The immutable or unchangeable laws originate in God's very substance or being, and His nature or character. These laws cannot change.

The Bible describes His substance. For example: (1) God is the Rock. [Deut. 32:15; Isa. 26:4; 1 Pet. 2:8]. (2) He is breath and Spirit, and the Divine Wind (same word – different meanings). [Gen. 1:2; Job 33:4; John 3:5-8 & 4:24]. (3) God is light. [Ps. 27:1; John 1:9 & 8:12; James 1:17] We see these as the laws of science or nature. Rocks, wind, and light all involve physical laws which are constants.

Looking at just one physical attribute is a lesson: God "dwells in unapproachable light"; and God is light with no darkness in Him at all. [Ex. 33:20; 1 Tim. 6:16; James 1:17; 1 John 1:5.] God is also a consuming fire. [Heb. 12:29] This explains why the Bible warns that no mortal flesh can see God and live. No travel agent books vacations to the sun – and God is far more powerful than our little sun.[4] Fire consumes flesh – a painful experience at best. Obviously, if you and I are to fellowship closely with God, we must be changed.

All immutable laws, like those of light, emanate from God's being, nature, or substance. These are the foundations of physical laws of energy, matter, and velocity — as well as spiritual laws governing character and behavior.

God's nature or character is also unchangeable. For example: (1) God cannot lie. [Num. 23:19] (2) God cannot be unfaithful. [1 Tim. 2:13). (3) Since God is love, it follows that He cannot be unloving. [1 John 4: 8 & 16] (4) God's Spirit is Wisdom, so God cannot be unwise or foolish. [Isa. 11:1; & Prov. 8:12]

Just as the leopard cannot change his spots, God cannot change — or He wouldn't be God! The Living God is the source of all immutable laws.

CHANGEABLE LAWS

The second kind of law may be changed. This type of law comes from God's will, His mind, or heart. For examples consider these:

(1) When God was going to destroy the whole earth, one man, Noah, caused Him to change His plan. [Gen. 6] (2) Abraham almost talked God out of destroying Sodom and Gommorah, where his nephew Lot lived. [Gen. 19:16-33] (3) When Moses was leading the Hebrew people from Egyptian slavery to freedom in Canaan, Moses was alone with God on the mountain receiving God's Law, the Commandments. The Lord interrupted their meeting and told Moses the people made and were worshiping a gold calf. Like a husband finding his wife in bed with another, God was furious. God decided to destroy the Israelites and start over. Moses talked God out of this plan and God changed his mind. [Ex. 32.1-14]

Therefore, God can change His mind or will. People who pray to God, especially intercessors or "prayer warriors," know that. So did Balaam's donkey. It's a heart thing.

COMPARING THE TWO LAWS

To illustrate, consider a parent disciplining a child about fire's dangers. Dad says, "Child, fire is hot. If you touch the fire, it will burn you." If the child disobeys, he or she is burned. Immutable laws are self-executing. Dad may say instead: "Play with that fire, and I will punish you." If the child plays with fire, then Dad has to choose to punish the child in a separate act. It's easy to see the difference. The first the parent cannot control, but the second, he can.

Both kind of rules train and protect. "Love" without limits is not love at all. Every child will test a parent, teacher, or other person in authority, to see where the limits are. Security lies within those limits. Most children and animals sense that.

Smart parents don't change such rules – unless wisdom and mercy demand it. Compromise sends the wrong message — the message that laws and rules may be disobeyed. Good parents do not compromise the law. Most criminals believe they will succeed in crime. They probably became lawbreakers because they got away with wrongdoing as children. God is a smart parent. God disciplines those He loves. [Heb. 12]

WHICH LAW FITS THE FIRST COMMANDMENT?

Was the first commandment, about the tree of knowledge, based on an immutable law or God's will? The Bible is not clear. Personally, I think it was a mix: Like the kid playing with fire, Adam got burned, so the punishment was built in. But there were elements of God's will in this first commandment which permitted God to act mercifully.

The Commandment said: In "the day" Adam ate the forbidden fruit, he would "die." Genesis 3:22 says God has the knowledge of good and evil. Evidently that knowledge can be as lethal as fire. When Adam ate the fruit, he took a destructive fire into his flesh. Adam was not ready to handle such knowledge, any more than an infant can handle fire. Fire and knowledge can be killers, as well as forces of good!

With that fatal disobedience, sin mastered man. Like a disease, it entered his vital parts. Sin attached itself to Adam's genetic essence, and began working death in all sin touches. A war started. First, war burned inside Adam. Then the war spread to all creation. It is a war of the good and holy against sinful, evil, destructive forces -- a battle between of the image of God in us against the serpent's lie that "I can do it my way. I can be my own boss or god"

Many have attempted to describe Eden and the Fall. For example, John Milton, in the 1600's, wrote the epic poem "Paradise Lost" – which is brilliant still. Yet, words are inadequate to describe what living humans have never known. How can one describe a rainbow or a rose to one born blind? Can you describe the melodies of birds or sounds of water to the deaf? Can you teach numb fingers how a baby's skin or silky feel of cashmere or cotton feels like? Can a man who has never left a desert understand what a rain forest looks and smells like? Adam's Fall makes us all blind, deaf, and senseless – dead men – lost without the Lord of Life and His Paradise. We do not truly know what human sin destroyed. Adam lost something wonderful, and we are still paying the price.

WHO OR WHAT WAS THAT SNAKE?

Who or what was that serpent? How did that crafty serpent react? I suspect the first sounds of devilish laughter were heard in the earth. Like shattering glass, Satan's mocking broke the tranquility of pristine creation. Satan surely laughed at man's foolishness to believe eating fruit could make man like God. (A created thing can never become the un-created Creator. Man cannot be God.) This sound heralded disaster. All creation must have given its first long collective groan. Or maybe it was a scream. [Rom. 8:22; Jer. 12:4 & 11]

The Bible identifies that serpent as *"Satan." "Satan"* is a Hebrew word. It means *adversary. Devil* is a Greek word for slanderer. These terms became the crafty reptile's names because it continues to deceive and torment humans. Satan nearly destroyed Job. [Job, Chapters 1& 2.] Jesus called Satan a "liar" and the "father of lies." [John 8:44] Satan appears as an angel of light, and his servants appear as righteous. [2 Cor. 11:13-15] Temptation, as Eve and Adam learned, was Satan's key to gain power over humans. Satan tried to gain control over Jesus Christ through temptation, just as he did the first man. [John 8:44; Matt. 4:3; 1 John 2:16] Thank God, Satan failed. What an animal!

The physical description of this ancient serpent is riveting. We don't know his size in Eden, but the Devil is no little humanoid. The Biblical Satan is not a red imp with horns and a spear. John, in Revelation 12, saw Satan as a terrifying being of immense size and power, a huge red dragon with seven heads, whose tail could sweep one-third of the stars from heaven. John said Satan has his own angels or messengers, and is "the accuser of the brethren" before God.

Isaiah described Satan as "leviathan," "the fleeing" and "twisted" serpent who "lives in the sea."; Isaiah also prophesied Satan's final destruction. [Isa. 27:1] The Psalmist said: leviathan is many-headed; and that it "sports" in the sea. [Psalm 74:14 & Psalm 104:26]. To Job, God described leviathan as a fierce, mocking beast, which no man can subdue or vanquish, and a being which the Lord made without fear, like nothing else on earth. This terrible beast is "king over all the sons of pride." [Job 3:8; & Job 41, especially 41:29-34]

Scripture describes Satan as a being which modern man has no record of seeing in the flesh. Whether fact or metaphor, the Biblical Satan is a powerful dragon-like beast[5] which no human can control or defeat. Did God create Satan – a superior animal -- to take down prideful disobedient humans?[6] It makes sense to me.

Only this serpent's Creator has more power over humans. The Bible says the devil's role is as the deceiver of man will stop only at the end of this age, when Satan will be thrown to doom. [Rev. 20:10]. Meanwhile, we must deal with this dangerous animal God's way, or be destroyed — just as Adam and Eve were.

THE EFFECT OF THE FALL ON ANIMALS

What was the reaction of other animals to the deceit of the Serpent, Satan? If those first animals were like the cows, horses, dogs and cats I've known, they would be following Adam around! The other animals were witnesses to the Fall of man. Did Adam's animal friends hear Satan's mocking laughter? Raucous laughter would have grated in their ears!

Were these animals ashamed that a fellow animal deceived their human friends? The animals who loved Adam must have been bewildered. Man, their master and caretaker, had fallen out with God, the Master and Caretaker of all.

When Adam and Eve turned from each other's nakedness and began the terrible game of hiding, how did it affect the animals? I think these animals smelled or felt the terror which overcame Adam as the forbidden knowledge was ingested. Didn't confusion beset the animals, too?

Harmony was replaced with discord. When the man and woman ripped leaves off branches to fashion crude coverings, did the birds in the trees twitter in dismay? When animals are confused or frightened, they tend to fight or flee. Don't you know the same darkness fell over the animals' souls and spirits? Some went wild — never again to trust humans and refusing to submit to man's tarnished authority. Some surely desired to help Adam. In the cool of that fateful day, how terrible it must have been for the animals! What disaster the Lord found when He came to walk with Adam and Eve that evening. [Gen. 3:8]

Surely, pandemonium broke out in the animal kingdom that day. John Wesley said the very foundations of animals' nature were put out of course, turned upside down. We still reap the fruit of Adam's disobedience.

It was horrible, the blackness which descended on hearts of man and beast. Adam hid from and blamed God and Eve for his sin. Eve passed the blame to the serpent. It was the darkest day of history. Sin destroyed the Garden of God.

Animal trainer, Vicki Hearne, surmises a loss of man's authority, an incoherence, which made most animals wild:

> *Then Adam and Eve themselves failed in obedience, and in this story to fail in obedience is to fail in authority.* **Most of animate creation, responding to this failure, turned pretty irrevocably from human command.** *The tiger, the wolf and the field mouse as well as, of course, the grasshopper refuse to come when called to recognize our naming. One may say that before the Fall, all animals were domestic, that nature was domestic.* **After the Fall, wildness was possible, and most creatures chose it, but a few did not.** *The dog, the horse, the burro, the elephant, the ox and a few others agreed to go along with humanity anyway, thus giving us a kind of second chance to repair our damaged authority, to do something about our incoherence.*[7]

I recall hearing Ed Cole, a Christian teacher, say that: Obedience is better than sacrifice, because we can never regain by sacrifice, what we lost by disobedience. A mirror, once broken, is never the same. Virgin creation was raped by man's Fall. Innocence lost is gone forever. One act changed the world. Peaceful paradise became a savage jungle — if not instantly, then certainly over time.

Look around. Isn't the Garden of God still lost? Man continues to disobey his Creator, still believing he can be his own god. The earth's ecosystems still real from man's lack of obedience to God. Animals reflect the same wildness and confusion at man's incoherent instability. Full of lies and inconsistent behavior, we are untrustworthy and, therefore, unloving. It's miraculous that dogs (and other animals) still choose to love and obey us.

WHAT COULD BE DONE?

If Adam's Fall took all creation down, what could be done? It looks to me like God was in a fix. While the Fall appears to be catastrophic, the Bible's God was not wringing his hands in despair. Disappointed, yes. Without alternative plans, no.

God plans ahead. The Lord had a Plan B (and maybe plans C through infinity)! God's attitude toward His creation never changed. God still loves us.

The first clue is: Why didn't God let Adam physically die on the day he ate that fruit of forbidden knowledge? This earth and mankind were masterpieces, and man was a lead actor in God's work. Adam and Eve had no children yet. All humankind was still in Adam's loins and womb.[8] Adam was created to become God's kids, His loving family. If Adam, both male and female, died physically on that fateful day, the Lord's plan would have ended.

The Almighty needed time to redeem fallen Adam. Man needed time and opportunity to grow into the kind of lover God created Adam to become. Mature love, like fruit, is produced only by mature persons. The Bible doesn't say love is a "gift" which we receive and suddenly we are perfect lovers. (When you believe in Jesus and ask Him into your heart to be Lord and Savior, Jesus gives you the power to become like Him Who is love. Biblical love is a fruit which must be cultivated to fruit-bearing maturity, and the living Word of God is the seed.) Real, Biblical love is a living thing, like a plant. Keeping love growing is like gardening in a desert -- if you don't take good care of it consistently, it will wither and die. Study the Bible to check this out. If we don't cultivate our love for people and animals, we and our relationships wither and die.

DEATH: WHAT DID IT MEAN?

Remember the broken commandment stated Adam would surely "die" "the day" he ate the forbidden fruit? Adam had no experience of death before they ate the forbidden fruit. Nothing had died. What did "death" mean? When did the first death occur? What was it like?

The Bible teaches that death entered the world through sin. [Rom. 5:12 & 1 Cor. 15:20-22]. Without sin, there was no death. Until he sinned, Adam could not have had a clue what "die" meant. The earth was fully alive.[9]

If you have tried to explain death to a child, you know it's neither easy nor pleasant. Did Adam ask the Lord what die meant? Sounds like a smart thing to do – before eating what you shouldn't. There is no record Adam or Eve asked God for wisdom about His Command.

How does the Bible define "death," anyway? Scripture teaches it has two meanings: (1) In physical death, the breath or spirit and/ or soul leave the physical body. [Phil. 1:20-24; Rev. 14:13; also John 5:25 & 1 Tim. 4:1] (2) In spiritual death, you are separated from God, who is Life. Spiritual death comes in two subcategories: "this life" and "eternal life." Disobedience kills our relationship to God. Some deeds kill like cancer, by degrees; others kill quickly, like cutting the jugular vein. [Eph. 2:1 & 5; also Luke 1:79; 1 John 3:14; Rom. 6:23; John 3:36; & Rev. 2:11]

Since the Fall, all humans suffer both kinds of death. In this life, we are dead to God, in relationship. [Eph. 2:1] After this life, the righteous who have physically died will be resurrected to live eternally

[Isa. 25:6-8; 26:19; Dan. 12:2; Rev. 20:13], and the wicked to eternal punishment. [Matt. 5:22, 30; 10:28; Mark 9:43-48; Jude 12-16; Rev. 20 & 21] [The Bible defines both "righteousness" and "wickedness," if you wish to study it.]

SPIRITUAL DEATH

Spiritual death entered Adam as surely as a child who falls into a fire is burned. Evidences of Adam's spiritual death are: (a) Adam saw his own nakedness; (b) he feared and hid from God; and (c) he lied to God. Adam quit walking with God. The man renamed the woman, Eve (Gen. 3:20), treating her as separate from himself. God still calls us, both male and female, "Adam." [Gen. 5:1-2.] The Bible says marriage makes male and female "one." [Gen. 2:24; see also Eph. 5:25-33.]

The Apostle Paul wrote we are all "dead in our transgressions and sins." [Eph. 2:1] Sin or disobedience kills trust and relationships. Adam's behavior, described in Genesis Chapter 3, proves the immediate separation of Adam from God. The relationships between God and Adam, and male and female, were broken. That's spiritual death.

Christians who have a regeneration experience through Jesus Christ describe the reversal of spiritual death as: Coming from darkness to light; from despair to hope; from loneliness to love; from being orphaned to adopted. A sign of this regeneration is a new unselfish love for God and others. Many new Christians also usually treat animals better (until they learn some Cartesian theology). This helps us understand life before the Fall, perhaps.

Like an empty field after harvest, we can glean only glimpses of what it was like before the Fall. It is impossible to imagine the changes sin and death brought to Adam and Eve — and to all creation. To be separated from God is to be separated from all that is good: love, life, light, wisdom, truth, joy, peace, and truth. God is the embodiment of these attributes. God is the source of all goodness.

WHY TWO DEATHS?

Why does "death" have two meanings? I think the Lord gave Himself legal options with the First Commandment. God ordained Adam's spiritual death to occur first for a reason. In that day of disobedience, Adam had to die [Gen. 2:17] or God would be a liar. God cannot lie. [Num. 23:19; Titus 1:2]. Some kind of death had to occur when the first humans bit into the forbidden fruit.(In my opinion, it was so Adam could procreate and the human experiment would survive.) God chose that Adam died spiritually the fateful day.

Being cut off from God meant being cut off from the source of all life. Like a branch cut off of a tree, Adam may have looked alive for a while, but he was not.

Evidences of this spiritual death are: Adam was ashamed of his nakedness; and he feared, hid from and lied to God. As surely as a child who touches fire is burned, Adam died. The Apostle Paul understood, as he wrote that we are all "dead in our transgressions and sins." [Eph. 2:1]. Adam and Eve were separated from God. [Gen. 3] The fellowship or relationship between Adam and God was broken. Man withdrew from the Lord God, his Creator. Man withdrew from the woman, renaming her "Eve"—treating her as separate from himself, rather being "one flesh" [Gen. 2:24 & Eph. 5:21]. God still calls them (us) "Adam" however. [Gen. 5:1-2].

We see as through opaque glasses, only glimpsing what the world was like before the Fall. But we do know that God is the embodiment and source of all good, of love, life, light, wisdom, truth, joy, peace, beauty, harmony and justice. To be separated from God is to lose all that is good. "Death" is the fruit or wages of sin, and encompasses a lot of bad things. It is the last enemy Jesus will conquer. [I Cor. 15:6]

ON THAT DAY, SOMEONE HAD TO DIE

God's law required a physical death that day. When Adam was cut off from God, another law was employed or instituted: The Right of Substitution. Justice required a death; but mercy allowed a substitute to die to spare Adam. Adam's physical death could be delayed by a stand-in. Ah! A brilliant solution.

Being a good Judge, Lawgiver, and King [Isa. 33:22], the Lord ordained God's "Plan B," in case Adam disobeyed, to keep Adam and Eve physically alive for a certain time. God fulfilled justice and gave time so the rest of God's plans could be completed. Like putting cut flowers in water so they would "live" longer, our gracious God stayed the execution of His lawless humans for His good purpose. This stay of execution was not without a price.

God provided substitute sacrifices to spare His children. Think about the implications of this verse:

For Adam also and for his wife, the Lord God made long coats (tunics) of skins, and clothed them.
                                      Genesis 3:21. [Amplified]

"Skins" became Adam's clothes. Skins are much different from leaves. Think about it. The word is "skins" — not "wool" or "hair." You do not get "skin" without killing an animal. Skins are taken off animals. Adam's coats were leather, taken from animals.

Notice the word is plural. More than one animal died. Animals were Adam's substitutes. Animals would die in place of Adam and Eve. God replaced Adam's "fig" leaves at a great price. The skinned animals in Eden were first of many substitutes for man's sin. The first animal sacrifices.

Think about it. The skin is both the largest organ and the organ with the most nerve endings in all warm-blooded animals. The skin is where sense of touch is exhibited. Lovers love to touch and be touched. Hugging, stroking, and kissing are skin activities. My animals loved to be scratched, rubbed, and otherwise touched. To be burned, whipped or skinned alive are cruelest of tortures. Lose enough skin, by fire or other means, and death results. Therefore, the merciful always humanely kill an animal before skinning it. Those first skin coats give us a lot to ponder, don't you think? What price sin?[10]

ONE DAY IS AS A THOUSAND YEARS

Adam had to die spiritually *and* physically. Adam's spiritual death was immediate. Through the animal sacrifice it appears God delayed Adam's physical death. Adam did die physically on the "day" he and she disobeyed. How? God controls time. The Bible tells us, "one day" is as a "thousand years" to the Lord. [Psalm 90:4; 2 Pet. 3:8] The Lord used His time, not earth's, to calculate the "day" of Adam's physical death.

A thousand earth years is a very long day. God planned that option. Adam would have time to procreate. God could work on man's education and training on how to handle the knowledge of good and evil. The Lord could start to make lovers out of His selfish man-child. God could have His Son, Jesus Christ, be born of a virgin, live fully as a human, and die on a tree for man's sins, in the fullness of time, i.e., begin to execute His plan of salvation.

Scripture bears this out. Adam and Eve had many children. Spiritual death was evident when Cain murdered Abel. [Gen. 4] Each of Adam's offspring physically died before they reached 1000 years. [Gen. 5] Adam died at age 930 years. Adam's immediate offspring lived exceedingly long. None, not even Methuselah, lived longer than 1000 years. All of Adam's offspring have died within God's "one day."

After the Great Flood and Noah, our life span became like today. At age 130, Jacob told Pharaoh his years "were few and unpleasant" and he had not "attained the years that my fathers' lived." [Gen. 47:9] Today, it is more common for people to live beyond one hundred years. However, most find the thought of living hundreds of years the realm of fiction.

We don't think eternally. Thank God He does! His plan allowed Adam's seed to survive. God has hopeful plans for the human race.

GOD'S JUSTICE

Why didn't the Lord just forgive and forget? Why did Adam have to die? Why did the animals have to be sacrificed?

All creation watched to see what God would do with His disobedient humans. If God let man get by with his first offense, what would happen? Would the "fire" of sin spread destruction? Would God be sending a message for all creation "to do your own thing, baby!"?

While some think God has since fallen down on the job, let's just address the first crime here. God had to make Adam and Eve an example. Justice required it. Love demanded it on behalf of all Adam's future offspring — and all creation.

If the Bible makes anything clear, it is that God is just, holy and righteous. [Jer. 9:24; Ps. 89:14] You cannot separate love and justice. Love, i.e., God, is just and righteous. Therefore, God could not leave Adam (or the future generations in Adam's genes) in death and disobedience. God's nature, His love, compelled Him to have other plans.

Think about it. We humans have not conquered death and sin in thousands of years. Would Adam have changed on his or her own? Would Adam realize how his/her action affects others on their own? Adam and all their seed or offspring are locked into a genetic predisposition for sin, aren't we? What if Adam ate the Tree of Life in their estranged condition? Without God's help we would be eternally trapped as creations separated from our loving Creator, wouldn't we? Leaving Adam in his sin would not be kind.

We are in an age where "love" is too often defined as a license to do what we want. Moral and ethical behavior are thought foolish or irrelevant. So, let me speak a word about justice. As a lawyer, I hope I have gained some understanding of justice -- although that is not the key. Proverbs 28:4-5 are clues to the key.

Only evil people hate God's laws. Love is the foundational law of God, a royal law. [Lev. 19:18; Deut. 6:5; Mark 12:30-31; James 2:8]. The Ten Commandments and other laws derive from one Royal Law. Justice and righteousness are critical elements to preserve a free society. Without law and order, there is anarchy. In lawlessness, people live in fear and doubt. Neighbors or strangers steal, maim, or kill each other. Commerce is killed. You keep life, limb and property only as long as you can protect them. "Survival of the fittest" describes anarchy. Law-abiding citizens and good government are essential requisites for a prosperous, secure society. History proves that societies which keep God's commandments thrive and know peace and security.

Real love is just and treats others right. Criminal justice requires the innocent's swift acquittal and quick punishment of the guilty. Civil justice rewards righteous deeds and penalizes unrighteous ones. The apostle Paul recorded: "The wages of sin is death, but the free gift of God is eternal life in Christ Jesus our Lord." [Romans 6:23] Justice is balanced and instructive.

If God meant to redeem man and have redemption "stick," He had to teach the man and woman the cost of sin. Humans must know and remember it forever. It would be very *unloving* to leave humankind as they were — deceived, ashamed, afraid, liars, and cowardly "buck-passers." Mercy tempers justice, so Adam got to live and fulfill his days, but not without punishment. God had to address Adam's sin, a killer-cancer to them and all God's creation. The judgment of death had to happen on the very day Adam and Eve took that first bite of forbidden fruit. Death was in that bite and all the consequences of sin.

ADAM'S SUBSTITUTE

The Bible says in that first 24-hour day, God provided substitutes to bear physical death for Adam. The substitutes are called "sacrifices". The first sacrifices were costly, even priceless.

This first sacrifice set a precedent. Since Adam, each sin must be paid for by an acceptable substitute for the sinner's life. Under the Covenant with Abraham and Moses, Jews offered lambs, baby goats and bulls to God (until the destruction of the temple in Jerusalem about 65 A.D). God told Abraham to sacrifice his son, Isaac, but had Abraham substitute a ram God provided. [Gen.22]. Isaac was a foretaste of the sacrificial substitute of God's own Son, Jesus of Nazareth, some 2000 years ago.

Which precious animals died because of Adam's sin? Did the Lord require Adam to choose the animals? Imagine having to choose the first sacrifices. Other animals must have been there. Animals love to be with us, and I'm sure they loved to be with the Lord and Adam and Eve. As the Lord God stroked the animals, tears of grief must have run down His face. How terrible a grief to know —as only He could know — what was to come on both man and all creation.

Curiosity, blended with an unfamiliar dread, must have filled the animals' hearts and souls as they gathered around God and Adam. Did they want to comfort God? My animals always want to comfort me.

The Lord surely must have taught them, man and animal. Explaining the need for a sacrifice to stay the full penalty of sin would be hard, wouldn't it? (Good parents instruct as part of discipline.) God may have explained the life or soul of the flesh was in the blood. And why blood alone could atone for or cover sin. "...For it is the blood by reason of the life/soul that makes atonement." [Lev. 17:11] Without shedding of blood there is no forgiveness. [Heb. 9:22]. God probably told them this was a temporary fix. The blood of bulls and goats could not cleanse the human conscience or make man alive spiritually. Another sacrifice, a perfect, obedient, innocent human, was required. God would become man and come in the fullness of time — when the human race was truly ready. [Hebrews 9 & 10]

Adam and his wife must see their substitutes die. The animals Adam and Eve had once stroked, petted, and loved would now become their clothing. They would wear those skins as a constant reminder of the cost of sin. All creation would witness the execution of justice. It could not be a pretty sight.

WHAT ABOUT FAIRNESS?

"Not fair!" That's right. Adam was not fair when they ate the fruit. Adam was unfair to disobey and bring death into Eden. Life has never been fair since Adam ate the forbidden fruit.

Was God unfair in treating His animals this way? Don't they have rights, too? Sin and war are never fair. Innocents often are injured or die in war. Adam's sin brought on war between good and evil.

God's unchangeable laws had to be fulfilled. Real justice is consistent. God is love, therefore He is just. [1 John 4:8 & 16; Ps. 89:14]. Understanding justice is key to knowing God, I believe. [Prov. 28:4-5] God is a God of justice and peace. Justice brings peace. Justice always rewards right behavior and punishes lawbreaking. If the criminal changes his way, there is peace; if not and the violator of God law is executed, there is peace. When the righteous are vindicated, there is peace. The righteous never need to fear judgment, as it brings them rest. Mercy or leniency is only wise if the lawbreaker chooses not to break the law again. It is foolish to be merciful to a hardened criminal or unrepentant offender. That endangers good citizens. God is never foolish. Mercy tempers justice, but never foolishly.

ACCUSTOMED TO DEATH

Through history run rivers of blood, shed because of human disobedience. Daily, humans and animals give their lives for others. The altars of sacrifice are often outside of temples. Homes, streets and battlefields can be counted as "altars," I believe. Yet, many are so accustomed to it we don't think it terrible. Even our entertainment reflects a love of bloodshed.

Also, most Americans and Europeans are sheltered from the death of both humans and animals. We have no time for death. We die in hospitals and nursing homes, if possible. We buy meat killed and cut up. Pets are "disposed of" by veterinarians or humane societies. We try to keep death from dirtying our homes and hearts. While we often view death in movies, we are emotionally removed from it.

Road-kill (animals killed on the highway by speeding vehicles) is the closest many of us get to real death. We speed by it on our way to somewhere else.

I'm being harsh only to illustrate my point, not to condemn. I pray the Lord will give us each grace to face death for what it is — and what His sacrifices mean.

Go with me, with prayerful imagination, back to the Garden on that fateful day. Let me warn you, the descriptions are graphic.

THE FIRST DEATH, THE FIRST SACRIFICE

The time for the killing came in Eden. God and Adam were there. You know the animals were gathered, too. All creation must have watched, listened, and smelled, tasting the air.

Imagine Adam's experience. No human had ever seen death. None had ever killed before. Nothing had died.

What animals were the first sacrifices? There were at least two animals — maybe more. There had to be enough skin to make two human size garments. Two garments can take many skins. The Bible and many traditions hold that the earth was filled with giants before the Genesis 6-9 Flood. If Adam and Eve were giants, a number of skins would be required, unless those first animals were also oversized.

These animals would have come willingly to the people they loved. God's love was the essential atmosphere of Eden. These animals trusted Adam. Adam knew these animals intimately, knew them by name. The first humans and animals knew each other better than you or I can imagine.

I believe God required Adam and Eve to participate in this first slaughter. This is based on His commandment that the sinner must choose and offer animal sacrifice himself. [Lev. 4:2-4, 13-15, 22-24, 27-29 & 32-33] The sinner had to bring a live animal before God's altar. The animal had to be that person's best — a choice animal, a favorite. Then, the sinner had to lay his or her hand on the animal's head and kill it. This was in the presence of the priest. The priest's role was to oversee, to pray and put the blood on the altar to atone for the sins. Note that the sinner killed the sacrificial animal, not the priest.

Adam and Eve probably had to lay their hands on the sacrificial animals. Imagine how you would feel. This was like killing your pet. As they felt the animal's life in their hands, Adam and Eve's thoughts must have been full of sorrow and remorse, even fear. These animals were their companions. Did Adam call them by the names he had given them? Did they speak to the animals as their hands touched them? Did they apologize? Or did they harden their hearts and ignore the animals because of guilt?

Killing an animal has always been difficult to me – and I've never done it for my own sin! Putting my hands on that sacrificial head and praying that God transfer my sin to an innocent animal would break my heart. As a veterinarian's daughter I saw many sick and dead animals. The times I have had to kill an animal, it has been extremely difficult for me. I have never gotten used to it. If I thought an animal died for my mistakes, I would be devastated. And that's how it should be. If you enjoy the killing, something is terribly wrong.

HOW WOULD YOU FEEL?

There would be no struggle. Eden's animals surely came willingly to the people they loved. Was the animal silent? I think so. How like the Lamb of God [John 1:29; Acts 8:32-35; Matt. 27:11-14], these first sacrifices must have been. Isaiah 53:7 says:

> *Yet He did not open His mouth; Like a lamb that is led to*
> *slaughter, And, like a sheep that is silent before its shearers,*
> *So He did not open His mouth.*

Did the first man and woman then try to get out of this terrible task? Did they ask to die as they deserved? Wouldn't you? God is a good parent. In His infinite wisdom, He knows the right discipline necessary to teach the consequences of our actions.

To refuse is only to make matters worse. Sin affects the human, and all under his or her stewardship. Refusal means sin continues to reign in the sinner. To refuse is further disobedience. It makes the heart callous to God and to others. God's protection and provision cannot operate. Death has an immediate continuous claim to sin not covered by repentance and blood. God knows only the substituted blood can stop the deadly consequence of sin. If the sinner wants to live, he must kill his sacrifice as God prescribes. God accepts an innocent animal in the sinner's place. This is what the Biblical sacrifices meant.

Do you think the priests told the sinner to look into the animal's eyes? Have you ever looked into the eyes of a lamb or goat kid, or a calf? The eyes of young animals are beautiful — soft and brown, so innocent and trusting. Touching and looking at the animal who is about to die for your sin must be very difficult!

Have you ever killed an animal? By hand? Have you ever watched it done? The first time makes most people sick. Only mentally ill people enjoy killing animals -- and they usually end up killing people, too. While people can become callous to butchering animals, it wasn't meant to be pleasant. Sacrifice is not meant to be enjoyed.

To be "kosher," sacrificial animals must be killed quickly and cleanly, and bled immediately to ensure merciful death. When Adam took the knife, did his hands tremble? Was Eve able to follow God's instruction to make the killing stroke quick?

Did Adam find himself weeping, his eyes blurring as he cut his animal friend's throat? Did man and animal exchange one long last look, as the killing blow fell? Was it very quick or was Adam clumsy, having to cut more than once?

BLOODY SACRIFICIAL DEATH

Blood would have spurted everywhere. Slicing the throat, which severs the jugular (a major artery), kills in less than a minute – really in seconds. Blood shoots outs, as the heart pumps its last. The killers are apt to become bloody, too. Fresh blood smells, too. Sacrificial death is not a pleasant, clean affair.

As that first life ebbed out, what was it like? Horrible, I'm sure. Did Adam and Eve keep a hand on the animal friends' bodies? Were Adam's and Eve's ears troubled by the gurgling noise the animals made as they died? Did the smell offend their olfactory senses? Did these first humans feel the life leave? Did they watch or turn away as the first deaths claimed their pets? When their furry friends' bodies crumbled to the ground did Adam's and Eve's hearts crumble, too?

The warm red life would have spattered and stained Adam and Eve, dripping down their leaf-covered nakedness. What did these fallen humans feel and think? Knowing the animal's soul was in that blood, did the terrible cost of sin impact them? Did they see the animal's eyes, full of life, darken and glaze over, as its breath, its spirit, left those perfect, beautiful bodies? Were they horrified at their sin, the cost of their disobedience to God's simple command? Did Adam understand God's grace, the blood covering of Adam's sin?

The eerie feeling, as death swallows life, is unforgettable. Probably these sin-stricken humans saw — and smelled — the bodily functions of the animal fail. The animal's clean coat would be soiled by its own blood and by the involuntary discharge of bowels and bladder. Some have smelled Death itself, usually described as a sickeningly sweet aroma. The soul-life fled. Only an empty shell remained.

Did Adam see the strange jerking dance of death in those bodies? Did Adam feel the body heat leave as the corpses grew cold? The muscles freeze into rigor mortis after a while. Could Adam easily forget those sacrifices? As Adam's offspring, we should not.

I think the good Lord designed physical death to look, smell and sound like a hellish nightmare. The Bible makes it abundantly clear that the living God wants His creation to have life, abundant life, eternal life (remember God's Tree of Life in Eden?). Because of Adam's disobedience, there is now a terrible price for such life.

Death, the absence of life, is a horrible thing. There is nothing good about death and its companions, decay, disability and disease.

HORRIBLE! HOW CRUEL!

"HORRIBLE!" "CRUEL!" you may cry. I agree. Genesis 3:12-13 indicates Adam showed no real remorse for disobeying God. Animals died because of Adam's sin. The bloody sacrifices were surely meant to be a cure of that callous lack.

"It's God's fault! Surely God could do something!" If we blame God for death and cruelty, we twist and blaspheme the truth that God is love. It is man who chose deadly disobedience. We are the guilty ones. Is God to blame because He gave us free will, and did not make us robots? It was Adam's choice. Adam and Eve were solely to blame.

God's law, His commandments, are perfect and good [Ps. 19:7; 1 Tim. 1:8]. Don't blame the God or His law. That is "passing the buck" — blaming someone else for our faults. It only makes things worse. Facing the truth makes life a lot easier and more pleasant in the long run. Adam wrote the animals' death sentence when he disobeyed God. Adam – not God – killed those animals.

God *did* do something. Holy justice requires a life for a life. God extended His hands of mercy to pluck Adam from the fatal judgment fire. God stayed Adam's execution to delay Adam's physical death. The price was costly – the lives of precious animals -- but necessary.

"Couldn't God do something?" Wait until the puzzle is put together. We don't yet clearly see God's love and His marvelous relationship with His creation. Looking at the pieces alone can be confusing. God's masterpiece, even if some scenes are unpleasant, is wondrous in its whole. God had a plan for the animals, too — even the serpent, Satan, and his kind.

NOT MEANT TO BE EASY

The first sacrifice was meant to be difficult for Adam and Eve. I hope Adam and Eve killed their substitutes with absolute horror and great remorse. I hope they begged God for help, for another way, even to die themselves instead. Adam named these animals. These were friends and companions. Adam cared for them, talked with them, and saw each other daily. Don't you think the first humans lost their breakfast, lunch and dinner? I wish they'd vomited up that forbidden fruit.

But it was too late. Sin and death had arrived on planet earth.

GOD CLOTHED THEM

The Bible says, God clothed Adam in skins. Can you see God tenderly, even reverently, picking up the fallen forms, and beginning the unpleasant task of skinning them? The Lord may have done the skinning. Or He may have supervised Adam, making the man and woman do the unpleasant task.

Whoever tanned the skins had a nasty task. Tanning is a smelly, messy business. First, you must skin the animal. Then you have to scrape the skins until they are "fat-free," before you stretch them to dry. In warm weather, the odors become obnoxious. Eden would be agreeably warm, don't you think?

Have you ever seen an animal skinned? I have. Beneath the skin are wonders of a body put together in awesome complexity — muscle, nerves, tendons, bone, interconnected organs. God's creation is fearfully and wonderfully made! Did Adam notice? Was Adam and Eve further shamed and nauseous at seeing the bare remains of an animal which gave life and skin to cover their nakedness?

Did God require Adam to burn the animals' bodies? This would be in line with the Mosaic law of animal sacrifice for sin. Did He require that Adam and his Eve eat the sacrificial meat before Him? In every bite was a reminder of the beloved animal, its life and name. How costly those first long leather clothes were!

I believe the Lord wept as He fashioned Adam's twin set of clothes from these precious leathers. How did this "fashion" feel to

Adam and his wife when they put it on? I've lived where animal fur seems like the only way to keep warm in winter. Did Adam and Eve experience that? Did warm furs truly cover their cold naked souls? Did the remorse nearly kill them, too? Did they feel God's grace as their sins were covered by their companions' blood?

What a cost – to wear the skin of one of their animal friends! Did the name of this animal scream within Eve? That scream seems to echo still, to me. Every time they touched that soft leather or woolly coat, it was meant as a reminder. Precious companions died so Adam could live. Adam's clothes were mute testimonies that the wages of sin are death. [Rom. 6:23]

That is what animal sacrifices were all about. Animals gave their lives to satisfy holy justice, to spare humans for enough years from death so God could begin to work His redemptive plan.

Do you think Adam ever spoke those animals' names in the years they wore those skins? Was Adam grateful? Or did Adam and Eve suppress the memory?

FORGETFUL HUMAN RACE

Adam's race has proven forgetful. Gratitude is not a normal handmaiden of a sinful heart. It's hard to understand, but true. Mom told me about desperate young women she helped during the Great Depression. Without needed jobs, only prostitution or suicide was left. Mom arranged for many women to get food and shelter, coached them enough to get decent work, and helped them find jobs. Later, if she'd meet them again, she said most would pretend they did not know her. Mom said she understood. I never have.

We humans have "forgotten" what Adam learned about animal sacrifice. We suppress painful memories – especially of our own failings. As Adam's offspring, we tend to blame others or blame circumstances. Unfortunately, we forget the good things, not only God's sacrificial giving, but His blessings and promises. We avoid the only person in the Universe who can help us regain Eden.

EVICTED FROM THE GARDEN

Spiritually dead, Adam had to be evicted from the Garden of Eden. The Lord sealed Eden's entrance. The Lord had a good reason. The way was blocked to the Tree of Life by human disobedience:

> *Then God said, "Behold, the man has become like one of Us, knowing good and evil; and now, lest he stretch out his hand, and take also from the tree of life, and eat, and live forever," therefore the Lord God sent him out from the garden of Eden, to cultivate the ground from which he was taken. So He drove the man out; and at the east of the garden of Eden, He stationed the cherubim, and the flaming sword which turned every direction, to guard the way to the tree of life.* Gen. 3:22-24 [NASV]

Until the Fall, the Tree of Life had never been forbidden to Adam. Now the way is barred. Why? Life and sin are incompatible. Love would not let man live forever in his sin, his disobedience. Adam's sin affects all creation. So, God had a plan.

Adam now faced life as a struggle. If living a hundred years seems long to us, how about the prospect of nine hundred years? Was that long enough for Adam to learn anything?

Adam and Eve surely retained indelible memories of Eden's beauty and wonders. Genesis is a record of their memories of that naming party and what those animals were all like before. Choosing the created (i.e., your own or another's ways) over the Creator was a terrible mistake. Did Adam remember his own betrayal, disobedience, and fear? Did he try to forget the unspeakable horror of death? Did Adam think of the animals' sacrificial love? Did the rest of creation remember? Is that memory in the DNA of all creatures?

The knowledge of good and evil came with a high price. The forbidden fruit proved a poor counterfeit for what they lost. Did all seem lost forever?

THE FALLOUT; THE PAIN OF ALL LIVING THINGS

Adam's Fall had a painful fallout. Man "died" – first spiritually, then physically. Death, disease, and disharmony entered all creation. Also, Adam's deaths affected man's relationships with God, as well as with all animals. Adam's fall in bringing death, must have brought the fear of man to the animals. the friends of those who died. Death creates a terrible loss for those left behind.

How can we even begin to imagine what the Fall meant to the animals? We know animals grieve when a loved companion dies.[11] Elephants,[12] primates, like gorillas and chimpanzees,[13] have been observed as grieving the death of companions. Other animals, such as dogs and cats, clearly experience grief and loss when their human or companion pet dies. Owls have been observed grieving over the loss of mates, being very angry at humans at fault for the death.[14] Many species are either too different or the evidence is not gathered, as to whether they grieve. We simply don't know much about the inner lives of hedgehogs, ants, and crickets.

Mom knew dogs grieve. Mom (relunctantly) sold a puppy to a lady with a terminal disease. The woman lived years longer than predicted — reportedly because of that dog. The dog was pregnant when her mistress died. Her husband returned the dog when the woman died. The dog came to Mom a nervous wreck. (I'm sure being pregnant didn't help!) I didn't like the dog. Mom told me the dog was grieving and to give her a year. Mom was right. After a year, the dog became one of the best dogs we ever had. Mom knew dogs. Many of you reading this book have also witnessed such behavior.

I believe those first animals grieved for Adam, at the Fall of man, and his spiritual death. I believe the good animals grieved over the animals who died. Don't you know that the animals offended by the Serpent's betrayal — felt unspeakable sorrow?

The Hebrew people have an interesting phrase, *za'ar ba'alei hayyim*. It means "pain of living things."[15] Rabbinical tradition has it that Rabbi Judah ha-Nasi was punished by the Lord because he did not show mercy to animals; when he changed his attitude, the punishment was removed. The rabbis note that Moses and David became leaders only after being shepherds. God's mercy to animals is given prominence in rabbinic literature, and along with it, man's duty to not cause animals pain. Even inflicting of necessary pain is frowned upon.[16] How wise!

> *"...the rabbis based a great deal of their legislation and interpretation on the principle of za'ar ba'alei hayyim ["the pain of living things"]. ....(Shab.128b)."[17]*

The Jewish Torah, i.e., the first five books of the Bible, shows God's view on animals.[18] Jews (who wrote almost all the books of the Bible) teach that man is responsible to God for animals:

> *"Moral and legal rules concerning the treatment of **animals are based on the principle that animals are part of God's creation toward which man bears responsibility.** Laws and other indications in the Pentateuch and the rest of the Bible make it clear not only that **cruelty to animals is forbidden** but also that **compassion and mercy to them are demanded of man by God."[19]***

Genesis teaches that disobedience has a high price. Sin is the cause of the "pain of living things." Disobedience costs the lawbreaker, and all around him or her. Disobedience also costs those who love the transgressor. God feels that pain, too. That which affects what God loves hurts the Creator. God loves His creation. Oh, to be God's healer and comforter! To help heal His loved creation would be a joy! (Maybe we can do more toward that end that we realize now.)

What Adam lost, cannot be regained. But the Lord had a plan – which includes heaven. There is hope!

WHY? WHY? WHY?

Why did the Lord God require the death of those first animals? Love. God loved Adam and Eve. Made in His image, they were His children. His love compelled Him to do something to spare their lives – no matter the cost to Himself. Parents are like that. Love also meant teaching Adam the cost of sin. It was a hard, but necessary lesson. Love ultimately meant making a way for Adam to return to intimate relationship with God, to reopen the entrance to Eden again.

And the teaching of Adam was unspeakably expensive. "Sacrifice" means that it costs something valuable. Do you know about the conversation the chicken had with the pig about (a non-kosher) breakfast? The chicken was bragging about the eggs she provided. The pig replied, "You only make a contribution, but my gift of bacon requires total sacrifice!"

To spare Adam's life, cost both God and His beloved creation. It meant subjecting all creation to futility for thousands of years. It's price included precious lives of magnificent, beloved animals.

Ultimately, man's redemption cost the life of God's Son, "the Lamb of God who takes away the sin of the world." [John 1:29] The Lord loves us enough to sacrifice all it takes to rescue us from death's dominion and make us His again. God is not alone in that endeavor. Adam's Fall and his redemption caused unspeakable suffering to the Lord. But love doesn't let children grow up rebels. So God instituted substitute sacrifices. God gave the lives of His favored pets to save His sons.

God loves you and me. God won't spare the lives of others to gain your safety, to spare your life. This is not so alien to us. All the time, police and soldiers are ordered into danger for the safety of citizens (of all ranks and stations). Have you ever experienced that kind of love? Do you know, experientially, that God loves you?

The Lord wants you to walk with Him, with each other, and with His animals in a renewed Eden, in heaven itself. Have you ever considered that God uses animals to assist Him in achieving His goals. Let's explore that idea.

ENDNOTES:

1. Genesis 5:2 indicates God calls humans, both male and female "Adam." So some references herein to "Adam" include both sexes.

2. 1 Kings 8:62-63; 2 Chronicles 7:4-5, for example.

3. The "law of sensitive dependence upon initial conditions," known as the "butterfly effect" after Edward Lorenz, the physicist who postulated it, is presented beautifully in Andy Andrews, *The Butterfly Effect*, 2009, Simple Truth, Inc.

4. See the DVD featuring Louie Giglio: *Indescribable* (2009) which presents photos of the cosmos with a wonderful message about the Creator.

5. Many believe Satan was an archangel, and use Isaiah 14:12-15 and Ezekiel 28 as proof texts. Having searched Scripture, this author found no link between these Scriptures and the verses actually describing Satan or the Devil. Without that link, this author hesitates to ascribe to this belief as sound doctrine.

6. Why the Lord God Almighty, the One who is Love and Truth, would create such a creature is another issue. It is not necessary to Mom's question to address that question here.

7. *Adam's Task*, supra, pp. 47-48. (Emphasis supplied)

8. "God has created all mankind from one blood (Acts 17:26; Genesis 5). Today researchers have discovered that we have all descended from one gene pool. For example, a 1995 study of a section of Y chromosomes from 38 men from different ethnic groups around the world was consistent with the biblical teaching that we all come from one man (Adam)" http://www.eternal-productions.org/101science.html Fact #37

9. Some argue death must have occurred prior to Adam's Fall. This idea is belied by Genesis, and by 1 Corinthians 15:26, "The last enemy that will be abolished is death." See also 2 Tim. 1:10; and Rev. 20:14.

10. The effects of Adam's deaths are the subject of numerous sermons and theological works. We touch on them only as relevant to the answer to Mom's question.

11. *Mother Natures Greatest Hits*, supra, p. 72, 78-79

12. For evidence of grief in the death of an elephant see Cynthia Moss' *Elephant Memories: Thirteen years in the Life of an Elephant Family;* and Jeffery Mousssaieff Masson & Susan McCarthy, *When Elephants Weep.*

13. "Koko," a gorilla who was taught human sign language at the California Gorilla Foundation. Koko asked for a kitten for her birthday. Later, after Koko had bonded with it, the kitten was accidentally killed. Koko behaved with actions showing grief. When her trainer asked Koko questions about death, Koko sobbed, and signed "Sad/frown" and "sleep/cat." In sign language, the gorilla communicated that she understood death and could understand on her own mortality. F. Patterson & E. Linden, *The Education of Koko*, (N.Y.: Holt, Rinehart & Winston, 1981); & Jane Vessels, "Koko's Kitten," *National Geographic*, v.167, #1, P.110.

14. Carl Anderson, "The Obstreperous Owls of Hammel," *Animals You Will Never Forget*, (Reader's Digest, 1969), p. 109.

15. *Encyclopedia Judaica*, "Animals, Cruelty To"

16. Please refer to the *Encyclopedia Judaica* and other rabbinical literature for a more complete view of these lessons.

17. [Id.] (Emphasis supplied)

18. I prefer to learn about God from those who have spent centuries studying Him and His law – sorting out the good truths. Jews have been persecuted from time immemorial, and undoubtedly will be until the Messiah returns to rule and judge all men. So have Christians. Perhaps because they are different as God's chosen ones, set apart for service to Him and His world. If you do not truly love God, you will not love His people. The Bible states that those who fellowship with God, carry His presence. Those who love evil, hate the light of God's presence. They hate those who carry His light. (Christians, too, are persecuted. In fact, more were killed for their faith in the 20th century than in all the time since Jesus lived.) .

19. *Encyclopedia Judaica*, "Animals, Cruelty to" The Jewish laws regarding killing animals are the kindest. Slaughter houses in the U.S. are supposed to kill by humane methods, i.e., quickly. (Slaughter houses don't always obey the laws.) "Kosher" laws are based on Biblical principles. The Jewish methods are motivated by consideration for the animal. Jewish law requires the knife to be exceedingly sharp and without the slightest notch. The killing blow is to be swift. The animal must be bled immediately. Such methods ensure a quick painless death. According to the rabbis, "I will eat flesh, because my soul desires to eat flesh" [Deut. 12:20] has a negative connotation. Meat eating should be in moderation, so few animals would be killed. Proverbs 23:20-21. God's attitude toward His animals is one of mercy.

CHAPTER 8

WHO WERE THE
FIRST ANIMAL
SACRIFICES?

*How far the little candle throws his beams! So shines a
good deed in a naughty world.[1]*

*I see the lives for which I lay down my life, peaceful, useful,
prosperous and happy, ... I see that I hold a sanctuary in
their hearts, and in the hearts of their descendants, generations hence. ... It is a far, far better thing that I do, than
I have ever done; it is a far, far better rest that I go to, than
I have ever known.[2]*

H eroes come in all shapes and sizes – not just human. A stray
dog gave its life for my grandmother, Nella. Mom told me
the story. I suspect that dog came to Nella lost, half-starved, maybe
mangy. The dog became Nella's companion. One day, Nella went into
a field, possibly to pick something for dinner, like poke or dandelion
greens. Nella either did not know or had forgotten there was bull
in that field. (I've been chased by a bull. It is terrifying when a ton
of hoofed, horned aggression charges you!) The bull charged Nella.

Nella's dog got between them and the bull went for the dog. Nella got over the fence without harm. Unfortunately, the dog did not. That stray dog died sacrificially for its beloved Nella. History is replete with similar stories of dogs and other animals risking or giving their lives for humans – or even other species. Some risk life and limb for loved friends, and others do it for strangers.[3]

Pompeii, Italy, was destroyed about 70 A.D. when Mt. Vesuvius erupted. In an excavation, the body of a dog was found covering a child – apparently trying to protect the child.[4] In modern times, firemen found a German Shepherd, it's dead body covering a toddler.[5] The toddler was alive! The child survived a house fire with only minor injuries – because of the dog. Susan McElroy, reporting about the German Shepherd giving its life for the toddler, said:

> *What has always struck me most about these kinds of stories is not how they occurred, but that they occurred. There is enormous importance in the notion of another species voluntarily defending us, sometimes with its very life. We treasure these heroic animals and their uncompromising devotion. ... Yet, ironically, humans who are willing to return the favor ... are frequently perceived ... as lunatics or fanatics.*[6]

Such animal heroism is actually remarkably common.[7] Most of us have encountered reports of all kinds of animals showing compassion, loyalty and self-sacrifice. After the 2011 Japanese earthquake and tsunami, a video of a half-starved shivering dog was shown. The dog stood amidst debris on a little piece of land of misery. Then as the camera got closer, another dog became visible, as it lay nearby. The first dog was protective and would not leave the injured dog. The reporter choked up as the story unfolded and reported both dogs were rescued. The gift of self-sacrifice is truly a common trait among God's creation, isn't it?

Are you as surprised as me at the many accounts of wild animals which become heroes or rescuers of both humans and other animals? I like the one about a wild eagle guiding a lost hiker to safety.[8] The woman had turned wrong and hiked about two miles the wrong way in the mountains when a gray eagle started squawking, and swooping at her. Finally, the hiker asked the eagle if she was going the wrong way? At that, the eagle grew silent and flew closer to the woman, holding itself still. The woman turned around and hiked back. This hiker got back just as a search party was ready to set out looking for her.

Leo Tolstoy, the famous Russian author, wrote an astonishing account of a falcon. Years ago, Tsar was hunting with his favorite falcon - a popular sport among the aristocrats of Tolstoy's day. The Tsar sought water, as he became thirsty. Finding a dribble coming down a hillside, the Tsar put his cup under the drip until it filled his cup. As the Tsar put the cup to his mouth, his falcon bumped it out of the Tsar's hand with its wings. Again the Tsar filled the cup and lifted it to quench his thirst. Again the falcon knocked the cup and spilled the water. When it happened a third time, the Tsar, in anger, killed the falcon. Meanwhile, the Tsar's servants had climbed up to the water's source. They returned empty handed, because they found a poisonous snake dead in the spring. The water was poisoned. The Tsar exclaimed: "Foully have I recompensed the Falcon; he saved my life, and I killed him for it."[9] How like Adam we all tend to be toward animals.

Badgers have a reputation for being fierce. Yet it's reported that in Canada in the 1800s, a badger took care of a lost boy for several weeks. The badger shared its den and brought the boy food. Wolves and other wild animals have adopted children, according to fable and historical accounts. For example, according to legend, a wolf raised abandoned twins, Romulus and Remus. The twins later founded Rome, Italy. Numerous accounts of wild animals assisting or adopting humans dot history. Sea animals have rescued humans, especially dolphins, too. There are abundant records of heroism by dogs, cats, mules, horses, pigs, birds, and other animals – for the benefit of humans. *Guideposts* and other publishers have books and articles with such anecdotes. Various organizations award animals for acts of heroism.[10] Animals freely demonstrate love, don't they?

Those first animals must have been the same. Why not? Our awesome God gave His only Son in total sacrifice by crucifixion to redeem humans from our sins. Why wouldn't God's creatures do like He does?

Viktor Frankl wrote that, in the German concentration camps, some would give away their last piece of bread, proving that the freedom to choose one's attitude, one's own way, is the last freedom man has.[11] "The greatest power that a person possesses is the power to choose."[12] Animals clearly have the power of choice. My pets choose to obey me – most of the time! Some choose to be mean, senseless killers. Some choose to be heroes – to live or die sacrificially – like my grandmother's dog.

OLD SOUP, THE ELEPHANT

An awesome example is found in the story of Old Soup, an elephant, owned by a Major Daly. In the summer of 1937, Old Soup was estimated to be about one hundred years old. Old Soup and other elephants were loading cargo, bags of rice, near Cawnpore, India. As in the past, Old Soup was delighted at the sight of the Major's young son and daughter. The children waved to Old Soup as they stood with their nanny, watching.

Suddenly, an angry sound tore the air. A young elephant went mad or rogue. It crushed its handler, smashed against the barge, broke rice sacks on his back and slung them like confetti. Trumpeting wildly, the rogue took off. The children were in his path.

The nanny started to pull the children to safety, but froze. The mad pachyderm spied them and charged. Old Soup pulled from his handler, trumpeted a challenge, lowered his tusks and headed for the rogue. The Major and his soldiers were too far away to help. Only Old Soup could save the children (and their nanny).

The earth shook as the elephants collided. The rogue turned again to the children, but Old Soup slammed him a second time.

Again, the rogue started for the children. Again, Old Soup trumpeted and lunged. The two gray mountains locked tusks and jabbed each other, blasting and pushing. Old Soup, his ears in tatters and his body battered, finally managed to catch the crazy young bull off-guard. His tusks gored the rogue's soft underside several times. The wounded rogue, then, attacked Old Soup with a vengeance.

Elephants rarely fight to the death. This proved to be the exception. The battle raged for more than an hour, as the children and nanny huddled nearby. Plunging tusks repeatedly into each other, one finally hit a vital organ. The defeated giant went to its knees and died. The victor raised his trunk and gave a long eerie blast. His right tusk was shattered. He was bloody from stab wounds. His ears hung in tatters.

The grateful children ran to the elephant. Old Soup was their savior! The weary bleeding giant extended his trunk and gently nuzzled the children. Old Soup did recover from his wounds. The Major retired Old Soup to his home as a treasured "pet."[13]

TWO KINDS OF ANIMALS

Old Soup and the rogue are evidence of two kinds of animals. First, are those who intelligently serve the God and man. The second is among those who insanely rebel and seek to kill and destroy. Consider Adam and the serpent. Eden's serpent was rogue, deceiving Adam, male and female, seeking their death. The first animal sacrifices were like Old Soup, willing to die to save the humans they love. Old Soup was willing to rescue human children, even fighting his own kind. What a price love will pay!

Who knows why some animals choose to love and serve humans, while others turn violent and become killers. While abuse can be blamed in many or most cases, sometimes it happens without human cruelty – as appears to be the case with the rogue. All we know is that some animals go "bad" – just as humans do.

Given that animals make choices, it may lie in that freedom. God gave humans and animals a choice. They can choose Him and His kingdom rule of love, or they can choose to rebel and be destroyers. Adam and some angels sinned against God. [2 Peter 2:4]. Clearly animals can rebel, also.

WHEN GOD CHOSE ADAM'S FIRST CLOTHES

That brings us back to Eden, when God called upon certain animals to provide skins for Adam's clothes. How do you picture that scene? Can you imagine what your pet would do if you were in Adam's shoes (or skin).

Like Old Soup and Nella's dog, don't you think the animals who loved Adam and Eve willingly gave themselves to God for man? I do. I believe some animals were willing to lay down their lives for the humans they loved.

Imagine, with me, different animals stepping before God, volunteering to die in Adam's place:

Lamb:

"Excuse me, Lord God, Your Excellency. May I please have a little time. I love Adam. I'm young and know I'm innocent. Let me die for Adam and Eve. Please, please, please! I know Adam made a dreadful mistake. It is simply terrible. If Adam must die, would you accept a substitute? May I be that substitute? My skin, with its soft wool, would protect and warm them. Let me be the sacrifice, please!"

Goat:

"You are so wise, just, and king in all your ways, Lord. You are good. This must be very difficult for you. You love Adam and Eve with all Your wonderful heart. I love them, too! Adam and I have really had some great times together, kidding around and stuff. I enjoy Adam and Eve (who is so very beautiful). My hide would be tough, Lord. I think Adam will need toughness now. Let us help. Please, Lord, let me die for Adam and Eve. And what is death

anyway?"

Pigeon:

"Father of all living things, Creator, how we praise You for giving us life! The joy of flying free, soaring over land and water into the clouds and above is fabulous. It is akin to fellowship with You. Adam is so like You that we would do anything for him. Adam and Eve have been very good to me. May I ask You if I could be one to die for Adam? While I'm small, my feathered skin would keep Adam and Eve dry when it rains, and it is beautiful and soft. Please let me be the one."

Bull or cow:

"Lord, Master of the universe, I am the one who should die for Adam and Eve. Adam takes good care of me and all my animal friends. Lord, I know he and Eve made bad mistakes. You are forgiving. I would do anything for Adam and Eve. The others are good to offer, Lord, but my skin would be the largest. It would make suitable clothing, which would protect and warm them, would be tough enough, yet soft, too, and is very handsome. It would be a privilege to die in their place, Lord. Please, I must be the one."

Just fantasy? While we don't know what happened, we can make an educated guess, don't you know? Let's see what else we know about sacrificial love of animals.

BIBLE ANIMAL HEROES

There is precedent for this idea in the Bible. The Bible has its rescue or sacrificial love stories featuring animals. Remember Balaam's donkey who interceded for the foolish prophet, saving him from the executing angel? (Numbers 22). Another example is the whale who swallowed Jonah (without chewing him up or digesting him) in obedience to God. [Jonah 2]. Think about the ravens who fed Elijah at the Lord's command – food those ravens might have enjoyed in the drought. [1 Kings 17].

Balaam's donkey served her master sacrificially. She took numerous beatings to save her master's life. That is love in any language. The donkey saw what Balaam did not – an angel with a sword intent on killing Balaam. That donkey could have chosen to leave the prophet to that angel's mission. Balaam never figured out what the donkey was doing, until the Lord opened his eyes! But greed and anger always dull human wits, blind our eyes, and stop our ears.

Included might be the fish which got a coin, of the right denomination, into its mouth and held it there until Peter caught it, so Peter could pay the taxed for Jesus and himself. [Matthew 17:27]. Somehow I don't think Peter, a professional fisherman, threw that fish back in gratitude. That fish sacrificed its life in service to the Lord, I think.

I find that I fluctuate between wondering what my animals see and hear that I do not, and sometimes being glad I don't know! I strive more than ever not to cause my animals pain due to my sin, my missing the mark.

A STUMBLING BLOCK

Animal lovers have stumbled over the blood sacrifices which God required in the Bible. Theologians struggle with the problem of suffering. In writing this book, new insights or ideas have occurred to me. Among them are that the first animals volunteered to die for Adam and Eve. I believe the Lord inspired this book and those insights.

Like a good lawyer, I looked for hard evidence which supports these theories. Your responsibility is to check out what is said here; to consider all the evidence before rendering a verdict; and then to render a verdict based on the whole of the evidence.

Why would an animal sacrifice itself for you or me? It has to be love, caring for another. Only lovers throw themselves into risk by choice. Enduring pain for the sake of something higher or greater. The fearful and selfish avoid such risk and pain. Throughout the ages, the best animal trainers understand that animals perform best when they love what they are doing, or when they are motivated out of love for the person asking them to take risks. Heroes lay down their lives for others because they care. Heroes love God, country, family and/or friends.

This may be what Vicki Hearne was talking about when she wrote about horses who will endure pain to work for us:

> *The horses ... embrace heroic precisions when they can... . What matters in an understanding of the horse' capacity for caring about beauty, precision, perfection of performance. This gives his or her pain meaning and context. ... To say that pain is meaningful is simply to say that for the creature experiencing the pain there is something that matters more than comfort, for the moment at least; something that is the ground of a certain creature's being, what it cares about, toward which it is oriented, in relationship to which pain isn't quite pain anymore, not anything that matters. This is probably not something anyone can make a judgment about for anyone else. My pain, like my death, belongs to me uniquely most of the time.[14]*

If this is the nature of horses, as it is humans and other beings, it helps us understand that the God of the Bible is a God of loving sacrifice. Little wonder that His creation reflects this trait. So, did God act cruelly in requiring the lives of animals for the preservation of Adam and Eve?

First, I do not believe that God forced any animal against its will to die for Adam. I think they went willingly. Why? One of the most telling things about animals – the thing which shouts of God's nature in them – is that cruelty doesn't work. A neglected, beaten, or broken-spirited animal neither performs well nor looks beautiful. The champions, the well-trained performers, do best because they are treated well.[15]

Mom's adage works: "God is love and if it isn't love, it isn't God" Animals, like people, response extraordinarily well to love, and generally return it. Isn't this mute testimony that a loving God created animals, since they reflect His traits of love and care?

Secondly, like Old Soup, when someone is in danger, those with loving hearts react instantly. They risk life and limb to try to save the endangered person. Self-sacrificing acts are not uncommon – among humans or animals. Some make careers of it, like police, fire, and military personnel. Others react according to the moment of need, like trying to stop terrorists, robbers or rapists, or just saving a person from drowning or other danger. Where did the idea come from that such behavior is "good"? It began in the Bible, in Genesis 3, I believe.

Saint Paul wrote in Ephesians 1 that "before the foundation of the world" (literally "casting down of the world"), the Lord chose us and preplanned our adoption as His children through Jesus Christ. In Jesus, God became man. Jesus laid down his life as a sacrifice for human sin, all the mistakes and cruel thoughtless things we've done. Jesus' death by crucifixion was so those who receive Him might live forever. Saint John wrote that Jesus became the "Lamb of God." [John 1:29]. God is the ultimate risk-taker for those whom He loves.

In Eden, after Adam and Eve ate the forbidden fruit and death entered into them, I believe the Lord may have explained to all creation His plan. That when the time was right, God would become man, take on Adam's sin and all the effects of disobedience in Adam's offspring, to fulfill justice and righteousness, so God and man could be reconciled. That includes your sin and mine. I believe the animals listened and understood God's self-sacrificing nature, the very core of real love. God made them to receive and give love. The animals understood.

Even if God never explained his plan back in Eden, His creation is programed to love, to give and receive as caring beings. It is little wonder that some, if not most of God's creatures choose to act like Him. For humans who have eyes to see, creation – even in its corrupted state – still reflects the nature of God.

GOD'S MERCY TO THE ANIMALS

The quality of mercy is not strain'd, It droppeth as the gentle rain from heaven
Upon the place beneath: it is twice blest; It blesseth him that gives and him that takes:
'Tis mightiest in the mightiest: it becomes The throned monarch better than his crown;
His sceptre shows the force of temporal power, The attribute to awe and majesty,
Wherein doth sit the dread and fear of kings; But mercy is above this sceptred sway; It is enthroned in the hearts of kings, It is an attribute to God himself;
And earthly power doth then show likest God's When mercy seasons justice.[16]

Shakespeare's words apply to animals, too. God Himself took the pain of death for those sacrificial animals, for the Bible repeatedly states that God is merciful. While Adam's Fall brought death and its associates (pain, disease and sorrow), God's grace and mercy poured out in answer. Adam and Eve did not know it, but animals whose throats are cut die quickly and without pain. There is much less suffering in violent death than humans realize. God was merciful. God gave sacrificial animals a gift "to die without pain." God gave them "shock." Isn't that just like our loving God!

In trauma, a natural powerful anesthetic literally floods the body. Mortally wounded people report feeling no pain. People may see their own blood before they know they are severely injured. Only if they survive until the shock wears off is pain felt. Animals appear to be similarly pain-free after severe injuries.

No matter how horrible the killing appeared to be to Adam, God's mercy covered the animals which Adam killed. God cares. He cared enough to alleviate the pain of all living things. He still does. This is another piece of evidence that God loves animals – as well as humans.

WHICH SPECIES WERE THE FIRST SACRIFICES?

Which animals did God choose or permit to be the first sacrifices? What skins clothed Adam? The Bible does not say. In Leviticus [chapters 4 and 5], God said bulls, lambs, goats, and doves or pigeons, were acceptable sacrifices for sin. Knowing that dogs, cats, horses and other animals have acted heroically, don't you know God had a lot of volunteers! For me it would have been hard to choose!

The lamb is the most likely. Lambs are innocent, and sweet. Lambs are a delight to watch. Their cuteness evokes a desire the cuddle and protect them. Lamb's wool is very soft. Abel was a keeper of sheep and he sacrificed a lamb to the Lord. [Gen. 4:4]. The lamb was God's choice for Passover, protecting the Jews in Egypt from God's judgment and preparing them to travel to the Promised Land, to freedom from 400 years of slavery. [Exodus 12]. Most important, the lamb is a symbol of the Messiah, Jesus of Nazareth. Jesus is repeatedly called the "Lamb of God." [John 1:29, 36; 1 Corinthians 5:7; 1 Peter 1:18-19]

PUTTING THE PUZZLE TOGETHER

When you put the pieces of Scripture together with other evidence, there is plenty to support the conclusion that God loves not only man, but animals. The sacrificial, love nature of the Creator is reflected in the behavior of many animals. The Love of God is shown by animal friends, both domestic and wild. So is the nature of Satan,

God's adversary, and the cruel effects of disobedience to the One Who is Love.

So we can begin to see the answers to such questions as: Why did God subject animals to the consequences of Adam's Fall? Why did God call for the sacrifice of animals for man's sin? Why is the Bible such a bloody book? There may be more the Lord wants us to understand. But this is a good start.

Writing about Adam's Fall and the animal's roles in it, has not been an easy task. I have wept as I prayed, studied, wrote and rewrote these words. I'm sure I could not have done it without the sustaining grace of my loving Lord. I've seen too clearly my own neglect, my blindness, and my insensitivity to God, His creation and my animal friends. How little I really know about them and God's plans for them!

Just as God volunteered to give his Son, Jesus, a sacrifice to redeem me for my sin, and bring me into His resurrection life now, I see that these animal friends volunteered to die for Adam and Eve. In doing so, they died for you and me, who are ultimately offspring of Adam and Eve. The motivation for these animals had to be that they loved Adam and Eve, just as Balaam's donkey loved the foolish prophet. Adam was made in the image of God. But man has no exclusive contract on God's nature and attributes. Animals love, care, think, share, have fun, enjoy life, and sacrifice. All creation reflects its Creator.

Animals throughout the ages have continued to be saviors, demonstrating the good news that God loves you and me. Even "wild" animals can teach us. Studies show, for example, that skunks make excellent parents. Domestic animals show God's nature in their patient service and forgiving affection to human masters. Just as the animals responded to St. Francis of Assisi, don't you know that the first animals responded to Adam and Eve, and rejoiced at the goodness of God? Animals continue to "tell" us about His goodness today in their actions.

Adam knew God's attitude about His animal creation. God always gives His very best. His volunteers do, also.

While I have never had an animal give its life for me, I have known those who would. Noble animals, they were full of God's love. Why should we not wish such companionship in heaven? Why would we even think that God would exclude them?

What is God's attitude toward His animals? I think Isaiah was told something about that attitude in Isaiah 66:1-4. God does not take pleasure in the sacrifice of animals. Death is a curse.

Animal sacrifice was instituted to preserve human life until God's plans could be matured into fulfillment. Then animal sacrifice was no longer necessary. Historically, animal sacrifice under the Old Covenant ended with the destruction of the Jewish temple in Jerusalem in the first century after Christ's birth and death. Christians believe, based on the Bible, that Jesus Christ became the Lamb of God and His crucifixion ended the need for animal sacrifice. If you do not believe that, don't you risk the alternative or the consequences?

Looking at Scripture as a pattern, let us look for more evidence of God's future, eternal plans for his creation. The God of Love, the God of Life, is ultimately the God of sacrifice and resurrection. If anything shouts from the pages of the Bible, it is that Jesus Christ is Life, and Resurrection from death, of all sorts. We shall see that He is for all His creation.

ENDNOTES:

1. William Shakespeare, *Merchant of Venice*, Act V., Scene I, Portia's speech

2. Charles Dickens, *A Tale of Two Cities*, English novelist (1812 - 1870)

3. *Listening to the Animals; To the Rescue*, Introduction, [Guideposts, 1999]

4. *Compton's Interactive Encyclopedia*, "Dogs"

5. Susan Chernak McElroy, *Animals as Teacher & Healers*

6. Id., p. 54-55

7.   See *Animals As Teachers & Healers,* supra; *Listening to the Animals,* supra; and *Chicken Soup for the Pet Lover's Soul,* (1998), for examples.

8.   *Animals as Teachers & Healers*

9.   *The Great Fables of All Nations,* supra, pp. 439-430.

10.   *In Real Animal Heroes* [Signet Books, 1997], editor Paul Stevens identifies organizations which grant awards to animals which have demonstrated heroic courage, devotion and sacrifice for humans or other animals. Included are stories of the animals listed above.

11.   Man's search for meaning -- Quoted in *Chicken Soup for the Soul*

12.   J. Martin Kohe, from *Chicken Soup for the Soul.*

13.   *Real Animal Heroes,* supra, pp. 32-36

14.   Vicki Hearne, *Adam's Task; Calling Animals by Name,* pp. 153, 157-158

15.   From Xenophon, the ancient Greek who is the "father of training" to modern trainers, including "horse whisperers", all agree that genuine training occurs only when an animal is understood; when communication is established through respect and listening to the animal. This means good treatment, never cruelty.

16.   William Shakespeare, *The Merchant of Venice,* Act IV, Scene I, Portia's speech

CHAPTER 9

COVENANTS: BEGINNING WITH NOAH AND THE ARK

*"And as for Me, behold, I establish My covenant with you
and with your descendants after you, and with **every living creature** that is with you: the birds, the cattle, and
every beast of the earth with you, of all that go out of the
ark, every beast of the earth. Thus, I establish My covenant with you: Never again shall all flesh be cut off by the
waters of the flood; never again shall there be a flood to
destroy the earth.*
*And God said: "This is the sign of the **covenant** which I
make between Me and you, and **every living creature**
that is with you, for perpetual generations...*

Gen. 9:9-17 [NKJ]

D id you know that "every living creature" which was with Noah
has a covenant with God? That includes all species on the Ark --
as in cows and pigs, lizards and snakes, elephants and mice, peacocks

and sparrows, and bugs! The excerpts from Genesis quoted above are relevant to the answer to Mom's question. What other promises or covenants do you think the Lord made to or with animals? What do these promises mean? Do they relate to the question about animals in eternity?

WHAT IS A COVENANT?

Many people don't realize what "covenant" really means. The dictionary defines "covenant" as a binding agreement between two or more persons; a compact; or a contract. The concept of a covenant may mean little to one without knowledge of the ancient understanding of covenant — especially a blood covenant. Covenants usually involved each person speaking curses and blessing on the other. Breaking your covenant vows brought on the curses. Keeping covenant brought the blessings. Becoming "blood brothers" (or sisters) is an example of a covenant. When you covenant with someone, you are pledging to care for them and their interests as though they are your own for the rest of your life and theirs.

In Biblical times, covenants were serious business. They meant the makers were bound to each other for life or until the covenant was fulfilled. The Hebrew word for "covenant" is *beriyth*. It means "a cutting" from the ancient practice of passing between the divided portions of a sacrificial victim — as Abraham did in Genesis 15. (I believe the sacrifices to clothe Adam involved a covenant of redemption for all flesh.) If blood is shed, the makers are taking a holy vow which must not be broken.

"Testament" in the phrase "last Will and Testament," means "covenant." The Lord made two covenants with people: first with the Jews or Hebrew people; and second with all men who become disciples of Jesus Christ. [See Malachi 3:1] The Bible, accepted by Christians, contains "Old Testament" and "New Testament" books.

In theology, "covenant" represents the promises God makes with men, i.e., humans, with whom He has a relationship. A Biblical covenant is a promise or set of promises which last for life or eternity. When the Lord promises something, it is a sure thing. God never breaks covenant. God is Truth [Deut. 32:4; John 14:6; 17:17] and cannot lie [Num. 23:19; Titus 1:2] – or He wouldn't be Who He says He is! That is why one can trust the Bible, His Book.

Americans no longer have anything resembling an ancient covenant. Mere contracts are often broken. Adoption is the closest thing to a covenant we have in our Western society. (It is almost impossible to get out of a finalized adoption.) Marriage used to be an irrevocable covenant. Marriage has become a mere non-binding agreement, even with most Christians.

One never enters into a covenant lightly, since it binds that person to the other for life or eternity. Breaking covenant brings dire curses on the breaker. That is surely what Jesus addressed in Matthew 5:33-37, concluding that we should let our "Yes" be "Yes" and our "No" be "No" — without fancy oaths or vows.

The Bible records over a dozen covenants which the Lord God made. Some include animals. The covenant God made with Noah and "every living creature" is the first recorded covenant. Animals are important to the Creator or He would not have made covenants with them. In Genesis 9, the Lord repeated "never again" (or similar words) which made the promise to humans and animals eternal.

NOAH AND THE GREAT FLOOD

This chapter opened with a quote about the Great Flood or Noahic covenant — God's promise to Noah and all animals not to destroy this world with another flood. It may shock a few people to learn the Almighty enters covenant with "dumb" beasts. It's in the Bible, however.

While many have heard the story of Noah and the Ark as children, most have not studied it as an adult. I gained a new perspective when I did. Genesis, Chapters 6 through 9, covers the Noahic Flood. We recommend that you read these passages, paying attention to the references which include animals. The Great Flood and Noahic covenant involve important points and a pattern. These are keys to Mom's question. The Bible shows that the Lord uses earthly things to give man patterns, or types and shadows of heaven and the world to come. [Hebrews 8:5] Moses was given the patterns of things for the tabernacle of God. [Exodus 25:9 and 40, and Numbers 8:4] Solomon was given the pattern of things for the temple in Jerusalem. [1 Chron. 28, 11-19]

The term "all flesh" is a key phrase throughout the Scripture and includes animals. Knowing this is necessary to understanding God's plan for animals. Previously, I thought the phrase applied solely to humans. In some contexts that is correct; however, often "flesh" is an inclusive term for all creation. In Genesis 6 the Lord said "all flesh" had become corrupt and then sent the Flood to cleanse the earth. What do you think that means?

Believing in a literal Biblical Creation or Great Flood may not be essential to answering Mom's question. But then, it may be. Faith is a requirement in the Biblical plan. Ask yourself: "Do I believe the Bible is mostly myth? Do I believe we originated out of chaos, descending from apes? Or do I believe we are created in the image of the Un-created Creator, a Being of absolute power and goodness?"

Do not confuse the ability to "believe" (or think) as you wish, with the right to do so. We each have the capacity to do murder. No civilized society gives its citizens the right to do murder. If I understand the Bible, the final judgment of the Lord will involve what we believe, as well as what we have done. Choose what you believe carefully, friend! Beliefs govern actions. Love is the royal law of God, so whatever[1] is not loving is wrong.

God is interested in both man's beliefs **and** his actions. The Lord is a just lawgiver, defining what is right and wrong to believe and to worship. God is also judge and king or governor over all this earth. (Isa. 33:22). God is withholding judgment at this time, for His own good reasons. It pays to understand His laws, justice, and mercy.

Scripture was given by God to guide us into all truth. The "types and shadows" help us understand what we've never seen: the reality of God's heaven and eternity. Like blind men trusting the seeing, we need the Lord who sees and knows all.

Many believe Noah's Ark is a type and shadow of God's salvation. This type is fulfilled in God's Messiah, whom Christians know to be Jesus of Nazareth. Let's look closer at this type and shadow.

A CORRUPT WORLD

Only ten generations after Adam fell, humans had gone totally bad. [Gen. 5 & 6.] (I use the word "bad" in the pejorative sense of evil, wicked, corrupt, murdering and cruel, not a slang compliment.) It started when Adam and Eve's first two sons got into it and Cain killed Abel in a fit of jealousy. Abel's blood still cries "murder" from the earth. [Gen. 4 & Heb. 11:4 & 12:24] Only one and one-half of God's days, i.e. 1500 years, and man was very corrupt and wicked: "... every intent of the thoughts of his heart was only evil continually." [Gen. 6:5] The Lord was sorry He created us and was grieved. The Lord said:

> *I will blot out man whom I have created from the face of*
> *the land, from man to animals to creeping things to birds*
> *of the sky; for I am sorry that I have made them.*
>
> Gen. 6:7[NASV]

Animals were included in God's indictment. Why? Remember animals have choices, too. The old serpent fomented Adam's Fall. Satan must have led other animals into such insanity. It goes without saying that wild animals, especially carnivores, are "wild" because they are unpredictably dangerous to humans. "The survival of the fittest" is not the real rule of nature, but a sign of anarchy — of disharmony, of the loss of Eden for animals, too.

Even some domestic animals are "rogues," – irreconcilably dangerous. You might say they are like Satan, the evil serpent, who is the arch-enemy of man. Animal trainers agree that rogues occur infrequently. These are animals with the equivalent of a criminal personality. Both Monty Roberts, in *The Man Who Talks to Horses* and Vicki Hearne, in *Adam's Task*, speak of the rarity of horses who are man-killers. When a half-ton or more of horse is pure meanness, it is indeed dangerous. "Wild" animals are not rogues in this sense, although some may be.

This is **not** to say all animals who injure humans are rogues. Most animal experts agree that most animal injuries are because the animal is acting naturally. For example, most dogs bite or harm humans for reasons perfectly understandable to a dog. We should examine our behavior to find out if we are doing something to make the animal bite, kick, or otherwise do harm.[2] Even though animal rogues are rare, just as with human homicidal maniacs, they do exist. Imagine the earth filled with such humans and animals!

The Bible says that the "earth was *filled* with violence." [Gen. 6:11-12] "It was corrupt – depraved and putrid" [Amplified Bible]:

> ...*for **all flesh** had corrupted their way upon the earth. Then God said to Noah, "The end of **all flesh** has come before Me; for the earth is filled with violence because of them*; and behold, I am about to destroy them with the earth."*   Gen. 6:12-13

I'm glad I missed that era of history—although today all flesh is getting pretty bad!

GOD'S JUST JUDGEMENT

Man, therefore, was not the only "flesh" which the Lord said was corrupt and violent. "All flesh" in Genesis, Chap. 6-9, included both man and animal, because both were destroyed.

In some cases it is not clear if "all flesh" describes only humans, or includes both humans and animals. See for example, Gen. 7:15, 16 & 21; Lev. 7:15-21; 17:11-16; Num. 16:22; 18:15; Job 34:15; Ps. 56:4, 65:2; 136:25; 145:2; Isa. 40:5-6; Jer. 32:27, for a partial list.[3]

The prophets, Isaiah, Jeremiah, and Ezekiel, used "all flesh" when speaking of God's judgment and destruction on sinful nations, tribes or peoples. We know from Joshua, and from Jonah, those judgments included animals, as well as people.

Why would God, a loving and good God, order the destruction of children and animals? Are they not innocents? Not always. Also, Christians need to realize that passing from this life can mean a release. See Isaiah 57:1-2. As a lawyer, I have learned a bit about the effects of severe abuse. For example, adoptions which fail often involve children severely abused prior to the adoption. Abuse has long-term effects. The younger the abuse occurs, the less likely there will be recovery, according to some experts. A local faith-filled Christian family adopted an infant who had been burned repeatedly by cigarettes (among other abuses). In spite of coming into a loving and nurturing home, this child grew up a criminal. As an adult, he became a danger to his adoptive mother and family. Violence ended his life. In one sense, his death was merciful, as his behavior was uncontrolled. Think of a whole society filled with people severely abused as children! Such a society would likely be violent and a threat to others.

A television program reviewed the deprivation of orphaned and fatherless children in post World War I Germany. These children were discontented and dysfunctional. They became the men and women who brought Hitler to power. They formed the cruel SS troops who enjoyed torturing and killing for the Reich.

Psychologists, sociologists and criminologists find that young children who are abused repeatedly, physically and/or sexually, can be difficult, if not impossible, to rehabilitate. This is not to say that we should not try. Nor is it to say that there are no success stories. God can and does heal emotions as well as bodies. This is merely to acknowledge that the ability and resources to help the severely abused are limited. The failure rate is dismally high. Such children can be "dead" inside — to love, trust, relationships and everything good. Tragically, they are very dangerous to themselves and others.

The same holds for animals that have been terribly misused or abused. Some go crazy and are dangerous to have around. The movie, *The Horse Whisperer*, deals with a horse crazy with fear — due to severe injuries – not human abuse. If cowboy and horse-gentler (Robert Redford) had not been able to get through to the horse, it was scheduled for destruction. Death can be merciful to those animals who cannot recover from injury or abuse. It can be the only way to safeguard their potential victims. They are dangerous to themselves and others.

GOD'S "HOUSECLEANING"

Because of one man, Noah, the Bible says the Lord decided to only "clean house" rather than demolish the earth. If there had not been one righteous human, God would have trashed everything. The Lord God chose instead to keep on working to save, to redeem, all flesh from Adam's Fall. What a task God took on!

> *In the six hundredth year of Noah's life... all the fountains of the great deep burst open, and the floodgates of the sky were opened. and the rain fell upon the earth for forty days and forty nights. .. and the water increased and lifted up the ark, so that it rose above the earth ... and all flesh that moved on the earth perished, birds and cattle and beasts and every swarming thing that swarms upon the earth, and all mankind; of all that was on the dry land, all in whose nostrils was the breath of the spirit of life, died. ... Only Noah was left, together with those that were with him in the ark.*   Gen. 7:11 [NASV]

Did you know it had never rained on the earth before the Great Flood? Pre-Flood, the earth was watered every morning by a mist. [Genesis 2:4-6]. I had always thought it just rained. In the Great Flood, the Lord sent a great rain AND opened the "springs of the deep" for forty days -- that's lots of water! Waters burst from above and below the earth. It was cataclysmic. Think blinding rain plus a tsunami of huge proportions. For 150 days, the flood waters soaked and scrubbed the earth really good.

The Great Flood is not a myth – although some treat it as such. There is archeological **and** sociological evidence support the Flood. There is evidence showing a great flood happened an estimated 4,500 years ago in the Black Sea area. Some scientists agree there is geological evidence of this flood in rock strata around the world.[4] Most cultures have a Great Flood story, i.e., that there was a great flood which covered the earth and killed almost all human and animal life, including a race of giants. [See Gen. 6:4 re: giants.]

The Great Flood apparently brought major changes. The earth prior to the fall and Noah's Flood was a different place. Some scientists say there is evidence that the Earth, prior to the Great Flood, was like a huge greenhouse. Earth's land seems to have been one mass, with the current continents joined together. (The continents do look like puzzle pieces which would fit together.) After the flood, the earth was divided during Peleg's time. [Gen. 10:25.] Also, Genesis 1 describes earth's land mass as sandwiched between two bodies of water: the firmament or heavens, and waters trapped under the earth like a massive artesian well spring. The resulting greenhouse effect could have provided an environment for life forms to grow huge in size and to live longer than we can. The two bodies of water also would provide enough moisture to cover the earth in a Great Flood.

There is nothing in science which can provide us with accurate information about the Pre-Flood life. We can only speculate about Pre-Flood relationships between humans, or the relationships between animals, or the relationships between man and animals.[5] At this point, the Bible stands pretty much alone as a source to explore those relationships. Noah and his relatives were the only human survivors. Being very succinct, the Bible does not give us much info. Much of what we think is really speculation.

THE LORD'S GREAT PLAN

The Lord planned well for the saving of Noah and the animals. A hundred years before the Flood, God told Noah to build an ark, to gather pairs of "every living thing of all flesh." [Genesis 6:13-22 & 7:1-5] Everything was included: birds, animals, and "creeping things." Creeping things appears to describe insects and reptiles. (Some consider insects and reptiles very creepy!) Of the domestic animals and the birds, Noah was to take "seven sevens" of each kind, both male and female. The rest, i.e., the wild animals, came in pairs. Noah was to take food for himself, his family and all the living things. What a huge task!

God's interest and concern for each and every living creature is demonstrated in these detailed provisions. Every species was preserved, from aardvarks to zebras. All came to Noah from elephants to ants (and cockroaches). Dr. G. Thomas Sharp shows that Noah's ark was large enough to house dinosaurs, too![6]

GOD'S ARK OF SAFETY

The ark was a large structure: 300 cubits long, 50 cubits wide and 30 cubits high. [Gen. 6:15]. A "cubit" is the length between a man's finger-tips and elbow -- about eighteen inches. The Ark was at least 150 yards long, 25 yards wide and 15 yards high. (About the same numbers in meters.) Think of it! One-and one-half football fields long and 4 or 5 stories high! If Noah used a giant's cubit, it would be much larger.

It needed to be large. There had to be room and food for 75 people, plus all the land animals and birds.

LOADING THE ARK

And Noah did according to all that the Lord had commanded him. ... Of clean animals and animals that are not clean and birds and everything that creeps on the ground, there went into the ark to Noah by twos, male and female, as God had commanded Noah. Gen. 7:5, 8-10 [NASV]

How did Noah gather and load all those animals and birds? The Bible says **the animals came to Noah**, i.e., they *came* to Noah. Noah did not gather them. [Gen. 6:20; 7:8-9, 14-16.] The whole operation was a volunteer thing. The Lord undoubtedly called the animals; and the chosen ones heard and obeyed.

There is precedent for God's calling of animals and their obedience. Consider that ravens obeyed the Lord in bringing food to the prophet Elijah in the desert. [1 Kings 17:1-7] Lions obeyed the Lord in several different instances. [1 Kings 13 & Daniel 6]

There are numerous present-day accounts of wild animals coming to people as apparent answers to prayer. One that impressed me was about a young man was grieving over his mother's untimely death. Daily he took his grief to the Lord, as he sought solace at her grave. In the lonely cemetery, a hawk approached him. The man began to feed it and tried to entice it to his hand. Finally, the hawk alighted on his arm -- without hurting the man with its sharp talons. At that moment the man's grief left him. The hawk disappeared, as though its mission was accomplished.[7]

The Lord sent those animals to Noah, to fulfill His purpose. (I think Noah may have prayed for his animal friends.)

WHO WAS THIS MAN, NOAH?

I recall an insightful adult Sunday School lesson on Noah. First, Noah marked the tenth generation from Adam. Ancients believed ten was the number of "completion." Lamech was Noah's father. He named his first son "Noah" because it means "rest." [Gen. 5:29] Lamech prophesied Noah would bring rest to the earth in his time. Noah, as tenth from Adam, was expected to give people rest from the curse on the ground. Every time Noah heard his name, he was reminded of his destiny.

A reading of Genesis chapter 5 reveals the first generations measured their lives in centuries, not decades. Noah was born 1056 years after Adam was created. Six of his nine male ancestors were alive for years of Noah's life. Only Adam, Seth and Enoch were gone.

Noah's grandfather Methuselah lived until the year of the Great Flood – about 600 years of Noah's life – and knew all his forefathers. Noah would have heard stories about the beginning, Adam and the animals.

People still teach their children and entertain themselves with stories (in books, videos, etc.). Noah's grandfathers must have loved to tell about Adam and the early days on earth, the beginning and the Fall. Uncles, aunts and cousins likely joined in. Think of the tales Noah heard and the lessons he learned from them!

LEARNING ABOUT HIS PAST

Noah's grandfathers would likely have taught the young man much about his history and name, Rest or Noah. Noah must have heard details about the Pre-Fall world. God and Adam walked every day in that special Garden. What the "cool of the evening" was like in Eden. What the sound of God's voice was like. Noah likely heard about the incredible beauty of God as He and Adam were face to face. How would Noah's forefathers have described the fragrance of God's own being -- or the aromas of that perfect Garden, with plants and animals unmarred by sin and death? What words describe the perfect peace and joy brought by obedience to God's will? Noah must have gained precious insights into intimacy with God and God's creation.

Most youngsters love hearing about animals. Imagine Noah questioning his grandfathers about the animals! Adam clearly related his experiences with the animals to his offspring – how he learned to know them, name them, and fellowship with them as Adam tended the Garden. The peace, rest, joy which animals seem to produce in humans, and humans can give back to animals would have been unspoiled and awesome. Adam understood the language of the animals and communicated freely with these first friends. Legend says the animals could talk with humans. What conversations must have occurred? What would Noah have thought about never struggling with the curse of sin. How thistles and thorns made hard the growing food after the Fall. Noah would have learned of man's stewardship and authority over every living thing and how to exercise that authority properly.

In order to bring rest to the ground, Noah had to learn to walk with God as Adam had, and as Enoch did. Like Adam, Noah needed to know the animals, to know their ways, what they ate and drank, what activities kept them healthy and happy, etc. Noah had to know how to relate and command each of the animals. To do this Noah had to walk with God.

Compare Noah to St. Francis of Assisi, a man who preached to and lived with animals. Noah had to talk to animals and they had to respond (positively) to him. Noah and the animals were going to spend a long time together on the Ark!

THE HARMONY ON THE ARK

There is no record of anything but harmony on the Ark during the year Noah and the animals floated on the waters. What a lovely word, "harmony"! The Garden of Eden was a place of harmony. Noah's Ark was the same. Actually, so it makes sense. Where God rules and reigns, there is harmony and love. On God's Ark, built by Noah, there was no violence. The violent were, no doubt, not invited onto the Ark. Noah's rest occurred because the unrepentant wicked, those who trash peace, were destroyed.

"Rest" includes peace from striving for food and safety. The wolves did not eat or even growl at the caribou. The lion laid with the lamb. According to Scripture, man and animals were vegetarians. [Gen. 1:29; 9:3.] They would not have been tempted to eat each other, as there was no division into carnivore and prey. Even if the animals had divided into eater and eaten, the Ark would have the atmosphere of Eden, that of pure love. Grace to live in peace together would have been given to all. Don't you think the animals drawn to the Ark were lovers, exceptionally devoted to God?

What harmony the Ark must have had. Man loving animals. Animals loving man. All caring for each other. Hallelujah! The Ark would be a type of vehicle to gain God's heaven. Heaven is the place of ultimate rest, of love, of harmony. It's not a "rest" from all work because work is good. It's rest from the curse of toil. Heaven on earth is when we enter God's rest (Heb. 4), from human labor. Peace must exist for every living thing, great and small.

Agnes Sanford, a pioneer of healing in the 20th century, learned to pray for the earth and its creatures to live in harmony and peace. In the years she lived near the San Andreas fault in California, there were no major earthquakes.[8] Her garden was a wondrous place, where bees did not sting and flowers flourished. I like her theology!

Noah needed faith-based knowledge and skill to manage the animals on the Ark, so there was peace-full co-existence. What quarters did each need for comfort? How to provide exercise and entertainment for each species? You may know that bored animals, like people become unhappy, even dangerous.

Even the preparations needed such faith to know how and what to do. What were the best foods for giraffes and gorillas? How to best preserve foods so they were healthy for pandas and peacocks? How much would each need for the voyage? It was a huge undertaking. Noah had to know a lot about each animal!

Since the best of each species likely volunteered to come to the Ark, they must have helped according to their ability. It's easy to imagine the "beasts of burden" like elephants, horses and oxen, helping. Beavers could have cut trees and shaped logs. Deer could have stripped the bark off. Oxen and horses could have hauled them to Noah. Elephants could have lifted the wood, like living cranes, to the carpenters. Maybe gorillas and monkeys helped do some building. There are tools users among the birds, so they too could have played a part in building and loading the Ark. All could have helped gather and preserve food and bedding materials for themselves and others.

Birds, rodents and ants are great at gathering stuff! Parrots may have directed traffic or used their sharp beaks to cut things. Bees could have upped honey production so humans and bears could enjoy the sweet stuff.

Once afloat, the animals could have continued to help Noah and each other with everyday tasks of feeding, cleaning up, and entertaining each other, don't you think?

AFTER THE FLOOD

God used the Ark to preserve a remnant of people and animals to replenish the earth after its bath. Restoration is God's work. (See Psalm 91 and 1 Cor. 10:13.)

When the waters receded, Noah and the animals came out of the Ark onto dry land. Noah offered a sacrifice, before all disbursed. After the blood sacrifice, God spoke the following covenant:

*"Now behold, I Myself do establish **My covenant** with you, and with your descendants after you; **and with every living creature that is with you, the birds, the cattle, and every beast of the earth with you; of all that comes out of the ark, even every beast of the earth.** I establish My covenant with you; and all flesh shall never again be cut off by the water of the flood, neither shall there again be a flood to destroy the earth." God said, "This is the sign of the **covenant** which I am making between Me and you and **every living creature** that is with you, **for all successive generations**; I set My bow in the cloud, and it shall be for a sign of a covenant between Me and the earth.*

Gen. 9:9-13 [NASV] (Emphasis supplied.)

Every time we see a rainbow, we know it is a sign God keeps His promises. The promise to never destroy the world by a flood is a beautiful promise, good forever. Like the promise of redemption from death through a Messiah, it is a promise not just to humans, but every living creature. No matter what you have been taught, read the promise again for yourself. The Ark is a symbol, a picture, of God's salvation or redemption of the world. (Most of the time, ministers speak only of humans in this plan of salvation. However, a careful and fair reading of the Bible shows that animals are included. The Lord's covenant is with both.) The Noahic covenant is for man and animals throughout their generations. It is an eternal promise. There is nothing in the Bible which excludes the animals. God is inclusive of all His creation who choose to come to Him through His proffered vehicle of salvation.

ALL FLESH

The word "flesh" is not limited to humans in the Bible. That's true in modern English. Speaking to the inhabitants of the Ark, God said "all flesh" – not just human flesh. The same Hebrew word is used for human flesh [Gen. 2:21, 23] and animal flesh [Exo. 12:8; 16:3; Lev. 7:15; Num. 11:4 & 13]. In the New Testament, Paul wrote:

> *All flesh is not the same flesh, but there is one flesh of men, and another flesh of beasts, and another flesh of birds, and another of fish.*   1 Cor. 15:39 [NASV]

"Flesh" in the Bible has several meanings. One use is for muscle, sinew and skin, as in "mortal flesh." Another is for "soulish desires," i.e., behavior that is selfish rather than pleasing to God. God's permissive will (if there is such a thing) tolerates man and animals who do fleshly things, without immediate or perhaps severe consequences. (There are always effects or consequences for every action.)

Following the Flood, God's permissive will or law changed. Man and animals were permitted to eat flesh. Meat eating was "legalized" in God's earth. Obviously, carnivores and omnivores came into being.

After the Flood, the eating of meat remained surrounded with many restrictions.[9] Jewish Rabbis taught against wanton killing and causing needless pain to an animal. Meat was to be eaten in moderation. The Biblical basis for these rabbinal teaching or laws includes:

Every moving thing that lives shall be food for you. I have given you all things, even as the green herbs. But you shall not eat flesh with its life [Hebrew "nephesh"], that is, its blood. Surely for your lifeblood I will demand a reckoning; from the hand of every beast I will require it, and from the hand of man. From the hand of every man's brother I will require the life of man. "Whoever sheds man's blood, By man his blood shall be shed; For in the image of God He made man. [Gen. 9:3-6]

The rabbinal teaching drew seven rules or laws from God's words to Noah. One law, from the Noah covenant, prohibited eating anything still alive. Also, the blood was and is never to be eaten by anyone, including Christians. [See Acts 15:29.] (I have never knowingly eaten blood pudding or other dishes made of blood.) It is not hard to figure out that God forbids humans to partake of the blood of animals because the soul, the life, is in the blood. If there is anything to the old saying that we become what we eat, that would help explain God's law about not eating blood. We are not vampires. We are not to take the souls of humans or animals into us. Religions and cults which partake of blood break God's law and commandments.

As we mentioned earlier, God graced both carnivores and their prey. Usually carnivores kill very swiftly. They are equipped with sharp teeth designed to bite deep, or the raptors have both sharp beaks and talons. Shock, that blessed anesthetic, and a lack of fear of death, are gifts of God to prey animals, gifts which prevents real pain when becoming dinner.[10] God is love and mercy is His way.

As we shall see further on, eating flesh will not happen in heaven. Don't worry, you won't miss eating meat. I have every confidence that heaven's feasts will be indescribably delicious to our changed bodies. [Although, only God could make eggplant taste as good as a good steak!) We will be happy there or it would not be heaven to us.

ANOTHER COVENANT WITH CRITTERS - THE FARMER'S BLESSING!

Noah's Covenant is perhaps the most important for Mom's question. But the next covenant God made with living things is astonishing.

In that day I will make a covenant for them With the beasts of the field, With the birds of the air, And with the creeping things of the ground. Bow and sword of battle I will shatter from the earth, To make them lie down safely.

Hosea 2:18 [NKJ]

God made a covenant with insects! And wild beasts! It's in the Bible! Why? So they would not destroy crops grown by God's chosen people. It's a blessing on faithful farmers who honor the Lord.

Isn't it interesting that God made the covenant not with man only, but also with the insects and wild animals? I think that covenant means He promised something to the grasshoppers, deer, rodents, rabbits, etc., – as they can be very destructive to crops. Some can destroy entire fields in short order.

Do you wonder what the Lord promised to do for these critters? Hosea did not record the answer. Maybe it was good things to eat, protection, and cozy dwellings. Perhaps it was heaven.

IMPLIED COVENANTS - GOD'S PROMISES TO ANIMALS

There are other scriptures which imply covenants, even though the term is not used. For example, on God's command, ravens fed the prophet Elijah while he hid by the brook from King Ahab and Queen Jezebel. [I Kings 17]. God likely made a covenant with those obedient ravens. (I like to think those ravens picked choice food from Ahab's table or kitchens!) Assuming this verse is not metaphorical, birds have the nasty task of "picking" the eye of a mocker. [Prov. 10:17.] God is a very, very good employer, so it is likely He promised good things to those birds.

Jesus said that not a sparrow "falls to the ground" without God seeing, and that God feeds the birds of the air. [Luke 12:24; Matt. 10:29-31; Luke 12:6-7; see also Job 38:41; and Ps. 147:9.] It is God, not man, who cares for the wild animals and supplies them with the necessities of life. His love and compassion extend far beyond humans "made in His image." Philosophers note that God cares for beasts in areas where humans are scarce – if I recall my college philosophy classes.

In truth there is much evidence that indicates animals know and obey, even love their Creator. Consider that Jesus rode an untrained donkey's colt, from a small town into a city, with crowds shouting, and the crowds also threw things in front of the donkey. There is no report the donkey acted up once. [Matt. 21:1-7; Mark 11:1-10; Luke 19:29-38.] Hungry lions shut their mouths in the presence of Daniel for a whole night, but quickly devoured his accusers. [Dan. 6:16-24.] Another awesome example is the lion which executed a prophet who disobeyed the Lord – yet the lion did not kill the prophet's donkey. Both that lion and the donkey stood by the prophet's body until people came and took the corpse away! [I Kings 13]. Birds sent from the Ark brought back an olive branch to Noah. [Gen. 8]. Don't you know the Lord rewarded such obedience!

Loving humans echo this in their care of animals. We spend hard-earned money on food, toys, vet bills, and even funeral arrangements for our loved pets. It is not hard, because our animals love us so very well. There are many people who know the love of God through animals and respond. Some even find their animals' love and loyalty superior to humans they have known – a sad commentary on human relationships.

Possibly this is why many of us enjoy fantasies and movies featuring some intelligent animal or animals. Somewhere inside us we recognize the truth in these tales – that animals have souls and spirits, being clever, loving, even heroic (or the opposite).

ANIMALS FASTING

In the Bible book of Jonah, we learn animals fast and repent and God forgives, not just people, but animals. Whatever Nineveh's sins were, God had a "belly-full" and judged the Ninevites. God's judgment was for execution so the whole city had become very corrupt and depraved, and likely very violent. Being merciful, God sent His prophet Jonah to Nineveh to warn them.

> *Jonah began to enter the city on the first day's walk. ....*
> *he cried out ...* "*Yet forty days, and Nineveh shall be over-*
> *thrown!*" *** *Then word came to the king of Nineveh; ...*
> *And he caused it to be proclaimed ...throughout Nineveh by*
> *the decree of the king and his nobles, saying, "Let neither*
> ***man nor beast, herd nor flock, taste anything; do***
> ***not let them eat, or drink water.*** *But let man **and***
> ***beast*** *be covered with sackcloth, and cry mightily to God;*
> *yes, let every one turn from his evil way and from the*
> *violence that is in his hands. Who can tell if God will turn*
> *and relent, and turn away from His fierce anger, so that*
> *we may not perish?" Then God saw their works, that they*
> *turned from their evil way; and God relented from the*
> *disaster that He had said He would bring upon them, and*
> *He did not do it.*   Jonah 3:4 & 6-10 [NKJ]

Jonah was angry about this. Then the Lord asked Jonah:
> *And should I not have concern for the great city of*
> *Nineveh, in which there are more than a hundred and*
> *twenty thousand people who cannot tell their right hand*
> *from their left—and also **many animals?***"
>   Jonah 4:11 [NIV]

Have you ever heard of animals fasting and crying to God or turning from evil and violence? The animals of Nineveh did. The Hebrew term includes horses, donkeys, camels, cattle, goats, sheep and other domestic animals. Why would animals need to repent? Well, consider that like humans, animals can be stubborn, mean, moody, cantankerous and even dangerous. In cultures like Nineveh, they could be involved in bestiality, i.e., depraved sex between humans and animals. They needed to repent – which simply means "change your ways; do a 180° turn in behavior and attitude."

While the Jonah passage struck me as novel when I first read it, it does make sense. I have watched my animals' body-language show guilt, as they know they've done something wrong. I've seen them change their behavior to please me. I have to forgive my animals' disobedience, too. Don't you?

GOD'S CARE FOR ANIMALS

God recognized and honored that fast of Nineveh's animals (and people). That's proof God's mercy is not only toward humans but also toward animals. Maybe when animals "go off their feed" and don't eat, they are fasting and crying to God for a purpose? Why not? I read of a cat who quit eating when its dying master did, and followed him in death days after he passed. People have told me they felt their pet joined them in prayer at times. It makes sense that animals can fast and cry out to God in their own ways. In some cultures, there is a belief that pets can ask to die in place of a sick human, because of instances where a very sick human lived but their pet sickened and died. (I don't know if it is true or not.)

It makes sense that God answers the petitions of animals, as well as humans. God loves all His creation. There is a whole lot we do not know about God and His living creatures! So why not?

GOD, THE COVENANT KEEPER

The God of the Bible is a covenant maker. Since Noah, there has never been another flood to destroy the earth. The rainbow which appears with rain is a constant reminder. The Jewish people have enjoyed the next longest covenant with the Lord. It's fundamental to the Jewish faith that Jews and God are eternally joined through covenant.[11] In defining the nature of a covenant people, Arthur Hertzberg said that when the people God has chosen obey His divine commandments, they experience His nearness greater than any other peoples; God is not a divine despot, so obedience to Him is not slavery, but the way to a recurrent encounter with Him. [12]

Christians are also a covenant people. Too few of us really understand what that means. Real faith is based on and grows from informed obedience to the Lord and His truth. The more we know of Him, the more our belief grows. The more we trust and obey, the more God can entrust to us. The more God trusts us, the more the benefits He can bestow. In fact, that is true of human relationships and human-animal relationships.

We can be like Noah, who trusted and obeyed God, in spite of persecution and being called into the unknown. Noah was a bearer of rest or peace, and a buffer between sinful violence and God's just judgment. He was a gateway of sorts to the (truly) good life. We can be the same to all creation. Isn't it clear that is God's commission for Adam and Adam's offspring?

To people who are in covenant with God, there are paradoxes. By analogy, consider becoming an artist, musician or scientist. To become a master takes not just talent, but slavish devotion and obedience. The best human and animal performers spend much time perfecting their skills. One cannot but wonder what animals who have obeyed God, enjoy as a result of such covenants between them.

This study is at least legal proof that God does not think of animals as existing solely for man's use and pleasure. God created animals for a purpose. God instructs and uses animals, blesses them, judges them and rewards them. It has been exciting to learn that the Lord established irrevocable, eternal covenants with animals! Words cannot describe my feelings about this and the possibilities it opens. I know God loves you and me. Now I know the Lord God loves all flesh, all creatures.

These covenants are a major piece of Mom's puzzle. Mom's question is turning out to have interesting answers. Keep in mind that we are still building a case, precept by precept, to see if the Bible says whether animals go to heaven. We may still be considering earthly things, but all signs are pointing toward a good answer. I only wish the animals could tell us more about their relationships and communication with the Lord, their Creator.

Aren't you glad we – and animals -- can be joined in covenant with the Living God? Noah's covenant is a wonderful promise for eternity. There is a way to salvation and safety, to provision in the midst of judgment and storms of life.

What do you think King Solomon meant when he wrote: Anyone who is among the living has hope — even a live dog is better off than a dead lion! [Eccles. 9:4] Perhaps Solomon was encouraging the living to be sure to enter covenant with God, the source of all life for eternity.

ENDNOTES:

1.   This is not to say I am for governments legislating what beliefs their citizens must hold. Only God has that right. Only God is all knowing and wise enough to have such a right. The First Amendment rights of freedom of religion were bought with the lives and fortunes of the founders of this nation. The right to believe what you wish without government interference is an essential freedom for a just society. (Separation of church and state is another issue, altogether.)

2.   For a good discussion, see the chapter on "Crazy Horses" in Vicki Hearne, *Adam's Task*, supra, especially at pages 145-146, where she quotes from William Steinkraus' book *Riding and Jumping* – Steinkraus was a renowned horseman and trainer. While I have not read Ms. Hearne's book *Bandit: Dossier of a Dangerous Dog*, about a pit bull which injured or killed, I have seen an article on it. In it, I understand, this trainer addresses issues of truly bad animals, and those who have behaved badly without necessarily being truly mean or evil.

3.   This is confirmed in *Gesenius' Hebrew-Chaldee Reference to the Old Testament*, p. 146, Strong's #1320.

4.   Let me repeat that I approach evidence as a lawyer. The scientific arguments and debates about Creationism vs. Evolution rage about us. Scientists are just as likely

as lawyers to utilize or manipulate the evidence to support their personal biases or the case they wish to make. What such debates usually come down to is: What you are willing to believe? The truth is that our origins and the history of the earth are un-provable as "scientific facts." To accept the evidence of Creation science means acknowledging the God of the Bible. That logically requires facing God's commands and claims. Some are rebels. Some just are not willing to face God.

5.   I recall in college learning about archeological evidence of huge cities dating 3000 or 4000 years before Christ, in India, and in South or Central America. There massive mortar-less stone structures which are air-tight — a feat beyond our modern engineering and technology. Human skill and knowledge must have been much higher the closer you get to Adam to engineer such structures and cities. What they did technologically had to have been destroyed in the Flood or later cataclysmic events. (Maybe that race of giants had giant brains, too!) However, technological skills don't teach us much about relationships, i.e., how they got along with each other. The U.S.A. has advanced technology, but as a lawyer I can tell you people don't get along that well!

6.   See www.creationtruth.com. Dr. Sharp spoke at Victory Christian Center, Tulsa OK on 2/26/2012

7.   Reported in *Guideposts*, February 1999 issue

8.   See Agnes Sanford's *Creation Waits*.

9.   See *Encyclopedia Judaica*, "Animals, Cruelty to and "Dietary Laws."

10.   *Healing the Land*, supra, pp. 97-101

11.   Rabbi Yechiel Eckstein, *What Christians Should Know About Jews and Judaism*, (1984), p. 53

12.   *Judaism*, p. 8

CHAPTER 10

JOB AND OTHER OLD TESTAMENT NUGGETS

Listen to this, O Job, Stand and consider the wonders of God. ... The wonders of one perfect in knowledge ...
Job 37: 14 & 16

Touching the Almighty, we cannot find Him out; He is excellent in power; and to justice and plenteous righteousness He does no violence [He will disregard no right].
Men therefore [reverently] fear Him; He regards and respects not any who are wise in heart [in their own understanding and conceit].
Job 37:23-24 [Amplified]

Already we have seen much. Are you as amazed as I am at how much the Bible says about animals? When we speak often about something that usually is a good measure of its value to us. For many, that is evident because of how much we speak to and about animals. It was not until I studied to find an answer to Mom's question that I saw that animals are vital to God's plans. Animals are important in the Bible. But there is more to learn (always).

In the Book of Job are significant passages about animals. Job is considered to be one of the oldest books of the Bible. Job dates back to the early Biblical patriarchs, perhaps as early as 2000 Before Christ.[1] In my opinion, Job is a key book to understand the Lord God, our Creator. Yet, like Revelation, Job can be an extremely difficult book to comprehend. Why?

JOB AND HIS FRIENDS

Job walked with God. The first chapter describes Job as "blameless and upright" before God. One day, Satan, the devil, came into God's throne room and received permission to test Job severely. Satan destroyed everything Job had except his wife and life. All Job had was wiped out in a series of disasters – Job's children, wealth and health. His wife suggested Job "curse" God and die.

Job's best friends, Eliphaz, Bildad, and Zophar, who also knew the Lord well, condemned Job. You can tell by studying Job (such as Job chp. 4-8). Job's complaints are debated with Job by his three friends. Each tries to reason why disaster after disaster has struck Job, and how Job could get back in God's good grace. These friends all assume Job has sinned because of the bad things happening. Job complains also against the Lord's treatment. Both Job and his friends make statements filled with truths about God. Each clearly knew a lot about their Creator. These friends however, condemn Job – without answers or solutions. [Job 33:3]. The term "Job's comforters" comes from how these three spoke to Job. Isn't it true today that one's family and friends are the first to condemn us? Strange, isn't it? Job's friends' wisdom is at times rather pithy humor, I think. For example, Zophar tells Job:

> *An idiot will become intelligent when the foal of a wild*
> *donkey is born a man.*   [Job 11:12]

The reason Job is difficult to understand, I believe, is because Job and his three friends' speeches are a mix of truth and error about God. Truth and error are tangled together like two balls of yarn after a kitten has played with them! It is difficult to unravel! Job and his three friends are like most of us today. Most Christians have truth and error mixed and tangled, so it is difficult to unravel. Sorting the good from the bad takes the help of God. I know that's true for me!

Unless you understand God better than Job and his friends, you can't unravel Job. Even in knowing Jesus experientially, being a Spirit-baptized person, with all the advantages that brings, and having access to many Bible translations and other resources, I'm sure I don't know God the way Job and his friends did. [See Col. 1:27; John 14:16-21; 17:12-24.] This God loves to reveal Himself and His truths to those who really trust and seek Him (and are trustworthy). (James 1:5.) God has given me great insights into His kingdom – in part so I can share them with others. My prayers include Exo. 33:13, to please and know God more and more. Following Jesus is a great adventure! I love it that. Don't you?

ELIHU, A KEY TO JOB

In Job 32 through 39, we meet a fourth man – Elihu. Most Bible commentators ignore Elihu, or consider him an arrogant, angry young man. I, however, believe Elihu is a key to unraveling the Book of Job. (You can and should test all interpretations, including this one.) Elihu is not mentioned as a friend of Job in Job 2:11 or Job 42. Elihu's first mention identifies him as a young man, waiting to speak after his elders have had their say.

So these three men ceased answering Job, because he was righteous in his own eyes. Then the wrath of Elihu, the son of Barachel the Buzite, of the family of Ram, was aroused against Job; his wrath was aroused because he justified himself rather than God. Also against his three friends his wrath was aroused, because they had found no answer, and yet had condemned Job. Now because they were years older than he, Elihu had waited to speak to Job. When Elihu saw that there was no answer in the mouth of these three men, his wrath was aroused. Job 32:1-5

Who was Elihu? Was his anger (and theology) correct? The first clues lie in Elihu's name and genealogy. Sometimes in Biblical interpretation names tell us a lot. "Elihu" (in Hebrew) means "God Himself" or "God who is." (Who else in Scripture is known as God Himself?) By translating Elihu's forebearers' names, a larger picture emerges. "Ram" means "one who came from on high." "Buzite" means "one despised and shamed by men." "Barachel" means "one blessed and anointed by God." Who fits the description of a young man, who came from on high, was despised and shamed by men, and was blessed and anointed by God?

Jesus Christ is God Himself, the *I AM* of the Bible [John 1:1-5, 14; 8:55-59.] Jesus came from on High [John 3:16; Eph. 4:8]. Jesus was despised and shamed by men [Luke 22:63-65; Isa. 53:3-4]. Jesus is also the Christ[2], the blessed Anointed One [Ps. 2:2 & Acts 2:36]. Jesus' ministry started when He was young just as Elihu was. It is safe to conclude that Elihu is either a type of Christ Jesus or was an Old Testament appearance of Him. You determine for yourself if this is a logical and a Biblical conclusion.

There are other things which point to Elihu as a type or shadow of the Messiah, the savior and judge of all. [Acts 17:22-31; Matt 25; James 4:12.] Job told God he was afraid to speak freely to Him, and wished God was a man so Job could go to court against Him, or have an umpire. [Job 9:32-35]. Elihu identifies himself as a man the Spirit of God made – so no fear of him should terrify Job. [Job 33:1-8]. Elihu was the answer to Job's wish.

Another clue is **why** Elihu became angry with Job. Job 32:2 says Elihu's anger burned against Job because he *"was righteous in his own eyes."* Other translations help with meaning: *"even made himself out to be better than God"* [Amp.]; or *"thinking he was right and God was wrong"* [Jerusalem]. Now, Job is described as "righteous" and "blameless" in Chapter 1. But as disasters and pain assailed Job, he began to mix complaints and judgments against God in with his praise of and hope in God. Job believed God had turned away from him and did not answer his prayers. [See Job, chp. 19, 23, 27, and 30] Job even wanted never to be born [Job 3:30] - a suicidal thought. So Job ended up sinning against God – for Job thought God was wrong and Job was right. That made Elihu mad at Job. Elihu defends God as always righteous (as He is). Elihu spoke to set Job straight. [See Job 36:2 & 4.] If you want to know more, prayerfully study Elihu.

So looking further at Elihu, we see God's care of animals in Job 36. Elihu speaks of storms, lightening and snow sent some times "for His world."

[Lightening's] noise declares His presence; The cattle also, concerning what is coming up. Job 36:33

For the snow He says, 'Fall on the earth.' And to the downpour and the rain, 'Be strong.'. . . Then the beast goes into its lair and remains in its den. *** Whether for correction, or for His world, Or for lovingkindness, He causes it to happen. Job 37:6, 8, 13

From these verses, we know the Lord lets animals know things before they happen – like storms. Many have noticed that animals sense storms coming long before humans. The Lord does the same for humans in tune with Him. [John 16:13.] Animals, some of them, appear to prepare for future events. Consider the animals who prepare for winter by storing food, like the ants, squirrels, etc. Did you know all this was in the Bible? Wow!

In England, during World War II, people observed their cats seemed to know exactly when and where German bombs were coming and even where they would land.[3] One cat moved her kittens, and a bomb landed right where they had been! "When" could be explained by cats' acute hearing, as the cat could hear the planes coming before humans. But not the "where." That would take the Lord telling the cat "where."

Pets have been upset hours before earthquakes. Dogs have alerted when their master or mistress was going to have a heart attack, diabetic coma, or seizure, and even accidents. Some go to the door or window only when their owner is returning, so have prescience (foreknowledge) that can only be explained supernaturally.

A coal miner in West Virginia fed a rat while he was down in the mine. One day the rat ran around in a frenzied manner until the miner followed him. Behind them, the mine roof collapsed right where the miner had stood.[4]

It is not clear how animals know such things. Why wouldn't the Lord speak to animals to protect them and those with them, especially humans?

OUT OF THE WHIRLWIND

Elihu's speech brought Job into God's presence. [That's why Elihu is key to the Book of Job. Neither Job's words, nor those of his friends brought the Lord's answer.] When Elihu stopped speaking, the Lord answered Job "out of the whirlwind." [Job 38:1.]

In Job 38 through 41, the Lord told Job off or at least instructed Job. Through a series of questions to Job, the Lord described His acts of power and beauty.

"Where were you when I laid the foundation of the earth?
Tell Me if you have understanding."   [Job 38:4]

The Lord clearly exults in His creation as He instructs Job. This awesome God describes the measurements of heaven and earth – something still beyond human abilities. I love the Hubble photos of the galaxies – but it cannot show all the universe. Consider that Job 38:31-33 described space thousands of years ago. For example, the Lord asked Job if he could *"bind the chains of the Pleiades or loose the cords of Orion,"* or *"lead forth a constellation,"* etc. Then, in Job, the Lord comes to earthly things, like: *"Can you hunt the prey for the lions."* *"Who prepares for the raven is nourishment?"* [Job 38:39,

41]. *"Do you give the horse his might? ... Is it by your understanding that the hawk soars...?* [Job 39:19, 26].

The Lord continues through a long list of animals, such as mountain goats, wild donkeys, wild oxen, ostriches, behemoths (which was likely a dinosaur, given the description). The final animal the Lord described was leviathan. Most of the Lord's speech was about animals. Why? Perhaps because God loves and makes living things, vital beautiful beings. The Lord is the consummate artist.

How interesting that the Lord corrected Job with questions which point to animals. *"Go to the ant and learn her ways."* [Prov. 6:6]. Who has not been fascinated by animals and nature stories? How like God are people who love animals and nature. We love stories, movies and films featuring animals – real or fictional. We learn from animals. When we actually care for animals, we learn the most, I think. The animals are good teachers about God.

In Job, it appears God is instructing us about man's relative importance in the grand scheme of things. Creation is very much on God's mind. Animals have a huge part in God's work and plans. God gave Job an earful. Then the Lord said to Job, *"Will the faultfinder contend with the Almighty? Let him who reproves God answer it."* [Job 40:1-2.] Job learned that justifying himself rather than God was not very smart. Sometimes after we have walked in intimacy with the Lord a while, we get too cocky, to sure of our own righteousness. The Lord loves us enough to correct us.

Modern Christianity has brought a wonderful intimacy with the Lord – as father, brother, husband, and friend. However, we can get too casual and even disrespectful. Like Job, when bad things happen to us, we can question, complain, even get angry with God. Rather than a fearful respect, awe, and reverence, we "make ourselves out to be right and God wrong" – not a good thing! We should be trusting and defending our loving Creator, rather than complaining. Remember His speech to Job, that song of creation which demonstrates God's love and power.

THE MAJESTIC HORSE

As a horse lover, I rejoice in the Lord's bragging about His majestic horse:

"Do you give the horse his might? Do you clothe his neck with a mane? "Do you make him leap like the locust? His majestic snorting is terrible. "He paws in the valley, and rejoices in his strength; He goes out to meet the weapons. "He laughs at fear and is not dismayed; And he does not turn back from the sword. "The quiver rattles against him, The flashing spear and javelin. "With shaking and rage he races over the ground, And he does not stand still at the voice of the trumpet. "As often as the trumpet sounds he says, 'Aha!' And he scents the battle from afar, And the thunder of the captains and the war cry. [Job 39:19-25]

This passage is a wonderfully poetic description of a horse – a war horse. Horses are fine, good animals, capable of protecting those whom they love. Job 39 presages the second coming of the Messiah, the Word of God, described in Revelation 19. The King of Kings returns to earth a mighty warrior on a white horse. Jesus' armies follow on horses. When these horses hear the last trumpet, proclaiming that the world has become the Lord's, don't you know they will be ready to fight the last battle against evil! What a terrible thing to be opposed by such fierce animals!

Many people have little contact with or knowledge of horses. While we can watch movies and read about horses, it is not the same. Standing near a horse, touching them, watching them in action is another experience. There is nothing like having a good relationship with a good horse.

As the daughter of a small town veterinarian and mom who loved horses, too, I grew up with my own horse or horses. I still love to be around horses. As a child, I discovered a book about "haute ecole" – French for "high schooling" horses. The book was filled with photos of muscular white horses doing things I did not know horses could do.

Dressage and "airs above the ground" meant the horses were trained to "dance" to make controlled leaps into the air, to precisely move in various directions. I loved it! The elaborate maneuvers are an art form – as much as human gymnastics and ice skating. Beautiful to watch, haute ecole has been called the ballet of equine performance. Some of these movements, I understand, were useful in battle before vehicles replaced the horse. When I read the description of the horse in Job, I am reminded of these white stallions.

For thousands of years, horses served man in war and peace. Xenophan, an ancient Greek military genius, wrote the first known manual on training horses, including war horses. Some of Xenophan's wisdom is still used today by trainers. Don't you wonder if Xenophan ever read Job?

Alexander the Great (356 to 323 B.C.), a king of Macedonia, had a most famous war horse. Legend has it Alexander chose and mastered a great stallion when Alexander was only twelve. Alexander was reputed to be the only person who could ride Bucephalus. Fearless in battle, the horse was very protective of Alexander. The stallion became indispensable to Alexander as he conquered most of his known world. Greece, the Persian Empire (most of the Middle East) and Egypt fell to Alexander – before he died at age 33. Bucephalus died of battle wounds in Alexander's last battle.[5]

War is certainly not the only or most important role horses play. Being mounts for war, including the Messiah's last battle to retake earth, are brief events, taken in historical perspectives. Horses have played a greater role as peacetime transportation. Look at the role horses have today – primarily as pleasure animals, used for riding, racing or horse shows – at least in industrialized societies.

Horses are fun companions. I never had a horse that was not a tease, who enjoyed making people laugh. Usually my horses also enjoyed exploring, and we rode together for hours all over the back roads of Indiana. My horses were compassionate when I was sad or hurting, too. To this day, a ride on a good horse is both enjoyable and restorative. As a child, I boasted I would live to be 127 and ride horses before I died. That statement tells how much I love being on a horse!

Today, horses are serving as therapy animals. Case studies show remarkable healing or improvement comes from riding, and interacting with horses for those with schizophrenia or psychosis,[6] from multiple sclerosis,[7] and other illnesses. Horses have very sensitive skins. Contact between horse and rider can be healing, therapists are learning. Riding can be relaxing, yet invigorating. It is little wonder to realize that the Lord created the marvelous horse as part of His healing arsenal.

LEVIATHAN, THE GREAT SERPENT

"Can you draw out Leviathan with a hook, Or snare his tongue with a line which you lower?

* * *

Lay your hand on him; Remember the battle — Never do it again! Indeed, any hope of overcoming him is false; Shall one not be overwhelmed at the sight of him? No one is so fierce that he would dare stir him up. Who then is able to stand against Me?   Job 41:1, 8-10

Why did the Lord use Leviathan to end His discourse with Job? What was the Lord saying? It seems important that the last creature God describes to teach Job is Leviathan.

Scholars disagree as to what Leviathan is. Some vote for the crocodile of the Nile. Crocs are not taken by fish hooks, to my knowledge. Sometimes men make a sport of wrestling in various parts of the world.[8] So the croc cannot be Leviathan. Others think Leviathan is a sperm whale. Others think Leviathan is an unknown sea serpent, like the Loch Ness monster. As we discussed in the chapter on "The Fall of Man and the Animals," a thorough Bible study points to Leviathan as being Satan, that Great Serpent. (See

Revelation 12 and Genesis 3.) If so, God's closing words to Job was a naming of Job's greatest enemy, the devil himself.

Nothing on earth is like him, One made without fear. He looks on everything that is high; He is king over all the sons of pride. Job 41:33-34

Was God showing Job the "king over the sons of pride" so Job would not to justify himself before God? Most teachers use the end of a discourse for emphasis. The Lord was correcting Job, warning him against pride. Satan loves to tempt man into prideful behavior and deceive man. If we fall into Satan's trap, we believe we can do a better job running our lives (and the world) than God can. We believe are as good as or better than God, than we are right and God is wrong. When we buy Satan's deception, we fall under his dominion. Who is your king? Who are you justifying?

The Book of Job opens with Satan gaining permission to destroy everything Job had except his life. Near the end, God describes Leviathan, a powerful reptile – an animal of great power and cunning, an animal against which man is no match. God's message to Job becomes clear: "Avoid thinking you are more righteous than God. Avoid pride, especially spiritual pride. Otherwise, your king will be Leviathan or Satan." Such pride puts all creation at enmity with us. Leviathan is God's tool against human arrogance. Only God can and does control Satan or Leviathan. There is nothing created which compares to God. [See Jer. 9:23-25].

OLD TESTAMENT AND JEWISH NUGGETS

The kind man feeds his beast before sitting down to dinner. [Hebrew proverb[9]]

The world has not always been kind, especially to animals. For example, it was not until 2002 that Oklahoma passed legislation banning cock-fighting. In cockfighting, the birds are equipped with sharp steel spurs and fight to the death. It is a cruel "sport" (if it can be called "sport"), and not the only one using animals to fight to death (or severe injury). People who follow Biblical principles are kind to animals. The laws of the Kingdom of Heaven make people different than the values of the world.

Two-thousand years ago, Jesus of Nazareth, a Jew, lived, died and was resurrected. At that time, Greeks and Romans held everybody and everything – except themselves – in contempt. Max Dimont, in *Jews, God and History*, compared the Jewish and Graeco-Roman cultures. Dimont wrote that the reasons the Romans and Greeks gave for holding Jews in contempt are irrational. Romans nailed people to die tortuously on crosses and called it justice. Yet, Romans expressed horror at Jewish circumcision of baby boys. Romans threw humans to wild beasts and called it amusement. Yet, Romans viewed the Jewish Feast of Passover as barbaric because lambs were sacrificed – never mind the lambs were killed with merciful quickness. Comparing the two cultures, it is it is the Jew who has the most kindness for less privileged humans and for animals.

The Greeks and Romans, who mercilessly worked man and beast seven days a week and called it industry, looked with scorn on the Jewish practice of a day of rest every seventh day for freeman, slave and animal. [10]

Humans and animals should give thanks for the Bible and Jewish teachings about kindness and rest. Thank God for those who obey His laws and, thereby, benefit every living creature.

Unfortunately, by the end of the first century after Christ, Gentile and Jewish Christians were divided. The Church thereafter lost the benefit of Rabbinal teaching and Jewish understanding of God and His Scripture. Only in the latter part of the 20th century has an examination of "Jewish roots" become acceptable to many Christians. In my experience, both sides have something to contribute to the other. I, for one, am willing to learn from anyone who truly knows our Creator and Lord. How about you?

Let's look at the understanding about God's plan for animals from the Hebrew or Jewish perspective. After all Jews wrote the Book. (If you have any anti-Semitic views, it is time to reconsider. Take it up with God.)

A SABBATH FOR ANIMALS

The Biblical Sabbath laws require rest every seventh day for not only man, but animals. *Thou shall not do any manner of work ... nor thine ox, nor thine ass, nor any of they cattle.* [Exo. 20:10 & Deut. 5:14]. *Six days do your work, but on the seventh day do not work, so that your ox and your donkey may rest, . . .* [Exo. 23:12 [NIV]]

The origin of a seventh day of rest is when God rested after six days of creation. [Gen. 2:1-2]. The only work the Lord permits is for tending basic needs of humans and animals, or to relieve suffering. It would be cruel to not feed or water an animal or to save a life. Cruelty, including to animals, is prohibited, Biblically.

It is a good law. Labor laws and Sunday closing laws (which once were common in the U.S.A.) find their origins in the Bible. At one time, a day of rest of man and beasts of burden was the norm. Sunday was a day to worship and rest. The oxen, horses and the like, which pulled wagons, plows and other implements got to recover their strength. In recent years, this practice has greatly eroded for the humans, and the few animals who still bear burdens. Yet science has proven that efficiency drops dramatically without that day of rest.

The man or animal who does not rest will get sick, or burn out. Real strength requires periods of rest. It is foolish and even wicked to work man or beast without rest. As we have moved away from the Lord, and the Bible, we have tended to work ourselves (and others) to death.

KINDNESS TO ANIMALS

The Hebrew consideration of animals is based on a number of Biblical commandments. Practicing Jews learn to praise God as the

One who satisfies all living creatures, and for giving food to the beasts and the birds. [Ps. 145 & Ps. 147:9]. Based on the verse, *"I will give grass in thy fields for thy cattle, and thou shalt eat and be satisfied,"* Rabbis taught for thousands of years that: *It is forbidden for a man to eat before he has fed his animal because the animal is mentioned first.*[11]

This duty to feed your animal before you is also supported by the Bible verse in Proverbs 12:10: *A righteous man has regard for the life of his beast, but the compassion of the wicked is cruel.* The New Living Translation puts it this way: *"The godly care for their animals, but the wicked are always cruel."*

Out of the same verses, Rabbis legislated that "a man is not permitted to buy animals unless he can properly provide for them." Today that means if you cannot pay for food, shelter and vet bills, don't acquire or get another home for the animal. These principles also find a basis in the Hebrew expression: "the pain of all living things" – which is an acknowledgment that both humans and animals suffer in this life, so we should not add to such suffering.

God's compassion for animals is evident in the Bible. Farmers are prohibited from muzzling an ox as it threshes grain. [Deut. 25:4.] A few mouthfuls of grain rewards and energizes a working animal, and doesn't significantly diminish the farmer's yield. This is similar to the rule that a worker is worthy of his hire or wages. [Deut. 25:4; & 1 Tim. 5:18.] Also, acts of kindness beget loyalty and productivity. The Jewish Torah says that one must not slaughter an animal and its young on the same day – a recognition that animals grieve. [Lev. 22:28]. Exodus 23:5 states that: *"If you see that the donkey of someone who hates you has collapsed under its load, do not walk by. Instead, stop and help."* [NLT] A parent bird must be released before one takes her young. [Deut. 22:6-7].

Several other Scriptures promote conservation as part of man's stewardship. Grain fields must lie fallow in the Sabbatical or seventh year. That same year, the land and workers (human and animals) get to rest. [Lev. 25:6-7.] Modern practices which do not allow rest violate this command.

DO UNTO OTHERS

The Golden Rule of Jesus, "*do unto others as you would have them do unto you,*" according to rabbinical teaching, applies to animals as well as humans. [Matt. 7:12; Prov. 22:8; Ps. 126:5; Gal. 6:7.] God's treatment of each of us will be according to our treatment of animals under rabbinical doctrine. This a belief both of Rabbis and in other religions. To the rabbis, the promise of long life is related to the duty (mitzvah) of sending the parent bird away before taking the young.

I find it terrible that many Christian theologians and apologists adopted an opposite view. Their Cartesian theology is unBiblical and cruel. If God is love, and He is, then which view would be truth? That's a "no-brainer" – isn't it?

Left without the disciplines of the Bible, and without the power of God to change human hearts, we are often the same as the Greeks and Romans. We have much to learn from and about animals. May the Lord help us to be better stewards and disciples. Are you willing to change your thinking and ways? I sure am.

ENDNOTES:

1.   See the Open Bible, introduction to Job; and the *Pictorial Bible Dictionary*, [1964] p. 433.

2.   "Christ" means "anointed one" in Greek.

3.   David Greene, *Your Incredible Cat*, [1984], pp. 85-88

4.   Stephanie Leland, *Animal Angels*, [1998], p. 100

5.   See   http://www.alexander-the-great.co.uk/bucephalus.htm   or   http://en.wikipedia.org/wiki/Bucephalus

6.   Adele von Rust McCormick & Marlena Deborah McCormick, *Horse Sense and the Human Heart*, [1997], pp. 33-46

7.   *Chicken Soup for the Pet Lover's Soul*, "Saddle Therapy" [1998], p. 123.

8. An Internet search for "crocodile wrestling" pulls up a variety of sites.

9. Robert Byrne, *Cat Scan, All the best from the literature of Cats*, [1984], p. 45

10. Max Dimont, *Jews, God and History*, p. 111

11. *Encyclopedia Judaica*, "Animals, Cruelty to"

CHAPTER 11

JESUS CHRIST AND ANIMALS

*Behold . . . on the first night of Christ's life, God honored
the animal creation . . . Was it not appropriate that He
should, during the first few days and nights of His life on
earth, be surrounded by the dumb beasts whose moans
and plaints have for ages been a prayer to God for the ar-
resting of their torments and the righting of their wrongs?*

. . .

*Not a kennel in all the centuries, not a robbed bird's nest,
not a worn-out horse on the tow-path, not a herd freez-
ing in the poorly-built cow-pen, not a freight car bringing
beeves to market without water through a thousand miles
of agony, not a surgeon's room witnessing the struggles of
the fox or rabbit or pigeon or dog in the horrors of vivisection, but has an interest in the fact that Christ was born in
a stable surrounded by animals. He remembers that night,
and the prayer He heard in their pitiful moan. He will
answer in the punishment of those who maltreat them.*[1]

Dr. DeWitt Talmage

As I finished the last chapter, the Lord gave me the impression that He wanted a chapter on Jesus' relationship to the animals. My first thought was: "What relationship?" As I explored the idea, I saw a lot more than I ever knew was in the Bible! (It was just more proof that unless we are truly looking, we are so blind.) So let's explore these ideas. Jesus relationship with the animals is very relevant to Mom's question.

Over one-hundred Old Testament prophesies foretell the birth, life, and death of the Messiah, and they are fulfilled in the man, Jesus of Nazareth – who really lived and died and was resurrected. God preplanned and orchestrated the whole thing – down to the last detail. The Roman census could have fallen at another time. Jesus' mother could have been a princess and given birth in a palace. Rich magi, wise men as powerful as kings, came and gave the infant costly gifts soon after His birth. Rich men and women later followed this rabbi, Jesus. Why was Jesus born in a stable – of all places?

A stable is dirty, with animals in it. Jesus was God. Jesus came to save mankind, didn't He? His titles include King of Kings and Lord of Lords. Why not in a palace or at least the best room at the inn? Jesus' birthplace was no accident.

Have you considered how often Jesus the Christ is likened in Scripture to various animals? Jesus is "the Lamb of God which takes away the sin of the world." [John 1:29] The Messiah is "the Lion of the tribe of Judah." [Rev. 5:5] Jesus said He was like a hen gathering her chicks under her wings. [Matthew 23:37 & Luke 13:34] Can we find anything in these references to help us answer Mom's question?

It was not by chance Jesus appeared as Savior first among the "brute creation." The Savior of the world (not just humans) was born in a stable – a place where beasts of burden find rest. Jesus came in the flesh as a helpless baby, into a mere carpenter's family. Jesus came as a Jew, a people despised by most of the world. Jesus was born in a little town, Bethlehem, in a tiny country, Israel. God loves the helpless, the poor, the despised. Jesus identifies with all who are like that. Any time you feel helpless, poor, or despised, think about that. Any time you see an animal abused or neglected, think about Jesus. Jesus chose to be born in that stable. To be born among the animals. That was God's choice – a choice relevant to Mom's question.

The world Jesus was born into was not a very safe place. The world has not changed much. As we mentioned, Noah's Ark is thought to be a type and shadow of the Lord's salvation. That Ark was really a huge stable. Likewise, that Bethlehem stable was afloat in a sea of sin, a world adrift in corruption and carnality. Yet, Jesus chose to be among the animals, just as the Lord filled the ark of old with all kinds of beasts. Does that mean Jesus loves to be among the animals?

Artists and song writers through the ages depict animals in the stable with the baby Jesus. A stable is rarely empty of animals. Cattle and camels kneel before the baby in adoration. Christmas crèches have sheep gazing on the holy Child. It has a ring of truth.

What other animals might have been in that stable? Donkeys, horses, goats, chickens, ducks, pigeons, dogs, and cats were common domestic animals in ancient Israel. Also, mice, spiders, sparrows, swallows, owls, bats, wasps, and fleas are often in or near stables. Maybe wild animals came, too. I have a Nativity statute with baby birds, squirrels, raccoons, rabbits, geese, mice, deer and other baby animals all around the Baby Jesus. Our Jesus would have loved them all.

Animals let others know when something new happens. Perhaps the neighborhood critters came too. Maybe garter snakes, so helpful to gardeners, slithered in to pay its respects. Why snakes? Not all snakes are as bad as the Great Serpent in Eden. Many nonpoisonous reptiles are handy to have around. Mom liked all kinds of critters, including snakes, and so do I. Snakes keep down the insect and rodent population, and some kill poisonous snakes. Snakes feel like cool silk to handle, and have an austere beauty.

The Nativity scene would not seem right without adoring animals gathered around the Christ child. Not just shepherds, but their sheep. Not an empty stable, but one with animals sharing their abode with the newborn King, Jesus.

A case can be made that Jesus is a fulfillment of the Noahiac covenant, the ultimate Ark which brings salvation to *all creatures*, not just humans. Let's see how the evidence stacks up.

IN THE WILDERNESS WITH THE BEASTS

The Gospel of Mark 1:13 records the beginning of Jesus' earthly ministry, some thirty years after His birth in that Bethlehem stable. After Jesus was baptized in water by John, the Baptist, John saw God's Holy Spirit descend upon Him. Then Jesus went immediately into the desert wilderness of Judea. Why?

> *And immediately the Spirit impelled Him to go out into the wilderness. And He was in the wilderness forty days being tempted by Satan; and He was with the wild beasts, and the angels were ministering to Him.*   Mark 1:12-13

In the original Greek manuscripts, the word translated "with" in the phrase "with the wild beasts" is a preposition meaning "in the midst of, amid." It denotes "association, union, [and/or] accompaniment."[2]   Jesus, at the very inception of His ministry as the Son of Man, was "with" animals.

How appropriate!   While Jesus was being tempted in the wilderness by Satan, that Serpent of Old, other wild animals were His companions. When the Great Serpent tempted Adam and Eve, it was in the presence of the animals. Now during the temptation of the second Adam, Jesus, animals are again witnesses. It gives meaning to the prophecy:

> *And all flesh shall see the salvation of God.*
>   Luke 3:6, Isaiah 40:5

Recalling our discussion of what "flesh" means in the Scripture, we know that this phrase "all flesh" includes both humans and animals.

Compare Adam with Jesus. Jesus is described as the "last Adam" in 1 Cor. 15:45. Both the first Adam and Jesus began in a place with animals which were all "domestic" or tame. Only after the first Adam fell, were animals divided into wild and domestic. The last Adam was born in a stable and then began His ministry in the desert with wild animals. Thus, Jesus reunited man with both domestic and wild animals. As both God and man, Jesus clearly had a great relationship with the animals.

This is not entirely surprising. Robert F. Leslie tells of meeting a bear, whom he named Bosco, in the Canadian wilderness. The bear sat beside him as he fished, and spent days as Leslie's companion. They ate and played together, and the bear protected him from other bears. When Bosco left, Leslie was "desolated." However, he treasured that brief relationship.[3] I like to think Jesus enjoyed the wild animals, too, before He came to minister to men.

Naturalists who have spent time with lions, wolves, gorillas, and other wild animals, tell of living among or with the animals without being harmed. Their stories are well publicized. For example, R. D. Lawrence, a Canadian naturalist, wrote on keeping wolves and rescuing injured wild animals such as mice, birds, lynx, bear, and moose.[4]

Lawrence and his wife lived and developed a relationship with many of them. Jesus' being "with the wild beasts" is not so different.

THE SALVATION OF GOD IS BROAD

It is reasonable to think that: Just as God ordered Noah to build the Ark for the salvation of man and animals, Jesus, the second Adam, came to construct – in His body, or flesh — an "Ark" for the salvation of "all flesh." Marks's Gospel ends, after all with Jesus' commission to all creation:

And He said to them, "Go into all the world and preach the gospel to all creation."

Mark 16:15

Why did Mark write "all creation?" What is God saying here? Why did Mark not write, "preach the gospel to all mankind?" We must be careful. The Bible commands us not to add to nor to take away from the Word of God. [Deut. 4:2; 12:32; Rev. 22:18-19.] Since all Scripture is inspired by God, then Mark wrote by inspiration of the Lord. [2 Tim. 3:16; 2 Pet. 1:20-21.] If we interpret "all creation" as referring only to mankind, are we not "taking away" from the words "all creation"? "Creation" includes all living creatures from amoebae to zebras.

Jesus Christ commanded His disciples to preach the good news to all creation. The Legends of St. Francis and St. Anthony support that animals are receptive to the gospel. We must address that issue. We must explore, prayerfully, what it means to "preach the gospel to all creation." If we don't, we may miss God's will, His best.

God created all animals and He cares for all flesh. Jesus came to reconcile all flesh. As we discussed earlier, St. Francis must have known this when he became a peacemaker between the town and the wolf.

Some Christians use Mark 16 as a basis to pray for animals to be healed. They combine the fact that gospel is for all creation, and that "believers" will lay hands on the sick [vs.18] (which does not limit healing to humans). I have used this combination, as well as Deut. 28:1-4, quoting Mark 16 in prayer, as I laid hands on my animals. The Lord has healed animals for which I have prayed, too.

Let me interject here that much of what I am writing in this book is new to me. Some of it stuns me. When uncovering new ideas, I tend to stare at them like a cow at a new gate. I've been researching and writing this for years now, but with every new revelation, I test and question and explore the idea as best I know how. The Lord has met me at every new turn, at every new question.

For example, after the troublesome question of why the New Testament seemed to say little about Jesus' relationship to animals, I found (in a rather miraculous way) this Third Century prayer attributed to St. Basil of Caesarea:

And for these also, dear Lord, the humble beasts, who with us bear the burden and the heat of the day, and offer their guileless lives for the well-being of their country, we supplicate Thy great tenderness of heart, for Thou hast promised to save both man and beast. And great is Thy loving kindness, O master, Savior of the world.. [5]

As you can see some of these ideas are not new, but old. They have just been forgotten or hidden for a very long time. In fact, as we are seeing, Scripture supports such a thesis. It is scriptural to say Jesus came to save both human and animal. There is more Scriptural evidence supporting this truth than not. The main obstacles are human pride and ignorance.

DOES THE LORD'S PRAYER INCLUDE ANIMALS?

Jesus taught us to pray, *"Our Father, who art in heaven, . . . Your kingdom come, Your will be done on earth, as it is in heaven."* [Matt. 6: 9-13 & Luke 11:2-4]

It dawned on me one day that I had no idea what His will in heaven was. If so, then I would probably refuse or reject His actions in trying to bring His will to pass on earth. My ignorance could block God's will in my life, my world.

What if God's will is (and has always been) to redeem **all** life from the Fall — not just humans? If we have no concept of God's plan, is it little wonder we treat animals with a lack of care and concern? We don't know their importance to God.

If animals are in heaven – and we already know horses are there – and, since heaven is a place without pain, sorrow or death, then we can pray for animals to have "heaven on earth" as well.

If we know we *can* pray that way, shouldn't we pray that way? In the Sermon on the Mount, Jesus taught about God's goodness to all:

Look at the birds of the air, that they do not sow, neither
do they reap, nor gather into barns, and yet your heavenly
Father feeds them. Are you not worth much more than
they?   Matt. 6:26

Many people enjoy feeding wild birds. I throw birdseed on my patio and enjoy watching sparrows, cardinals, mockingbirds, cowbirds, and blue jays come feed. This habit of feeding the little birds has also brought squirrels, hawks, and owls. It has been a postcard-pretty treat on a winter day to see a red cardinal tucked in my snow-dressed holly bush. We who love to feed the birds may be a partial answer to the Lord's Prayer – agents of God feeding His birds. I like to think so anyway.

In Luke's Gospel is a similar quote to Matt. 6:26, except the birds are identified as ravens. [Luke 12:24] Is not this also a statement about God's care for the birds? The fact that their value is less than humans is not an issue here. The fact is, they have value to God.

Jesus pointed to the Father's care of the little birds to teach us more than one lesson. Isn't it remarkable that in wilderness areas, without the interference from man, bird species thrive. Even in urban settings, many birds have adapted to urban sprawl. The law office where I work is on the fifty-ninth floor. I often see hawks, doves and buzzards soaring around near the building.

The Psalmist wrote: *"Let everything that hath breath praise the Lord!"* [Ps. 150:6] That's everything, folks! Why should "everything" (animals) praise the Lord, if this short life of pain is all they have?

St. Francis of Assisi reportedly had a contest with a nightingale in singing God's praises. The bird won! The nightingale had much to praise God for, just as St. Francis did. The birds have much to praise the Lord for because the Savior's loving-kindness and grace clearly belong to "every living thing." Jesus came to buy salvation for every living creature.

JESUS AND THE DONKEY'S COLT

While I never considered it before, look at this miraculous event. As the time came for his entry into Jerusalem a few days before His death, Jesus sent the disciples to bring a certain colt of a donkey — a colt which had never before been ridden. This is recorded in three of the four Gospels, showing its importance. [Matt. 21:1-7; Mark 11:1-10; Luke 19:29-38]. Jesus chose an unbroken donkey's colt for His ride into Jerusalem.

And as they approached Jerusalem, at Bethphage and Bethany, near the Mount of Olives, He sent two of His disciples, and said to them, "Go into the village opposite you, and immediately as you enter it, you will find a colt tied there, on which no one yet has ever sat; but untie it and bring it here. . . ." And they went away and found a colt tied at the door outside in the streets; and they untied it. ... And they brought to colt to Jesus and put their garments on it; and He sat upon it. And many spread their garments in the road, and others spread leafy branches which they had cut from the fields. And those who went before, and those who followed after, were crying out, "Hosanna! Blessed is he who comes in the name of the Lord; blessed is the coming kingdom of our father David; hosanna in the highest!" And He entered Jerusalem and came into the Temple;   Mark 11:1-11

There are some remarkable things about this event which tells us Jesus' relationship with animals is awesome. First, how did Jesus know where this donkey was located, and that it had never known a rider? Either Jesus knew the owner and colt, or something supernatural happened. Scripture does not say. (The willingness of the owner to release the colt on the words, "The Lord has need of it," is remarkable unless the man or woman knew Jesus.)

Second, this colt had never known a rider. This colt was from a small village, and Jesus rode the colt into the busy city of Jerusalem. Bethany and Bethphage were small towns during the time of Jesus. Yet this unbroken, small-town, donkey's colt willingly carried Jesus on his back into the bustling, noisy city of Jerusalem.

The crowds which welcomed Jesus were noisy. They were shouting "HOSANNA TO THE KING!" They were *throwing* garments on the road in front of the little colt on which Jesus sat. Many seasoned donkeys and horses would have been terrified and spooked by the commotion.

Can you explain how the donkey braved that much noise and motion? The donkey must have felt a calm emanating from the Prince of Peace which eliminated its natural fears. That young colt immediately trusted Jesus enough to let Him mount its back, ride through shouting crowd, into a big city. This instant rapport is remarkable. It is a statement of the relationship which this last Adam has with animals.

This is a significant event. The One who is greater than the first Adam, greater than Noah, greater than St. Francis, greater than any animal trainer who has walked the earth, rode that colt. Jesus (or if you prefer His Hebrew name, Joshua or Yeshua) is like His name. "Jesus" means "the Lord who saves, who brings Shalom, the peace and wholeness of God." This colt is evidence that Jesus is Lord and Prince of Peace to all creation. In an instant that nameless donkey knew Who and What this Man was. We should be as smart!

We could say Jesus was the ultimate "horse whisperer" and spoke "donkey." Men and women like St. Francis and Monty Roberts are not unique, nor are they simply "products of their time." As Creator, Jesus is the ultimate communicator with animals. He was and is God...[6]

That colt knew Who Jesus was. Like the animals in that Bethlehem stable, the donkey saw the One who is Love incarnate. That colt recognized God in Jesus and His love for all His creation. This intelligent animal gave Jesus instant honor and obedience. This was what all creation has been groaning for, isn't it? [Romans 8:22]

The young donkey must have gladly carried its loving Creator — through noisy crowds throwing strange objects into the pathway! Believing the little donkey was eager to please the Master is easy for most who know animals. Horses, dogs, cats and other animals perform tasks with obvious pleasure. I wonder if the colt knew what was ahead for Jesus? What a privilege to carry the Savior. What a burden to carry Him to His crucifixion.

Jesus began His human life in a stable, among the domestic animals. Jesus began His ministry as Savior in the wilderness among wild animals. Jesus began His journey to Calvary on a young, never-before-ridden donkey. Jesus will return as Lord of Lords and King of Kings on a horse, one day in the future. Perhaps very soon.

THE FISH WHO PAID JESUS' TAX

St. Anthony, if you recall, when he preached to those fish, told of a fish who paid Jesus' taxes. The account is found in the book of Matthew. Religious leaders had asked Simon Peter if Jesus paid the temple tax. Peter, without knowing the answer, said, "Yes." When Peter returned, Jesus spoke about the taxes before Peter could even tell Jesus question. Jesus then told this professional fisherman to go fishing:

> ... *go down to the sea, and throw in a hook; take up the first fish that comes up, and when you open its mouth you will find a shekel. Take it and give it to them for Me and for yourself.* Matthew 17:27 [Amplified]

Don't we all wish taxes were that easy to pay!

The miracle is how that coin got in that fish's mouth. One possibility is this fish found and picked up the coin; held it in its mouth without swallowing it; and looked for Peter to throw in that hook. Or, God could have created the coin in the mouth of the first fish Peter hooked. The first would reflect Jesus' ability to command the obedience of fish. The latter is a simple act of God. Both are miraculous. Both are possible with God.

Myself, I like the first. It is like the Lord to use animals. It is in keeping with the sacrificial service of God and His creation to man – a point we covered earlier.

JESUS SHED BLOOD - THE ULTIMATE IDENTIFICATION

Jesus identified with the animals' who were sacrificed for sin:

*For the bodies of those **beasts [“zoon”]**, whose blood is brought into the sanctuary by the high priest for sin, are burned without the camp. Therefore Jesus also, that He might sanctify the people with His own blood, suffered out-side the gate. Let us go forth with Him, outside the camp, bearing His reproach.*   Heb. 13:11-13 [NKJ]

The Greek word for "beast" or "living creature" has an emphasis we miss in our culture. The King James Version translated the Greek word "zoon" (Strong's #2226) as "beast." It is from "zoe" (Strong's #2222). We get the terms "zoo" and "zoology" from "zoe."[7] The King James is not wrong. It just loses something. According to *Vine's*, "zoon" is used primarily to denote a "living being," and *Vine's* is "stressing the fact that life is the characteristic feature." "Zoe" is the same word used in Revelation 4:7 to describe the four living creatures before God's throne — which we will discuss further on.

Do you see the implications? If the emphasis in "zoon" is life, what is the Spirit of Truth saying in Hebrews? Remember that the life is in the soul, and the soul is in the blood?

> *... and to Jesus, the mediator of a new covenant, and to the*
> *sprinkled blood, which speaks better than the blood of Abel.*
>
> Heb. 12:24

Abel's blood still speaks – although his body is dead. [See Hebrews 11:4 & 12:24.] That means Abel is alive and well in eternity! Jesus spoke of Abraham as alive and not dead in John 8:56-58 and Luke 16:19-31. These faithful one's spirits are alive! They are connected to the Source of all Life, God Himself!

Is the Lord saying in Hebrews that, while the bodies of these sacrificed animals are dead, they still live? Jesus identified with the animal sacrifices. The lives of these sacrificed animals are connected to Jesus Christ. He chose to die, to be sacrificed as the Lamb of God, in a place where animals were sacrificed. Jesus gave Himself to save humans, — just like every animal sacrificed since Adam and Eve.

The Second Adam loves and identifies with animals — especially animals who die sacrificially. How like God that is! It is not far fetched to think Jesus came to save all who live and accept Him.

JESUS HEALS ANIMALS AND THEY KNOW HIM

Animals know the Lord as Healer. Many of my animals have shown this sensitivity to His healing power. I frequently hear testimonies of God healing animals. The Catholic and Episcopal churches have had blessing services for animals for a long time. An increasing number of ministers pray for animals. I've even heard reports of animals being raised from the dead after prayer. Our God is a healing Savior for both man and animal.

A few years ago, on my radio program, a veterinarian and a children's minister who owned a dog were my guests. We discussed animal heroes and how Jesus heals our animals. The veterinarian shared a story of another vet she knew who was a new Christian. That vet had not thought to pray for animals. During an operation on a dog, the dog's heart stopped. The vet was frantically attempting to get medicine to try to stimulate the heart into beating again. The vet was afraid he'd lost the dog. At the time, the vet's office was being remodeled, and a workman there asked if he could pray for the dog. Distracted, the vet agreed. The worker prayed a simple prayer. The dog revived. The vet was astonished — and elated. From then on, prayer became a regular part of that vet's practice. I wonder how many veterinarians have experienced similar answers to prayer? I know many pet owners have.

My Siamese, "Kitty," loved the presence of the Lord and knew Him as her healer. She had a dramatic healing one day. Kitty liked to go walking with me. (Some cats like walks.) One spring day, I took her to a state park. A trail went up over small cliffs near a lake. At the top, Kitty explored while I sat and talked to the Lord. I noticed some insects buzzing Kitty. When I approached, I realized they were ground hornets or wasps. We both ran. When we stopped at the bottom of the cliffs, Kitty's little head and face were covered with bumps! The bumps were swelling, causing her pretty blue eyes to swell shut. I realized Kitty could go into shock and die from the hornet venom. Faith arose strongly in me. I pointed at her and commanded her to be healed in the name of Jesus. In seconds the swelling went down and the bumps disappeared. Kitty looked at me with those wonderful blue eyes as though to say, "Gee, thanks! Isn't Jesus great! I knew you'd take care of me." When in need, Kitty came to me for prayer like bears come to honey!

Gretchen, our German shepherd, developed a tumor-like growth on her lip. The Lord led me to curse the tumor and call it healed by faith. However, it grew bigger. Some friends, seeing it, were alarmed at its size. As I looked to the Lord, I felt just to keep calling the tumor gone, according to Romans 4:17 & Heb. 11:1-3. (I don't deny the tumor was real; it is just that faith calls those things that are not into being. Obviously you don't need faith for what you can see, touch, taste or hear.) After several days the tumor dropped off and a bloody place was left. I asked the Lord to cauterize the spot. The bleeding stopped. Later, I checked Gretchen's lip and could not even locate the place where the tumor was. Hallelujah!

When Gretchen was about two years old, she had a kind of doggy "myasthenia gravis," which caused her to stumble and be unsteady on her feet. The vet said this disease was progressive and fatal. While Mom owned her, Gretchen and I were bonded. I was also an intercessor, so I sought the Lord for Gretchen's healing. The Lord told me that my prayers would not heal Gretchen. Legally, she was Mom's dog. The Lord required Mom to pray for her. I had not known Mom to pray for healing before, so I wanted to panic. (Healing seemed to require a lot of faith. I had never observed Mom exercising that level of faith.) I cried and argued with the Lord, but He knew what He was doing. So I started believing for Mom's faith. Every time the phone rang, I'd hear Mom enlist others to pray for Gretchen's healing. (Our phone rang a lot.) Half of our town and lots of out-of-towners, too, must have joined Mom in praying for Gretchen! Gretchen got well and stayed well many years.

In 1998, a four-week-old Siamese kitten got under my long skirt. I stepped on him and squashed him. I was horrified to see him go comatose, and his bowels and bladder discharge. I knew enough to know he was dying. So I prayed fervently. I prayed all night over him. A few days later, he turned very yellow. The vet gave him little chance, as his little intestines were pressed against his backbone and his liver was huge. I had prayed through until faith arose in me and I had the Lord's peace. That cat is now thirteen! Jesus is a marvelous healer!

What Scriptures can you use to petition the Lord for healing an animal? You don't have to quote Scripture to get answers. God loves His animals. Scriptures build faith, and so you can "remind" God of His promises. Jesus is the Word [John 1.1] and the author of faith [Heb. 12:2]; and faith comes by hearing the Word. [Rom. 10:17] Praying the Spirit, i.e., tongues, builds faith [Jude 20]. The Lord often requires faith to do His work. [Mark 6:1-5]. Verses which I meditate on for faith, before I pray for my animals, include these:

> *Now it shall be, if you will diligently obey the Lord your God, being careful to do all his commandments which I command you today, the Lord your God will set you high above all the nations of the earth. And all these blessings shall come upon you and overtake you, if you will obey the Lord your God. ...* **Blessed shall be ... the offspring of your beasts, the increase of your herd and the young of your flock.**   Deut. 28:1-3

> *And whatever you ask in My name, that will I do that the Father may be glorified in the Son. If you ask Me anything in My name, I will do it.*   John 14:13-14 [NKJ]

> *Have faith in God. Truly I say to you, whoever says to this mountain, 'Be taken up and cast into the sea,' and does not doubt in his heart, but believes that what he says is going to happen, it shall be granted to him. Therefore I say to you, all things for which you pray and ask, believe that you have received them, and they shall be granted you.*
>   Mark 11:22-25

My veterinarian friend uses Mark 16:15-18 when she lays hands on sick animals for healing.

Whatever Scriptures are used, we know the Lord watches over His Word to perform it. [Isaiah 55] You may have an account of a healing or miracle relating to an animal. Such stories abound. Several magazines, such as the Readers Digest and Guideposts, regularly run stories about animals which have been rescued, protected or healed miraculously.

It would be interesting to gather more Bible verses which have played a part in the healing or protection of our animal friends. I wonder if heaven has a video-room where we can view things that happened, so we can review such stories. I never tire of hearing them.

GOD CARES

Jesus cares for our animals! The animals know it. Christ's redemption from the curse is broad. Jesus' blood was shed for redemption of all His creation. God's love is far greater than we imagine. How foolishly arrogant to think that God, who lovingly made every living creature, would care only for man.

There is a God-ordained kinship between all living things, as J. Allen Boone observed.[8] Most people treat animals as inferior and subhuman, far below the animal's capacity. Yet animals have character, intelligence, and accomplishments. Some people ridicule those of us who treat animals like friends. Such people refuse to think a "mere animal" can understand us, – let alone read our minds and intentions. That is ignorance "gone to seed."

How very poor in joy are those who have never been friends with an animal. Those who become friends with animals are the richest people I know -- blessed and real. Cultivate a friendship with an animal, if you haven't already done so. If you are faithful and patient, you will be rewarded beyond measure. Prepare to be humbled in the process. Animals are forgiving and yet know more of real dignity than most of us think. Jesus is their Lord and Savior, too. He gave great gifts to us in His animals.

Have you never observed the *joie de vivre* (joy of living) which animals display? When I've had a rough day, I can count on my animals to make me laugh and relax, and to possess and benefit from the "now." Animals enjoy life. Mine care enough to work at getting me to join in the joy of living. Daily, they teach me how to live better. Observe animals. Pay close attention. They will teach you – shout at you silently – of the really important things, of the care and plans the Lord has for all His creatures.

Animals are worthy of God's love and care. Animals, wild and domestic, have served humans, even with their lives. The dogs and other animals daily assist humans to health and better lives. Remember the story of Old Soap and the account of the gray eagle guiding the lost hiker? What about the dolphins, badgers, wolves, and others which have aided humans in the ocean and in the wilderness? Balaam's donkey was an intercessor who fought an angel for her master. What about my grandmother's stray dog which gave its life for her? Have you heard about an AIDS patient who wanted to kill himself after receiving that diagnosis, but, his cat wouldn't quit loving him.. That cat was the only friend who did not withdraw from the AIDS patient. That cat not only stayed, but drew closer to him, not fearing his dread disease. That cat was God's messenger of love to him.

There are many animal heroes. Most are unsung heroes. These heroes know the Lord. These animals serve His commandments of love, faithfulness, honor and courage. Their reward must be more than this life offers.

Jesus, like the Second Adam He is, includes them in His plans. He came to them, in the stable and the wilderness. He came for the animals, too. Do you see? Is the puzzle taking shape now?

ENDNOTES:

1. From *The Immortality of Animals and the Relation of Man as Guardian From a Biblical and Philosophical Hypothesis* by E.D. Buckner, A.M., M.D., Ph.D., [1903], at pages 62-63

2. *Thayer's Greek-English Lexicon of the New Testament*, [1977], Strong's #3326, p. 402

3. *Animals You Will Never Forget*, [Readers Digest, 1969], pp. 81-85

4. *The Zoo That Never Was*, by R. D. Lawrence, [1981]

5. Attributed to St. Basil of Caesarea, prayer A.D. 370 (The Washington Daily News, April 16 1971, P. 23). Source: *Respectfully Quoted; a Dictionary of Quotations*, edited by Suzy Platt [1993]

6. If you are either not certain or dispute that Jesus is God, then I challenge you to reconsider. Only after considering the evidence fully and fairly can you defend a position of faith, of doubt, of another religion, or of atheism, with intelligence and integrity. Read the New Testament; start with John's Gospel and Acts. Jesus is Word

of God, Word made flesh. John 8:58, identifies Him with the holiest name of God, the Name given to Moses in Exodus 3:14; the great "I AM." Repeatedly, Jesus is identified as the only Son of God the Father;. We become God's children only through Jesus. Study the Old Testament prophesies fulfilled in the life of Jesus relating to His birth, life, ministry, death and resurrection. There are good Christian books which address this evidence. Do it before you become locked in the position of a fool – which is what the Bible calls those who do not trust and obey God — Ps. 14:1 & 53:1.

7.   *Vines*, supra, "Beast" p. 53.

8.   J. Allen Boone, *Kinship With All Life*, (Harper & Row, 1954). Boone was inspired by the German Shepherd Strongheart, which was the first dog movie star, greater than Rin Tin Tin and Lassie.

CHAPTER 12

WHAT PARTS DO ANIMALS PLAY?

As the heavens are higher than the earth, so are My ways higher than your ways and My thoughts than your thoughts. ... My word that goes out from my mouth: It will not return to me empty, but will accomplish what I desire and achieve the purpose for which I sent it.

Isaiah 55:9 & 11 [NIV]

"But this is wondrous strange! There are more things in heaven and earth, Horatio, than are dreamt of in your philosophy."   Shakespeare's Hamlet

What would this life — or heaven — be like without animals? Imagine it: No bird songs or the sound of wings. No warm, fuzzy puppies or playful kittens. No doe-eyed cows; no milk or cheese. No chipmunks or elephants. No lions or pussycats. No aquariums with rainbow-colored fish and exotic shrimp. The earth is populated with animal life — from the tiniest amoebae to massive whales. What would this earth be without living things, both plant and animal?

Why didn't the Lord make us all machines? Evidence surrounds us that God made few machines. It is fallen man who "loves" machines more than animals, I think.[1]

Have you ever wondered why? I have, and I know that I am not alone! Without answers, don't we sit in darkness, ignorant of the stupendous beauty and plans which surround us?

> *Thou art worthy, O Lord, To receive glory and honor and*
> *power; For Thou hast created all things, and for Your*
> *pleasure they are and were created.*   Rev. 4:11 [KJV]

It gave God pleasure to fill this earth with life. God certainly chose to make a huge number and variety of living things. Some estimate there are in excess of 1,000,000 animal species, and there are over 10^{33} (as in 10 followed by 33 zeros) animals alive today. Researchers are still adding to the list of species a thousand per year![2] That doesn't count plant life.

Devices are not as interesting as living things. Machines are useful and the thrill of technological innovation is fun. But no machine compares to life. Living things have infinitely more diversity, flexibility, creativity, and other desirable qualities. Can a computer paint a Mona Lisa or a Sistine Chapel scene? Machines don't greet me at my door and clown until they make me laugh. No machine has voluntarily sacrificed its "life" for another being. Only living things can love you – as well as forgive you, trust you, and be a faithful friend. Machines cannot love and don't form relationships.

Our living loving Creator didn't want robots. God is love. His very nature made Him create other lovers. Contrary to fiction, machines cannot love you. God made living things to form loving relationships. The earth is truly rich with lovers living in harmony — in spite of sin's ravages:

The intricate and extensive web of animal life exhibits millions of creatures living together harmoniously, attacking one another only out of the necessity to eat.³

What fun He must have had making all living things! I believe the Lord would have made the living creatures even if He'd never made us humans.

Mom knew that God is love, and she knew God's love for all creation. Her favorite Bible chapter was 1ˢᵗ Corinthians 13 – Paul's amazing description of love. People and animals were drawn to Mom. Mom treated all animals, wild and domestic, like potential friends. For example, Mom fed black widow spiders (on a bet), had a pet racoon, and protected good snakes from being killed. 1 John 4:7-12 could have been written with Mom in mind.

Quite frankly, in spite of my life-long experience with animals, I had no idea the depth and width of God's love for all living creatures and their roles in His creative plans, until well along in this book.

TAKING ANIMALS FOR GRANTED

It is easy to ignore the familiar. We are so accustomed to animals working for us, we take them for granted. Animals have served the Lord, cooperating with humans since the Fall of Adam. Animals provide many services to man, in peacetime and in war.

Besides providing meat for our tables, they have worked for us. From ancient times, oxen and horses plowed our fields and hauled our wagons and carriages. In some places, it was (and still is) elephants, camels and llamas working as burden bearers. Dogs, cats, ferrets and others have killed rodents, guarded and rescued people and possessions. Dogs and horses help herd our flocks and cattle. Dogs and pigeons carried messages through enemy lines during war, and performed other heroic tasks. Today, dogs and other animals are service-trained to aid the disabled — the blind, deaf, paralyzed, and mentally ill. In truth, most animals love to work!⁴

Many people today are starved for physical affection. Medical research has confirmed that babies and adults who are never touched can have severe emotional and physical health problems. "Pet-able" pets like dogs, cats, even horses, readily give us something loving to provide touch. And yet, pets were never meant to replace married love. Also, animals cannot fulfill the loneliness that people have without a personal relationship with the Lord. The animals would cringe at the absurdity of the thought.

Studies have proven that people who keep a touchable pet live longer, healthier lives. Stroking a dog or a cat lowers our blood pressure. Pet owners recuperate from surgery and illness faster. In today's America many live isolated because of age, health, or single life styles. Our animals and I made sure Mom got touched many times a day. Now, as a single working adult with plenty of good friends, there are still days when the only loving touch I receive is from my animals. Pets provide needed companionship.

Parents keep pets because children learn lessons of responsibility, unselfishness, patience and forgiveness from caring for animals. C. W. Gusewelle wrote that some study the lives of saints to learn about forgiveness, "And some of us keep dogs."[5]

Animals are good for us! It is little wonder that the pet industry is a multibillion dollar business. Animals are not gods, but they are gifts from God to us. Praise the Lord for His good gifts, the animals.

LOVING IS HEALTHY

Animals are healthier for us than machines. Farmers don't love their tractors the way most used to care about a good team of horses or oxen. Computer games, and cyber-pets don't lower your heart rate or lengthen your life.

I wonder how many are saved from suicide because a dog, cat, bird, or horse loves them? I know of several. Even death has come easier because loving pets would not leave the side of their master or mistress. God loved us enough to surround us with lovers of all kinds and sizes! Think of the furry, feathered and fuzzy friends you have yet to make.

Yet, a cautionary word is needed. While God gave man dominion over all life on this planet, He did not mean for animals to be mere slaves. Your attitude about animals may be a test. Those who think animals are as disposable as a plastic toothbrush miss God's plan entirely.

When my parents gave me a puppy or pony, I became responsible for that animal. If I neglected or abused it, my parents would punish me, even to taking it away from me. That is Biblical. Nowhere does the Bible say that animals are enslaved, valueless, or mere disposable commodities.

A Tulsa pastor repeated this story on radio: A man liked the song of the mockingbird. Finding a baby bird, he caged it outside his dwelling so he could hear the bird whenever he liked. A few days later he saw the momma bird feeding the baby. The next day the young bird was dead. The man spoke with a noted ornithologist about the incident. The ornithologist told him that mockingbird mothers have been observed feeding their captive babies poison berries. It is as though the mockingbird believes a quick death is more desirable than slavery. Many animals cannot handle captivity. They die or become depressed, even infertile. The joy of living is killed by useless, boring captivity. What a lesson!

ANIMALS AS ENTERTAINERS

Some animals thrive on entertaining humans. Have you ever had a pet "clown" to make you laugh? If you have watched circus animals, like dogs, horses, lions and elephants, perform or seen whales, porpoises, walruses, seals, and otters act in marine zoo shows, then you know the delight of animal entertainers. For centuries, circuses used trained animals. It is "art" if the training is not cruel. If the activities cause many injuries it is not training. Real animal trainers do not cause pain or suffering. In truth, you cannot get the kind of performance you want with cruelty! Those who love, get lots better results.

According to trainers and other observers, performing animals clearly enjoy their work. (Entertainment is a type of work). Examples are trained bears, or mules jumping from up to 30 feet into a diving pool, or skunks which "drag-race," or squirrels which water ski.[6] These animals perform not out of fear, but love!

Doggie sports are recreational. (Check out the tv listings.) Besides obedience training and trials, agility, doggie Frisbee, diving, and a freestyle dog dancing are growing dog sports. Begun in California in the 1970s, dog relay races, called "Flyball," have been spreading. Owners are as avid as "soccer moms"![7] So, too, are therapy dogs. My friend has a tiny Yorkie, and has trained her as a therapy dog. Kids and adults enjoy watching the little lady perform (in costume) – and the dog knows well over 30 tricks! My mom's show dogs would strut their doggie stuff before the show judges.

The body language of working and performing animals shows they enjoy it. It is obvious the trained animals like more than just the food and affection from their trainers. Well-treated animals clearly enjoy their work.

Is that surprising? The Bible begins with God working six days. Then God gave Adam the job of tending the Garden of Eden. It stands to reason God would also give meaningful work to animals. Inactive animals show signs of boredom, even depression or other mental illness.

After Mom's death and my return to a law practice, her poodle, Samson, never quit grieving. He couldn't handle being left alone without human and canine company for long days. The fact that animals have emotions is accepted today. Counseling is available for emotionally disturbed dogs and cats, and medicines for their mental illness, too.

Zoos and animal breeding programs have been dispensing with cages and jail-like pens as fast as they can, opting for enclosures which emulate natural habitats as closely as possible. Innovative changes improve the mental and physical health of captive animals. They respond with behavior more like their wild relatives. One benefit is there are more successful breeding programs. It's more fun to observe animals who are contented and healthy.

ANIMAL TEACHERS AND TOOL USERS

God's creatures are remarkable. From earliest recorded records to date, the study of animals has produced life-lessons for the observant open-minded human.

No animal is an island unto itself; animal societies are astonishingly well-developed when we consider the general lack of conflict among different species even amidst the most adverse conditions for survival. The only enemies animals have are hunger, cold, and the predatory survival instincts of other species. Often, in fact, one species will help another, and some animals will even endanger their own lives for the sake of rescuing another. [8]

Man has no monopoly on creativity. Animals are creative, too. Consider the Bowerbird which creates an elaborate bower of plants and flowers to attract his mate. (Smart men know most women like flowers!) The Bowerbird truly "says it with flowers!" Chimpanzees, other primates, and elephants have painted canvases which art experts have found beautiful.[9] A dolphin has done paintings, standing on his tail with brush in mouth — and the zoo commands high prices for the art![10] The songs of certain birds, like the nightingale, are touted as musically exquisite. The song of the whales is hauntingly beautiful — recordings of whale songs are popular. The "dances" of certain birds and other animals speaks of artistic expression. Isn't creativity a mark of the Creator?

From birds to monkeys, tool-usage is common. Birds drop stones to break eggs, nuts and other encased goodies. Seals and sea lions use rocks to crack mussel shells. The beaver is an admired master engineer in making dams and canals.[11] Our animal friends are quite resourceful. It is little wonder the Lord God bragged to Job about the animals!

Saying these animals are "acting out of machine-like instinct," is like saying someone from a different culture and language group has no intellect because you cannot communicate with them. Absurd! People who say such things have never lived closely with animals and observed them honestly.

Most ancient cultures considered animals to possess many human attributes, including wisdom and foolishness, intelligence and stupidity, honesty and deceit, loyalty and unfaithfulness, wit and humor. The ancients also believed animals could communicate. Jesus, and other rabbis, delighted in teaching by parables — many included animals.

"Animal Tales" [the] "stories in which animals are the principal characters, with the plot revolving around them . . . [are] found at all culture levels in all periods." [12]

While the statement above is addressed to the Hebrew culture, it is true worldwide. For example see Aesop's Fables from ancient Greece, India's Pilpot. People have always used animals as the "stuff" of lessons for life. My mother read to me fables and other animal stories. Now I realize some of their significance. From stories such as the turtle and the scorpion, to the fox and the hare, many have learned moral and character lessons. Many are clearly fictional, although usually have some resemblance to animal behavior. Yet, each has a kernel of truth.

Remarkably, the Bible contains few, if any, "fables" of imaginary or fantastical animals. The Bible is history – and prophesy of things to come. The Bible animal stories are told as historical events. Only a few passages are allegorical, e.g., portions of Revelation. Rabbinical teaching, following the Biblical admonition to learn from the animals, includes this commentary:

Had the Torah not been given to us for our guidance, we could have learned modesty from the cat, honesty from the ant, chastity from the dove and good conduct from the cock.

[Erubin, 100b][13]

Animals seem to know their purposes and roles. Animals seldom trust people who treat them like slaves or furniture.

Western Christianity has a schizophrenic view of animals: A St. Francis attitude on the one hand; and a Descartes/B.F. Skinner arrogant cruelty on the other. Neither side trusts the other. Frankly every animal I've known votes on the side of St. Francis, by responding to kindness and avoiding brutality.

A chief problem with the Descartes side is the belief that: "The Bible says man is superior to every other creature because 'man was created in God's own image.'" Some Christians get very upset if man's superiority to animals is challenged. It is as though an identity crisis occurs.

Personally, I think it is exciting that the meaning of being "made in the image of God" is "up for grabs." I have confidence that God's definition is far more wonderful than man's.

Scientists still explore the unknown frontiers of animal behavior and intelligence. There already is plenty of data to prove that animals think, create, relate, and love. Animals have character and creativity. Humans have no monopoly on those abilities or attributes. Nor are the useful arts limited to man.

WHAT MUST WE LEARN FROM THE ANIMALS?

The Lord planned that animals would enrich our lives. Those who love animals are vastly the richer for it. God entrusted Adam with a stewardship over this earth and the animals in it. It was a healthy assignment. We have much to learn from creation. Many of us miss the important lessons the Lord wishes us to grasp.

Most animals are amazingly honest and discerning. They are amazing judges of character. Most seem to know instantly if a person can be trusted or not. I have learned to trust my animals' judgment of people and other animals. Animals show us truth.

Animals can show us the nature of God. Many animals are models of the Lord's character qualities: love, unselfish caring, faithfulness, devotion, patience, humor, joy, grief, anger, goodness, gentleness, kindness, self-control, and intelligence. Did you know skunks are better at family relationships than most humans – with no juvenile delinquency?[14] Without these important lessons, no man, woman or child is truly successful.

I never consciously applied Jesus' Golden Rule (i.e., do unto others as you would have them do unto you), to animals. [Matt. 7:12] This Rule was and is practiced by such as St. Francis of Assisi, Noah, Monty Roberts, native American Indians, and Bedouin sheiks who raise wonderful horses and camels. Among "primitive" peoples in Africa, South America and Asia are those who treat all life as a great kinship and all animals as "brothers and sisters" to man. Researching Mom's question has opened my eyes to amazing possibilities about human-animal relationships.

Wise humans in every culture have learned all life is interconnected. When we humble ourselves and listen with the heart and mind to the living things around us, we can learn much about what really counts. Often our own purpose comes in focus.

Like Balaam's donkey, there are animals who will love us enough to take our beatings so we can live.

May God show us, you and me, how to learn from His animals. May we know the animals' joy of living and the curiosity which keeps life eternally interesting for them. To learn to live in harmony and mutual assistance, with unselfish respect for all creation, is a great goal. God gave us role models. We have looked at some already. There are more who are unknown and unheralded. Some are close to us.

DISCERNING ANIMALS

This study made me realize how Mom may have come by her incredible discernment of human character. Mom could "read" a person's character within minutes of meeting them. She was rarely wrong. That was useful to me in business, in choosing friends, and in dating.

Various accounts report that most, if not all, animals have a keen ability to read people's thoughts and motives.[15] When a stranger approaches, most animals will size them up very quickly. There are even accounts of wild animals hiding long before hunters enter their territory — as though they read the hunters' minds as the humans decided to come killing.[16]

We are all mentally and emotionally naked before God — just as Adam was before the Fall. [See, Heb. 4:12-13; 1 Chron. 28:9; 2 Chron. 16:9; Ps. 94:11a; Ps. 139:2]. It makes sense that God would gift animals in tune with Him with insights into humans around them — for the animal's safety and service. It seems that the Holy Spirit's gifts of discernment of spirits, word of knowledge, and word of wisdom mentioned in 1 Corinthians 12 are not limited to humans. We seem to be mentally naked before some, if not all, of the animals as well.

Animals are remarkably in tune with humans they love. Consider an account of American pilots stationed in England during World War II who befriended a starving stray dog. "Bomber Dog" became a mascot who saw pilots off for each bombing run. One pilot became the dog's special friend. During one run, the dog suddenly became unusually dejected. Bomber Dog's friend was shot down and thought to be dead.

For ten days the dog didn't eat, continually watching the sky toward Germany. The captain then began recording the dog's actions. For six months Bomber Dog's behavior fluctuated from playfulness, to terror, to melancholy. At the last, the dog hid, shaking in misery. A few days later, Bomber Dog came out, exploding with joy. He barked as though he was trying to tell the men something. Then he raced out to the main entrance, and enthusiastically greeted an army truck. The truck carried his pilot.

The pilot's account of his escapades of danger and escape, hope and hopelessness behind enemy lines matched — day by day — the dog's moods.[17]

Recently I was told that during the Vietnam war, an American soldier's hound dog began baying (howling) strangely one night. His family felt to pray. The soldier's letter which arrived later told of his being under heavy enemy fire at the exact time his dog was sounding the alarm.

There are many accounts of animals returning home across hundreds of miles unknown territory, following their humans to locations where the animal had never been. Other accounts tell of animals sensing imminent danger or their owner's death, even at a distance.[18]

Frankly, these accounts make sense. We've examined Bible accounts of animals serving humans at the Lord's command. They need God's supernatural gifts sometimes.

As mentioned earlier, many believe animals "talked" before the Fall of Man. Some believe the communication confusion after the Tower of Babel [Genesis 11] may have affected man's understanding of the animals' language as well.

St. Francis' ability to communicate with animals appears to be more than legend. Some people say they "read" animals' minds or communicate "telepathically." This study has proved to me the concept is not necessarily unbiblical – although I expect the truth is different than most people think.

I don't know whether I've experienced knowing what an animal thinks or not - beyond reading body language and sounds. It's not something easy to prove or disprove. I admit to a desire for freer communication with animals. Love wants more.

Some seem to have enjoyed a communication with animals which approaches what Adam had. Such communication is not easy for humans. Trainers work on it more than most. Vicki Hearne's words are apt:

[M]ost of animate creation doesn't answer as loyally and with as much respect for ... the human landscape as dogs, cats and horses do. It is then the sacredness of answering, for a tribe as lonesome and threatened ... as ours is, that makes animals matter.

* * *

The animal trainer's version of Genesis ... must continue to be ..a picture of Adam and Eve leaving Eden accompanied by the few species who chose to share their lot, to accept human fate

* * *

... [W]e need [to do our part in] ensuring that animals are not denied their fundamental rights. This is a right that can be and indeed is violated continuously, ... but is un- alienable. This is ...the right from which all others follow, for them and for us, the right to be believed in, a philosoph- ical right to freedom of speech, the right to say things the philosopher has not taught them or us how to say. [19]

I find J. Allen Boone's books interesting because he said he successfully bridged the language gap between animals and humans which Adam's Fall produced. He credited the silent-movie dog, Strongheart, a German shepherd, for this feat. An accomplished dog in police and war work, the dog was the first famous canine movie star. In "sitting" for the dog, Boone was instructed to: (1) speak to Strongheart as an intelligent person; (2) never "talk down" to him like a "dumb animal" or "dog"; and (3) daily read something worthwhile to the dog. Prayer with the animal is also suggested.[20] Boone's record of his experiences with animals challenge me.

Key elements cited by those who have had a two-way conversation with an animal include: treating the animal as your equal, not as an inferior being; doing interesting things with the animal; and being totally honest. God gave animals the ability read our hearts. They are rightly alarmed at arrogant superiority, deceit and meanness.

When the communication starts, incredible lessons can be-gin. The differences offer exciting new vistas into another life. Just as it can be fun to learn and explore a different human culture, the world of each animal and its society, can be explored.[21]

I have always treated animals as persons and the rewards have been great. Animals have been my friends and teachers. Their body language can eloquently speak their thoughts. When I listen to the heart of each animal, I see my Lord.

Yet as I have researched and written this book, I have been challenged. Frankly, I had no idea what rich revelation this study would produce. I am humbled that the good Lord would entrust such a project to me. I am not worthy. I do not have the relationship with animals which God has shown me is possible. Frankly, the Adam-St. Francis relationship with animals is still beyond me. I feel like a child looking through the window of the candy store — with treats still beyond my reach.

J. Allen Boone summarized four essentials to worth-while living which he learned from animals in this credo: (1) Respect all life; (2) Be understanding and tolerant; (3) Never forget every living thing has a purpose, a particular needed job to do in God's plan; and (4) Whenever possible, lend a helping hand.[22] That sounds pretty Biblical to me.

AN ORCHESTRA OF PRAISE

All creation was made to sing the song of the universe, to extol the Creator God with all their being. (We humans often are either out of tune or absent.) The Lord conducts this living orchestra. The Master brings out the best from each. The results are splendid harmonies too glorious for words.

From psalms and church hymns we learn that praising God is something everything was created to do. Listen to creation's songs. Hear the eternal music, the praise of everything which loves life.

Praise the Lord! Praise the Lord from the heavens! ... Let them praise the name of the Lord, For He commanded and they were created. He has also established them forever; He has made a decree which will not pass away. Praise the Lord from the earth, Sea monsters and all deeps; Stormy wind, fulfilling His word; Mountains and all hills; Fruit trees and all cedars; Beasts and all cattle; Creeping things and winged fowl; Kings of the earth and all peoples; ... Let them praise the name of the Lord!   Psalm 148

We could learn to worship from the dog. The ancient Greek word for "worship" is *"proskuneo."* It is a compound word which may mean "like a dog." It is used in passages describing the worship God desires, like John 4:23-24 & Rev. 4:10. Dogs "kiss" their owner's hands and fawn or prostrate themselves before their masters.

Every dog I've known is a natural at praise and worship! Whether I am gone five minutes or five months, my dogs greet me enthusiastically. They want to be wherever I am. They watch me with adoring eyes and seek my approval in everything. Dogs respect authority, and adore masters who love them and care for them. When I think how they outdo me in worship, I'm ashamed! I am determined to improve. How about you? We can learn from dogs.

Healthy animals display an exuberance. They enjoy life! Isn't that a form of praise? As an animal lover, I've felt a warm glow inside watching my animals work and play in health and happiness. God must feel the same way.

By loving to please me, my animals praise me. The same principle works for praising the Lord. When I am enjoying doing the things God called me to do, I feel His pleasure. When His creation glows with health and harmony, He must repeat, "It is good!"

THE CHALLENGE

Through writing this book even to this point, my understanding of animals importance in God's plans has deepened immensely. Some truths have hit me like an explosion! I have fallen more in love with Jesus, my Lord and Master.

My prayer is that you, too, have been challenged. I pray you accept God's grace and choose to change. We need what God would give us through the animals. There are animals all around us as gifts. The Lord is faithful – as His animals demonstrate to us. Let's take His hand, and allow Him to lead us into wonderful adventures of life and learning! Hallelujah! Let everything which has breath praise the Lord! The good news, the Gospel, is for all creatures!

Praise God from Whom all blessings come;
Praise Him all creatures here below;
Praise Him above ye heavenly hosts;
Praise Father, Son and Holy Ghost.[23]

ENDNOTES:

1.   I like what machines can do and, like most Americans, I use lots of machines. But, I am aware of a loss. As an office-bound, working adult, I was largely divorced from nature.

2.   Warren D. Thomas, D.V.M. & Daniel Kaufman, *Dolphin Conferences, Elephant Midwives and Other Astonishing Facts about Animals*, [1990]., p. 17. See also, Dr. Bernard Heuvelmans, *On The Track of Unknown Animals,* third revised edition, [1955, 1995]

3.   *Dolphin Conferences, Elephant Midwives And Other Astonishing Facts About Animals*, p. 129.

4.   See Vicki Hearne, Adam's Task and Jeffery Moussaieff Masson, *Dogs Never Lie About Love,* for discussions of animals loving meaningful work.

5.   *Listening to Animals; Best Friends*, [Guideposts 1999], p. 82 [from C. W. Gusewelle, The Rufus Chronicle [1996]

6.   "The Last of The Politically Incorrect Country Fairs," *Wall Street Journal,* 7/24/98, p. W-1

7.   "Flyball Is A Sport People Really Sink Their Canines Into," by Tony Horowitz, *Wall Street Journal*, 8/5/98, p. A

8.   *Dolphin Conferences, Elephant Midwives and Other Astonishing Facts about Animals*, p. 71

9.   Desmond Morris, *The Biology of Art*, (N.Y.: Knopf, 1962), p. 151; D. Guewa & J. Ehmann, *To Whom it May Concern: an Investigation of the Art of Elephants*, (Norton, 1985)

10.   *Mysteries of Animal Intelligence*, supra, pp 101-103

11.   *Dolphin Conferences, Elephant Midwives And Other Astonishing Facts About Animals*, p. 106

12.   *Encyclopedia Judaica*, supra

13.   Rabbi Alexander Feinsilver, *Talmud for Today*

14.   J. Allen Boone, *Kinship With All Life*, (Harper & Row, 1954) pp. 111-113

15.   See J. Allen Boone, *Kinship With All Life; Language of Silence* [Harper & Row, 1970]; *Animals Tame & Wild*, edit. Gilbert & John Phelps [Topaz Publ. 1979]; Steiger's *Mysteries of Animal Intelligence*, supra; "Ben Got His Man" in *Animals You Will Never Forget*, [Readers Digest, 1969], for examples. J. Allen Boone and others have explored communication with animals and observed important things, even if their terminology and interpretations do not always appear Biblically sound.

16.   *The Language of Silence*, supra.

17.   *Language of Silence*, supra, p. 104

18.   For examples, see Vida Adamoli's *The Dog That Drove Home, The Snake-eating Mouse, And Other Exotic Tales From The Animal Kingdom*, [1989]; "Hector the Stowaway Dog" Animals You Will Never Forget, supra. Many of the books cited here have such accounts.

19.   *Adam's Task*, supra, p. 264, 265, 266

20.   As mentioned before, the Steigers successfully used these methods with their Rottweiler, Moses. See, *Mysteries of Animal Intelligence*, by Sherry Hansen Steiger and Brad Steiger, supra, citing J. Allen Boone, *Kinship with All Life*.

21.   J. Allen Boone said of a chemist, J. William Jean, who achieved results with microorganisms which others were unable to achieve, that the man lived the golden rule, by looking for the best in and assisting the other life form its fullest expression.

Millions of microorganisms visibly (under the microscope) turned to Dr. Jean with enthusiasm. The implications are vast. *Kinship with All Life*, supra, p. 115

22. *Kinship with All Life*, p. 116

23. Bishop Thomas Ken, *Doxology*, 1692

CHAPTER 13

ETERNITY: TWO DESTINATIONS

I have been warned not even to raise the question of animal immortality, lest I find myself "in company with all the old maids." I have no objection to the company. I do not think either virginity or old age contemptible, and some of the shrewdest minds I have met inhabited the bodies of old maids. Nor am I greatly moved by jocular enquires such as "Where will you put all the mosquitoes?" — a question to be answered on its own level by pointing out that, if the worst came to the worst, a heaven for mosquitoes and a hell for men could very conveniently be combined.[1]

The C. S. Lewis quote above humorously treats a topic many avoid — that of animal immortality. Actually many avoid the topic of their own mortality. "Eternity!" "Immortality!" From ancient times, people have speculated about what lies beyond this life. Like Shakespeare's Hamlet, some long for death and yet fear what lies beyond this life. What does lie beyond for us? Are we immortal? Or are we destined to be forgotten — merely worms' dinners? What lies beyond the door of death? If we cannot answer these questions for ourselves, how can be hope to address them for our animals?

Do Dogs Go To Heaven?

WHAT WE BELIEVE

According to popular polls in the 1990s, some ninety-percent of Americans believe in God. The overwhelming majority of Americans believe in heaven. A lot less believe in hell. Most believe — or hope — they are going to heaven when they die. Americans are now poly-cultural and have many non-Judaic-Christian beliefs or religions. "Heaven" and "hell" mean different things to different people and in different religions. Thus, the meaning of these poll results is in question. The culture of tolerance has influenced many churches to adopt some non-Biblical, usually Eastern, doctrines. There are important distinctions between Western Christianity and Eastern religions:

> *The real issue is one of metaphysical absolutes, or ground-beliefs. The East – ... Indian traditions in particular – does not honor the same ultimate values as does the West. By and large, the East claims finality for unity, consciousness, eternity, simplicity, soul. The West, in contrast, claims finality for love, plurality, community, diversity, com-plexity, time, individuality, separateness. When the East claims that All is One, it means just that. All is Brahma. This positions exalts unity over community, knowing over loving, eternity over time.*
> *But the God of the Bible incarnates himself in time and in an individual body. ... unity is no more absolute than is plurality, since God is both! ... God will be all in all, but he is also the God of eternally preserved individuals. ... It all flows from so simple a biblical claim as "God is love" (1 John 4:16). Love demands the plural.*
>
> * * *
>
> *Jesus' project in our fallen history was to bring about rec-onciliation, an eternal conversation between man and God, not an absolute identification. ... Such "news" goes beyond the ... mystical practice ... born in the valley of the Indus*

river ... The God of Israel and the Church is primarily con-
cerned about loving community, and loving conversation
between man and God. You and I, as persons, will be held
forever distinct in the loving regard of God himself.[2]

Again, this book answers Mom's question from a purely Biblical
viewpoint — as much as I am capable of doing so. What are your
absolutes? What are your images of eternity? Do you have an image
of heaven? Or hell? Why do you believe what you believe? What is the
source or authority for your beliefs? Do you know the truth? Many
scholars and saints have written about eternity. Some have raised
tough questions about the images the Bible gives us. Space is too
limited here to address such questions. There are many books which
provide well-reasoned, Biblically-sound answers.[3]

THE REALITIES OF HEAVEN AND HELL

The terms *heaven* and *hell* bring up a number of issues. First,
what are the meanings of these terms? Are they merely "conditions"
or are they real places? What is heaven like? Is it boring pleasantness
where you sing and play harps all day? (That's the picture I had as a
child.) What is hell and who is consigned there?

Another issue no sane person would avoid is: how can we be sure
we have a ticket into heaven, and insurance against hell? Eternity is a
very long time. This present life is indeed short. Can I ensure that my
loved ones, including my pet (or pets) go to heaven with me? What
about hell — do animals go there, too? Can I help them avoid hell?

Are you wondering why we have to discuss negative things, such
as hell? Look at it this way. If you saw a driver speeding toward a
washed-out bridge, wouldn't you shout a warning? Hell is a reality
that deserves a warning shout. Hell is an eternity of "living death."

TRUTH IS LOVE

There is an old saying: "Love without truth is license; truth
without love is brutality." We need to be honest with ourselves

and others. The Bible is abundantly clear that Heaven and hell are spiritual realities. If we love others, we cannot ignore the bad, or wrap the truth in soft lies. Someone will get hurt. Good parents teach their children that fire is real, will burn you, and can kill. If we fail to teach a child these lessons, we fail in loving them. If we fail to show others that un-repented sin has eternal fiery consequences, don't we also fail in being loving?

The Lord God is a good Parent. Just as He directs us how to come home to Him and to heaven, He places warning signs about a fiery hell all through Scripture — and requires each of His children to warn others. Love compels me to be a realist about heaven and hell. The Bible is clear that everyone not joined in loving relationship to the Living God, is unprotected. Holy justice does punish the foolish! Please understand, I don't serve God because I am afraid of hell or simply to gain heaven. I serve Jesus because He is the most wonderful person I've ever known and I want to be where He is.

I learned a lesson in such protection one day when I was walking with our pets. Accompanying me were Mom's two dachshunds, Choc and Kinder, along with my Siamese, Kitty. I felt a bit like a shepherd that day. Kitty and Kinder always stayed with me. Choc, on the other hand, was a law unto herself. Choc got out of my sight often and into trouble just as frequently. That day was no exception. I was sitting for a few minutes on the creek bank near a railroad overpass. Suddenly, Choc came floating past *in the water*! Her short legs were unable to fight the strong current. It pulled her toward the underpass where it was swifter and turbulent. Her face was frantic. I felt helpless – envisioning a drowned dog. I called to the Lord for help, praying in the Spirit. Suddenly the current brought the dog near the bank where I could grab her. I'm not sure Choc learned her lesson that day, but I learned one: Stay close to the protection of the Master Shepherd and don't be off doing your own thing!

WHAT DOES THE BIBLE SAY?

Because my readers' information and beliefs may be diverse, this chapter will look briefly at what the Bible says about eternity — and it says quite a lot. There are two poles in Christian doctrine about this life and the next: (1) one emphasizes that this life is temporal, and its pleasures will detour one to hell, as in *Pilgrims Progress*; (2) the other holds that the good things of this earth are proofs of a good and gracious God and heavenly blessings, which is popular today in most churches. Both have merit.

I encourage you to stop reading a moment and make a few notes of what you believe about *heaven* and *hell*. Do you know if your beliefs line up with the Bible? Check out the references I cite here. Check out the words heaven and hell, and their derivatives and synonyms in a Bible concordance and a Bible dictionary. Pray for accurate images and beliefs. Ask the Lord Jesus to help you. If praying to Jesus is uncomfortable, simply ask your Creator to show you the truth.

HEAVEN IS — WELL, HEAVENLY

There are more than 700 references to heaven in the King James Bible. That's about seven times more references to heaven than to hell. Jesus referred often to the "kingdom of heaven" —especially in the Gospel of Matthew. Repetition emphasizes a point. The Bible spotlights heaven.

Heaven is often plural, as in Gen. 1:1 — although you can't always see it in translations. There are at least three or four heavens described in Scripture. (1) The sky or atmosphere is one. [Gen. 8:2] (2) Outer space is another. [Gen. 1:14-18] (3) The "third heaven" appears to be the highest and God's current throne or residence. [2 Cor. 12:2 & Rev. 4:1-11] (4) Lastly, this earth and its heavens will be destroyed by fire on the "day of judgment and destruction of ungodly men" [2 Peter 3:4-7, 11 & 15; Rev. 20:11; Isa. 66:15; Daniel 7:9; Heb. 12:26-29; Haggai 2:6.] and, at that time a new heaven and earth will be created. [Revelation 21:1; Isa. 65:17; 66:22; & 2 Pet. 3:13]

When Bible-believing Christians refer to heaven, we tend to combine the heaven where God's throne is now with the "new heaven and earth" which will be created after the last judgment. We think of heaven as where the "dead in Christ" are with the Lord, now and for eternity. [2 Tim. 4:16] Wherever the living God sets up His throne is heaven to us – in this age or the next.

HEAVENLY VISIONS

From ancient times to date, people have had visions of, or visits to, heaven. The list includes heroes of the Jewish and Christian faith. Jacob saw angels coming and going into heaven. [Genesis 28:12] King David described heaven's splendor and music in psalms. [Psalm 8:3; Psalm 19] Isaiah saw God on His throne. [Isa. 6] Ezekiel saw God's form, His throne, and heard His voice. [Ezek. 1] Paul of Tarsus saw indescribable things in the third heaven. [2 Cor. 12:1-4]

Hebrews describes the heavenly city and some inhabitants, including Jesus. [Heb. 12:22-29] John described heaven and its inhabitants in vivid detail. [Rev.4-5 & 19-22] Even today, people have visions or dreams of heaven. Many are remarkably similar. Similarity in unconnected accounts lends credibility to such experiences.

Heaven is also called paradise. The repentant thief, crucified alongside Jesus, was comforted by Jesus with this promise: "Today you will be with Me in Paradise." [Luke 23:43 NASV] *Paradise* is used to describe heaven in 2 Cor. 12:4. The Tree of Life is there — a renewed Eden. [Rev. 2:7] The word *paradise* derives from a Greek word, with origins in ancient Persia[4] There is a similar word in Hebrew. This word was used for the Garden of Eden [Gen. 2:15 & 3:23]; and also gardens or parks of great beauty. That may be why Paul and John used it to describe heaven, a place of indescribable beauty and spiritual bliss. One of the enjoyable things about gardens are the flora and fauna — the beauty of things living together in harmony.

The last chapters of Revelation describe new heavens and a new earth coming at the end of this age. God's centerpiece is a city, the new Jerusalem, built by God and made of incredible wealth and beauty. Its foundations are precious stones. Its gates are huge pearls.

The streets are pure gold. It is a cube some fifteen hundred miles on each side. That's some piece of real estate!

HOME

Although God's presence is everywhere, heaven is His throne. In heaven we will be with Him forever – without the hindrances of this mortal flesh. It will be home. I will never again be separated from the Lord of Love and Life. That excites me so much I can hardly contain the joy!

To me, the most wonderful thing about Heaven is the Lord Himself. I will have a clear, unobstructed look at the Lord God — Father, Son, and the manifold Holy Spirit — face to face. The song *I can Only Imagine* by Mercyme, describes it well. Until I'm fully satiated, I will gaze at Him, and "drink in" His presence. His voice, like the sound of many waters, will be such music to my ears — unmuffled by this earth's sinful clamor. [Rev. 1:15] I will hug and touch my heavenly Daddy and my Jesus – in awe and honor. Waiting for that day requires His grace.

THE LIGHT

The light in heaven will be marvelous. "The Lord is my light and my salvation," Psalm 27:1 says. Heaven is illuminated by the very being of God the Father, and the Son. [Rev. 22:5] God is pure light with no darkness at all! [1 John 1:5] I have experienced this Light in a measure, and it is impossible to describe. Jesus is light. His light is the energy which is life. [John 1:1-4; & 8:12] His presence, this Light, feels to me like being immersed in pure, liquid love.

NO MORE CURSE

There is no curse in Heaven. [Rev. 22:3 & Zech. 14:11] God will:

> ... *wipe away every tear from their eyes. Death is gone for good – tears gone, crying gone, pain gone – all the first order of things gone.*   Rev. 21:4 [TMB]

Imagine what that means. To be sorrow-free and pain-free forever. To never lack for any good thing. The very air is life. There is no tiredness or weariness of heart, mind, or body. Everything is crystal clear and clean. We will think, understand, do things, and feel good – all without effort. Everyone loves everyone, for the royal law of love governs everything. [James 2:8] There is something in heaven for everyone. Real, everlasting pleasures and joys. [Ps. 16:11]

LIFE AND TRUTH

God's plan made Jesus the Way, "the ticket"or "the key," to entering heaven. [John 14:6] Jesus died and was resurrected to give us eternal life, abundant life. [John 10:10; 11:25; & Heb. 2:9-15] Those who confess and obey Jesus as Savior, pass from spiritual death into life. [Rom. 6:23; & John 3:14] Death is defeated and is no more.[1 Cor. 15:54-56; & Rev. 21:4] Life fills heaven.

Jesus is the Truth [John 14:6]. Truth is the atmosphere of heaven. There are no hidden agendas, no selfish thoughts or unholy ambitions. In the pure presence of God and His Christ, all you ever want to do is whatever pleases Him! Far from boring, Heaven is a place of unfettered and unmarred creativity. Our Creator God loves to work and to do new things! [Prov. 8:30; Isaiah 42:9; 43:19 & 48:6-7] Like a body in perfect health, all things in heaven work together in harmony. Everything is beautiful, perfect, and good.

I realize to some this may sound trite or simplistic. Describing Jesus and His heaven to some people is like describing a sunset to a person born blind, or beautiful music to a person born deaf. Such things must be experienced. Even if I have not seen it, I trust those in Christ who have described it. Simply ask the Lord to open your eyes and ears. That's His part of this message. [Prov. 20:12] Only our Lord Jesus can open the eyes of the blind and the ears of the deaf. He is more than willing to do so.

OTHER WITNESSES OF HEAVEN OTHER WITNESSES OF HEAVEN

Through the ages, Christians have described their visions and dreams about heaven or their visits to heaven. When Mom was dying, I asked her if she saw heaven and Jesus. Mom nodded, "yes!" Numerous books describe such experiences others have had of heaven.

Others have written "inspired imaginings." From the 13th century, we have Alighieri Dante's *The Divine Comedy*. In the 17th century, John Milton's epic allegorical poems, "Paradise Lost," describe hell, and "Paradise Regained," describes heaven. C.S. Lewis wrote *The Great Divorce*, an allegory about heaven and hell. *Pilgrim's Progress*, written by John Bunyan from an English jail, is an allegory of Adam's offspring traveling toward heaven and the difficulties encountered along the way. In 2010, *Heaven is for Real* relates the experience of heaven Todd Burpo's young son Colton had. The child saw things which the Bible describes.

Heaven is a real place. Heaven is a place where God is very present, uncloaked and unlimited. Therefore, heaven is a place filled with all God is: light, eternal life, love, wisdom, truth, goodness, peace, joy everlasting, beauty, music, grace, and every good and wonderful thing possible. There are several good books on heaven which are informative if you wish to learn more.

HELL, THE ULTIMATE TORMENT

If Heaven is real, then it only makes sense that there is a real hell. Jesus referred to hell in His teaching. He described it as a place of everlasting torment where the inhabitants are "gnashing" their teeth.

The real existence of hell is irrefutably taught in Scripture as both a place of the wicked dead and a condition of retribution for unredeemed man. ... The nature of hell is indicated by the repeated reference to everlasting punishment (Matt. 25:46); everlasting chains (II Thess. 1:8);

the eternal fire (Jude 7); the pit of the abyss (Rev. 9:2,11);
outer darkness (Matt. 8:12); the wrath of God (Rom. 2:5);
second death (Rev. 21:8); eternal destruction from the face
of God (II Thess. 1:9); and eternal sin (Mark 3:29).[5]

Hell is the absence of all that heaven is, just as darkness is the absence of light. [Matt. 8:12; 22:13; 25:30] There is a "horror of darkness." [Gen. 15:12] Such darkness can be felt. [Exo.10:21] Hell has chains of black, heavy darkness forever. [2 Pet. 2:4; Jude 6 & 13] Hell is a place for those who want nothing to do with Light and Truth, with God. [John 3:19; & 12:35-46] Hell can be understood as the total absence of all the benefits of the Light. It is the absence of the Lord's influence for good.

I meditated on the Scriptures which described hell. It was instructive if unpleasant. The Bible describes hell as a "lake that burns with fire and brimstone, which is the second death." [Rev. 21:8] In hell, the inhabitants swim in flames. Hell is not solid, but rather like "residing" in the Sun.

Human skin contains the most nerve endings in the human body. The pain of a burn is excruciating pain. (Ask a hospital burn nurse.) Residents of hell are in constant unrelenting pain covering every inch of skin. The consequences? They would never be able to stand being touched — no hugging, no kissing, no hand-holding. Starved for affection, but unable to endure being touched, their torture would be double – both physical and emotional.

Burning matter can be noisy. The roar of the fire, the popping and crackling of the "fuel" would be horrible. There would be no peace, no quiet, no pleasant sounds.

Brimstone smells like rotten eggs. In hell, you'd lose your appetite pronto. With burned, brimstone-filled mouths, nothing could be eaten without pain. Brimstone is nauseating, too. Inhabitants feel hunger gnawing at their insides, while nausea and pain prevent eating and drinking – if these were available.

In Luke 16, Jesus told of a certain rich man and poor Lazarus. The rich man died and went to hell, and begged Abraham to send Lazarus across the chasm that separated Hell from Paradise to give him just a drop of water. Abraham couldn't do it. (Fire evaporates water.) Hell's inhabitants would be thirsty. There is no relief there.

WHO INHABITS HELL?

The Bible is clear that the eternal hell is the place for the wicked. It's where rebels against the Lord reside. In a sense, hell is God's eternal prison for evil, mean persons. A list of those destined for hell (if they do not change their ways) includes:

... the cowardly and unbelieving and abominable [depraved] and murderers and [sexually] immoral persons and sorcerers [practicers of magic arts] and idolaters and all liars, their part will be in the lake that burns with fire and brimstone, which is the second death.

Rev. 21:8 [Amp.]

But without [heaven] are the dogs and those who practice sorceries (magic arts) and impurity (the lewd, adulterers) and the murderers and idolaters and everyone who loves and deals in falsehood — untruth, error, deception, cheating.

Rev. 22:15 [Amp.]

Hell does not exist to frighten sinners into serving God although some preachers make it sound as though it does. "Hellfire and brimstone" preaching leaves me cold. I cannot imagine someone serving God because that person was terrified of Him. I wouldn't want to give my heart to the Lord Jesus if He tried to frighten me into serving Him.

At the same time, I recognize that sometimes people are like the proverbial Missouri mule — you have to beat them over the head with a club to get their attention. Pain, or the threat of it, is a great attention getter. There are those who come to the Lord out of pain — but not because of the wrong kind of fear of Him. Jesus wooed me with gentle strength, patient love, and delightful humor. I ignored Him for years, enjoying the transitory pleasures of this world and serving other gods. Jesus persisted in love until I returned to Him. There were times I felt hopeless and worthless. I even wondered why my animals loved me. Now I know that even then Jesus valued me and kept believing in me. The Lord God is no respecter of persons. [Acts 10:34] He treats all of us the same. The real God is loving, patient, kind, humble, not easily provoked, longsuffering, unfailing, and One who does not think evil. [1 Cor. 13] It is a false Christ who would be cruel and oppressive.

God loves us so much He sacrifices the lives of animals who love us in order spare us. God sent His own Son to die for us as the ultimate act of unselfish love. The God described in the Bible is Love, Truth, Wisdom, and Righteousness. Along with love and wisdom comes justice. He had to satisfy the demands of justice when man broke the laws of God. Hell satisfies that judgment. Both those who choose right and those who do not (rebellious, evil people) receive their just rewards. Some receive their just rewards in this life. Some in the next.

No loving father enjoys having to discipline a child. Somehow, if we could feel the Creator's pain because of what we have done, I suspect we'd know real hell. I know when I have realized the pain and trouble I've caused the Lord (and others) by my mistakes, it has hurt. I'm glad to know that pain now, so I have a chance to change my ways! Search the Scripture and thoroughly study the character of the Lord God. I challenge you to find one act of clear-cut, unprovoked meanness on God's part recorded in the Bible.

HELL – ARE THERE ANIMALS THERE?

The Bible tells us that Hell's foremost prisoner is an animal – the Great Serpent, Satan. [Rev. 20:10.] Also, it will be the future home of the Beast. This Beast is described in Revelation 13:2 as being like a leopard, with feet of a bear and mouth of a lion. Hell was prepared for

God's adversaries. [Matt. 25:41] The principals destined to be there are the Great Serpent Satan, the Beast, the False Prophet, Death and Hades. [Revelation 19:20-21; 20:11-14]

Since we know animals have spirits, Job's description of the place or places of death includes both human and animal:

The departed spirits tremble under the waters and their inhabitants. Naked is Sheol [hell or the nether world] before Him and Abaddon [Destruction] has no covering.

Job 26:5-6 [NASV with footnotes interwoven]

ETERNAL JUDGMENT – GOD'S JUSTICE

Isaiah, Jeremiah, Ezekiel and other Bible prophets lived during times when ancient Israel and their neighbors worshipped of all kinds of gods. These idolatrous practices included orgies of sexual license and cruelties to children and animals. People gave lip service God's commandments, but they did whatever pleased them. Isaiah wrote:

Thus says the Lord, "Heaven is My throne, and the earth is My footstool.

* * *

But to this one I will look, To the one who is humble and contrite of spirit, and who trembles at My word. **But he who kills an ox is like one who slays a man; He who sacrifices a lamb is like the one who breaks a dog's neck;** *He who offers a grain offering is like one who offers swine's blood; He who burns incense is like the one who blesses an idol. As they have chosen their own ways, And their soul delights in their abominations, So I will choose their punishments, And I will bring on them what they dread.* Isaiah 66:1-3 [NASV]

Archeological evidence has shown that in Israel or Palestine, ancient idol worship included human sacrifice — some babies and children — and many animals, both clean and unclean. Bestiality and other cruelties to animals were part of this.

These bear little resemblance to the animal sacrifices discussed in earlier chapters. God's sacrifices restored a man's relationship to God and His Creation broken by sin (if only for a limited time). Killing was never designed to afford human's any amusement or to be mere ritual. God instituted rules ensuring that the killing of sacrifice animals was swift and painless, and very messy. There was no pleasure intended in sacrifice.

These sacrifices helped mankind understand the cost of sin and the price of peace with God. Man was to contemplate the animal's innocence and value time a sacrifice was required. To make any sacrifice to God, it must be with the right kind of animal and done in the manner God prescribed, or it was an abomination to Him.

Jude 10 says: *But these speak evil of whatever they do not know; and whatever they know naturally, like brute beasts, in these things they corrupt themselves.* [NKJ]. What does that mean? Going to the Greek text, the phrase translated "brute beasts" is "aloga zoa" "Aloga" means "without speech." "Zoa" is the root of the English word "zoology," and means a living being (of any kind), including its spiritual life[6] If I understand the text correctly, Jude 10 means some people only have knowledge of things like speechless animals do, by what their physical senses tell them alone. I think such passages, like 2 Peter 2:12 & 16 and Jude 10, describe corrupt evil people and contrast them to animals because such people live carnally, by "instinct," not the law of love. Any other interpretation does not fit with the whole of Scripture. One should not to interpret Jude 10 as consigning all "dumb animals" to this life alone, nor to the same fate as the human brutes described in these passages. There are too many Scriptures to the contrary. "Dumb animals" (meaning speechless, not brainless) have stood by as silent witnesses while mankind behaved badly through the ages.

The subject of judging and judgment is a huge topic in the Bible. When I was just out of law school, I served as an administrative law judge. During this time, I committed my life to the Lord; therefore I was interested in what the Bible said about being a judge. It says a lot! Especially the points about being just, and not showing partiality to rich or poor. [Gen. 18:25;-26; Exo. 23:1-9; Deut. 16:18-20; Lev. 19:15]

God will surely judge both the righteous man and the wicked man, for a time for every matter and for every deed is there. Ecclesiastes 3:17

God Himself is the Judge over all the earth. [Gen. 18:25; Ps. 50:6; Heb.12:23] The Lord is Judge, Lawgiver, and King, and that is how we must know Him for full salvation. [Isa. 33:22; Matt. 25:31-46; James 4:12]. God is the Judge over the living and the dead [Acts 10:42; 2 Tim. 4:1; & 1 Pet. 4:5] and knows and judges the secrets in our hearts. [Rom. 2:16] At the last judgment, the Great White Throne judgment, everything will be judged and separated into hell or the new heaven and earth. [Rev. 20-21] God is a just and fair God. First He gave us the law, the commandments. The law is "genetically" programmed within every human. These commandments were written in our consciences when the first Adam ate of the fruit of the tree of the knowledge of good and evil.

A just judge applies the law, not his own standard. To invent new rules when the accused stands before the judge is unfair and unjust. Justice requires certainty. That's why the Bible says that where there is no law, there is no sin or transgression. [Rom. 4:15] God holds the world accountable because of the law. It's because of the law that the knowledge of sin comes. [Rom. 3:19-20] Those who keep the law, whether they know what is right through hearing God's word or simply because of their conscience, are rewarded. [Ps. 58:11; Rom. 3:25-29] Those who don't keep the law, are subject to the penalty of sin. Sins penalty is poverty, sickness and eternal death. [Rom. 3:10-18; 6:23; Deut. 28; Rev. 20:13-15.] No human has been able to keep the full letter of God's law, since Adam's Fall. That's why Jesus came. Jesus becomes the Way home to God and heaven.

DO "BAD" ANIMALS GO TO HELL?

A classified ad:[7] *"Damnation puppies, 8 weeks old, $45."*

In spite of this ad, I don't think there are a lot of animals, especially dogs, in hell. But what about the bad actors, the mean or killer animals? Do they go to hell?

We have already established that animals have souls and spirits. Animals show their ability to make moral and rational choices. Observant pet owners have seen their animals act either defiant or guilty when disobedient. Animal trainers understand this.

All of us who spend time with animals have been bitten, scratched, stepped on, thrown off, knocked down, or otherwise injured by these animals. But such injuries are nearly always accidental (without malice) on the part of the animal. If you have a good relationship with the animal, that animal most often acts profoundly sorry that you were hurt. Also, injury may occur if the animal is protecting itself or someone else.

Most animals are good — just like people. Some are good because it's as natural to them as breathing. I've seen animals suffer unspeakable cruelty and still offer love and forgiveness to the person hurting them. Animals often love people as Mother Teresa loved — without prejudice and without being repelled by a person's condition. Such animals don't care if you are unwashed, covered with putrid sores, or dying. They still give love. If there's a heaven for such saints as Mother Theresa, surely God has rewards in eternity for loving animals.

On the other hand, some animals would rather bite than love. Anyone who has lived and worked with animals knows there are a few truly "bad" or evil animals, just as with humans. Some turn bad.

They may turn bad because of severe abuse from humans. Some are subjected to hell-on-earth. Some may go bad for other reasons.

Usually people and animals "go bad" by choice. The Bible says all of us have broken God's Laws, and we all are criminals deserving of punishment or imprisonment. God, being just, must judge all according to our deeds. Sin is often the easier choice. Sin is like weeds which pop up voluntarily, then take over. Good character, like good crops, takes cultivation. Being good demands work. It's impossible without help from God – which is called grace.

While many wish to avoid issues regarding a place of eternal punishment, I am too much of a realist to do so. The matter becomes personal to me. If my dog can go to hell for a bad attitude, doesn't the same apply to me?

Just like the human arena, the animal world has its bad characters. Adam's Fall was influenced by an animal — the crafty serpent. I believe that the Bible teaches that certain animals will go to hell — just as certain people will. I base this in part because God's judgment falls on both man and animal in this life.

Earlier, we ascertained that judgment came on animals *and* humans in Nineveh before Jonah arrived. The domestic animals such as cattle, were subject to judgment and responded to Jonah's preaching with fasting and repentance just as the humans did. Before Moses led the Children of Israel out of Egypt, the Egyptian animals suffered and died from the plagues right along with their owners. At the same time the Hebrews and their animals remained untouched. [Exo. 8:17; 9:1-12, 25-26; 11:4-7; 12:29-32] Pharaoh's army with their horses were destroyed in the Red Sea when they went after the Children of Israel. [Exodus 14-15] Everything that breathed (humans *and* animals) was destroyed when the land of Canaan was given to Abraham's descendants. [Deut. 7:1-2; 20:10-20; Joshua 6:21] Let's clarify what is meant when referring to bad or evil animals deserving of eternal punishment. This does not refer to animals which injure or kill to protect themselves, to protect others, or their territory. It does not refer to animals reacting in fear, or killing to eat. It does, however, refer to the rare animal which intentionally hurts or tries to kill humans or other animals out of pure meanness, out of bitter, unforgiving hatred or "just for sport." The hell-bound animal is surely the one bent on injuring and hurting others without good cause -- as did the Serpent in the Garden, Satan. They are (or would be) killers. Fortunately there are few of them. Are there consequences for animals who are truly mean, or are killers because they enjoy killing? In Matthew 25:31-46, it says that the Son of Man will judge all nations, dividing them into "sheep" and "goat" nations. Those who were kind to strangers, prisoners, and the destitute are sheep, and those who were not are goats. The former are to be with Jesus in eternity; the latter burn in hell. We already know from the examples of the judgment in the Old Testament, that a judgment on a nation is a judgment on men, women, children, and *animals*.

The Bible does not say there are any excuses or defenses available in the last judgment. We cannot stand before God and say, "The devil made me do it" or "It's my parents' fault," or "It's the environment I grew up in." Nor can any animal, I dare say.

But faced with a clear choice some animals — like those in Nineveh at Jonah's preaching — change. Some call this *retraining*. The Bible calls it repentance, which means to change direction and go another way.

ENDNOTES:

1.　C. S. Lewis, *The Problem of Pain* (Collier Books, 1962), p. 136-137

2.　U. Milo Kaufmann, *Heaven, a future finer than dreams*, [Light and Life Press, 1981], p. 13-14

3.　See for example, Grant R. Jeffrey, *Heaven the Last Frontier*; and W.A. Criswell and Paige Patterson, *Heaven*; U. Milo Kaufmann, *Heaven, a future finer than dreams*, [Light and Life Press, 1981]. Heaven; *Close Encounters of the God Kind* by Jesse Duplantis is another. I would also commend to the reader the sermons of Charles G. Finney, a lawyer turned evangelist in the 1800's, and Watchman Nee, the great Chinese teacher-evangelist. See also, William F. Buckley, Jr., *Nearer, My God,*

[Harcourt & Brace, 1997]. Among others too numerous to mention, I believe these have an understanding of God, man and our eternal destination which illumines many dark questions.

4.   *Pictorial Bible Dictionary*, supra, "Paradise", p. 622

5.   *Pictorial Bible Dictionary*, p. 346

6.   See George Ricker Berry, Ph.D., *The Interlinear Literal Translation of the Greek New Testament*, [Zondervan, 15th printing 1974]

7.   Times-Gazette, Ashland, Ohio, reported in *Readers Digest*

CHAPTER 14

THE RESTORATION
OF ALL CREATION

A stork that was present at the song of a dying swan told
her 'twas contrary to nature to sing so much out of season;
and asked her the reason of it. "Why," says the Swan, "I
am now entering into a state where I shall be no longer in
danger of either snares, guns, or hunger; and who would
not joy at such a deliverance?"[1]

The warm Indiana morning was green with life when my father
asked me to join him in a drive to the county incinerator. Doc
(as everyone called my father) took dead animals to the incinerator.
(It was the safest way to kill any disease the animal might have had.)
Doc had put a client's old dog to sleep as I recall, and its body needed
to be cremated. This dog had entered a stage when pain was more
common than comfort, and romps in the fields were only a memory.

I climbed into the front seat of Doc's car. As a child, going
anyplace with my busy father was a treat. Immediately I began asking
questions. My parents never discouraged my questions. (Often their
answers were to give direction on how I might find the answers
myself, so I learned to research early.) I still love asking questions.

As we drove down the country road, I studied my father's tanned, intelligent face. As I did, an interesting question popped into my head. I was young and believed Doc knew just about everything.

"Where is this dog now?" I asked him.

"Its body is covered with a tarp in the trunk," Doc answered. Doc's car was his mobile veterinary clinic out of which he doctored farm animals.

"Did this dog go to heaven? Do animals go to heaven?" I wanted to know.

Something like surprise flickered swiftly across Doc's face. He paused. Doc was a deep thinker, but I don't recall him talking about God. But then, I was taught not to "pry" into people's religion (and some other topics). Doc's interests were science, history and world events.

"I'm sure there is a heaven for dogs," he told me.

The answer came in a matter-of-fact way. It filled my young heart with confidence and peace. I was satisfied that there was a heaven for animals. Doc said so. A quiet, shy man, Doc was a man of few words, but I knew him have integrity and be very honest. I could trust anything he said. I imagined a heavenly meadow with dogs playing with joy.

As children, my brother and I held funerals (with Mom's help) for our little furry or feathered friends. Doc's words completed the picture for me. There was something more than this brief existence for them. A promise of a beautiful place with endless comfort and pleasure for my animal friends was a certainty. Doc said so. Therefore, I never again thought about the issue of animals going to heaven — until Mom asked all those ministers her question.

AN AFTERLIFE FOR ANIMALS?

Throughout history, people have believed in an afterlife for animals. Ancient Chinese and Egyptians killed both servants and animals of their deceased, powerful, wealthy masters and buried them in the same tomb. They believed the masters needed and wanted the animals in the next life. (These ancients believed they could "take it with them." Talk about keeping the same lifestyle!) We should be repulsed by the idea killing servants and animals just because their master died. Yet we can sympathize with the hope of an afterlife for all of them. The servants may have been willing to die with the prospect of the afterlife more attractive than this life. Whether they joined their master or mistress in Paradise or in Hades is the question! The animals had no choice. Some animals choose to die when their human master dies. That is different than being killed for that purpose!

The belief that there is an afterlife for humans and animals is common today among those of many religions and philosophies. Books and magazines discussing animals' importance in our lives, line the shelves of bookstores and libraries. Pet-loss became a hot topic in the 1990's and still is in the 21st century.

As adults, we usually re-examine things we were told as children. Believing alone does not make a thing so. Otherwise, the tooth-fairy would be real; Santa Claus would come for every good child with presents on Christmas; this world would have already ended; and politicians would never be guilty of lying. What is the truth about animals? Is there a reliable source? Was Doc stating a truth or was he telling me a fairy tale? What in my childhood was truth and what was fiction? Could the living God have put words in Doc's mouth? Does the Bible back up Doc's statement? Or does the Bible disprove his reply? Whether Doc believed what he said or not, something in him moved him to speak those words to his child.

ANIMALS GRIEVING

We know by observation that animals grieve over the loss of loved ones. It is well documented that both domestic and wild animals grieve, some to the point of death or suicide, over the loss of a loved mate or master.[2] Mom and I observed our animals grieve over such losses.

Arthur Schopenhauer, a German philosopher, said:

Animals have these advantages over man: they never hear the clock strike, they die without any idea of death, they have no theologians to instruct them, ..., and no one starts lawsuits over their Wills. Animals hear about death for the first time when they die.[3]

That sounds wise and wonderful, but is it true animals "die without any idea of death"? How would Schopenhauer explain some animals' actions which show they have some understanding of time and death? Could Schopenhauer explain the behavior of pets which act strangely just days and hours before their owner dies? What about the film of a hippopotamus trying to rescue a young antelope from death? The antelope was seized by a crocodile. The crocodile let her go when the hippo charged. The hippo nudged the antelope up the river bank, helped her to her feet, and opening its huge mouth, repeatedly breathed warm air on the dying impala before leaving her.[4] Or wild geese who clearly were upset at the death of a mate? Or Koko the gorilla who learned sign language, and expressed grief when her kitten was killed? What about the dying cat who managed to find a human to feed her while she was pregnant, and hang on just long enough to wean her kittens before expiring?[5] What about the famous Syke terrier, Greyfrier's Bobby, a shepherd's dog, who in 1858 followed his master's funeral procession and stayed by the grave until 1872 when the dog died?[6] In Scotland, the Greyfrier's churchyard has a statue inscribed with a tribute to the dog's faithfulness. Consider the 7-year-old Siamese cat who quit eating when her dying master lost his appetite two days before he passed on; the cat died 18 days later.[7] Mom's toy poodle appeared to understand when Mom passed on. Samson quit going to her side of the car to look for Mom and looked very sad.

Who would not hope the Lord rewards such love in eternity!

CHRISTIAN THEOLOGY IS A HISTORY OF MIXED BELIEFS

Now we come to the crux of Mom's question. What is the will of the Creator God? What is heaven really like? Who is there? Are animals included? What animals? Is there a resurrection for our earthly animal friends, as the Bible says there is for human believers? Or does heaven contain no earth-born animals? Do you pray the Lord's Prayer, saying to God: "Your will be done, Your kingdom come, on earth as it is in heaven" as I do? Do we realize what we are asking? What is in heaven? We need to know.

In earlier chapters we saw that a half-dozen ministers gave Mom many different answers. Viewpoints are a mixed bag of beliefs about animals in heaven. Forgive me if I sound harsh, but some viewpoints are ludicrous. In spite of the prevailing theology, through the ages, people have clung to the idea that animals are in heaven. An Inquisition[8] document describes heaven with "beautiful groves with singing birds." Yet, this rural image of paradise was frowned on by church leaders in the twelfth and thirteenth centuries.[9]

Thomas Aquinas, the Dominican, and Bonaventure, the Franciscan, did not believe there were animals in heaven.[10] (Isn't it ironic that a disciple of St. Francis did not believe animals went to heaven.) These beliefs are expressed in Dante's description of heaven in the Divine Comedy.[11] Dante's heaven is pure light; no animals dwelt in that pure light; and only redeemed human spirits and God were there. This is in keeping with the belief that animals lacked souls.

The Reformation saw new theologies — which included animals in heaven. Believing the Lord would purify the earth and heavens in the last judgment, Martin Luther taught that everything in the original Eden would be in the refashioned heaven and earth: "all creatures most beautiful," even insects and unpleasant creatures will be transformed and fragrant.[12] There is hope skunks and stink bugs will smell beautiful!

Puritans and other ascetic reformers, however, retained something of Aquinas and Bonaventure. The Puritan hereafter was viewed to be a purely "spiritual" realm, without much resemblance to this material world.[13]

John Wesley, the Anglican priest and the father of Methodism, held a God-centered (or theocentric) view of heaven, like most reformers. However, Wesley made a very strong argument for animal immortality.[14] Wesley must have known and loved dogs! The Lord has always had His witnesses who shine as one lone candle in a great darkness.

ANIMALS IN HEAVEN NOW

As wonderful as space ships might be, Jesus doesn't return to earth in a mechanical contraption. In John's Revelation, he foresaw that Jesus, as the Messiah, the King of Kings and the Lord of Lords, will return in the flesh mounted on a white horse, with His calvary behind Him. [Rev. 19:11-21] Consider that carefully.

The Lord's first coming was as a servant, a holy sacrifice, riding humbly on a donkey. Jesus' second coming to earth is as a conquering hero, riding a war horse. I love that Jesus' comes on a magnificent stallion. I imagine the stallion looks something like Pegasus. (Pegasus was a gorgeous winged white stallion of Greek mythology.) Whatever the horse looks like, it will be an impressive event! I am glad the Lord loves horses since they have been such special friends to me. Beautiful horses put a song in my heart. They are as refreshing as the mythical waters Pegasus's hoof print was said to bring. I agree with Trish (Chapter 2), that heaven would not be heaven to me without horses.

THE WONDERFUL CHERUBIM

When I was writing this chapter, I felt to study the cherubim. ("Cherub" is the singular of "cherubim.") Turns out these beings may be very important to Mom's question. Archeological findings of figures in the Near East have led some to conclude cherubim look like winged sphinxes.[15] This does not fit with accounts in the Bible. Sphinxes have a lion's body, a human face and two wings. Many western artists portray cherubim as fat babies with wings. Biblical cherubim are **not** cute little baby angels.

What do cherubim really look like? Looking to the Bible, the prophet Ezekiel is our main source. Ezekiel had several visions which included cherubim. Ezekiel first saw cherubim at the river Chebar (likely northwest of Babylon). [Ezek. 1]. Ezekiel saw the "glory of the Lord" arrive at the temple at Jerusalem being carried on cherubim. [Ezek.9:3]. The cherubim were in (or causing) a great storm, flashing with lightings, having glowing metal in the midst of it. Wheels whirled. Above was the throne of God. Pretty exciting! Ezekiel's cherubim had four different faces. Each had a man's face, with a lion's face on the right and an ox or bull's face on the left, as well as an eagle's face. In Hebrew thinking, the ox, eagle and lion, combined with man, symbolized strength and wisdom.[16] The cherub's legs were straight, but its feet were like a calf's hoof, and looked like burnished bronze. Cherubim had four wings, with human hands under the wings. Cherubim covered themselves with wings. Ezekiel always saw the cherubim connected with whirling wheels, as though they were part of each other. Their whole body, hands, wings and wheels, were full of eyes all around. So God's cherubim are powerful complex beings.

THE PURPOSE OF CHERUBIM

What purpose do cherubim have? What does the Bible say? David sang about the Lord riding on cherub's wings. [2 Sam. 22:11 & Ps. 18:10]. King Hezekiah acknowledged that the Lord dwelt among cherubim. [2 Kings 19:15]. Ezekiel saw the Lord above or in the midst of flying cherubim. [Ezek. 1 & 10] God stationed cherubim with a flaming sword at the entrance to the Garden of Eden after Adam's Fall. [Gen. 3:24]. Ezekiel saw a cherub put his hand into fire, and put coals of fire into the hands of an angelic man to scatter over Jerusalem in judgment. [Ezek. 10:6-7] In addition, the glory and presence of the Lord are associated with cherubim:

> *Then the glory of the Lord went up from the cherub to the threshold of the temple and the temple was filled with the cloud, and the court was filled with the brightness of the glory of the Lord. Moreover, the sound of the wings of the cherubim was heard as far as the outer court, like the voice of God Almighty when He speaks.*   [Ezek. 10:4-5]

From these descriptions we see that these many-eyed, fiery immortals are intimate with the Almighty. Cherubim are beyond any ancient Icarus[17] and modern science fiction space craft! Cherubim guard things holy and precious to God, like great watchdogs. Cherubim have to be pure spirits to stay close to the Almighty. God is pure Light and a consuming fire! [Ps. 27:1; John 1:1-9; John 14; 1 John 1:5; Heb. 12:29]. (Mortal flesh cannot handle the presence of God any more than we can vacation on the sun.)

Cherubim must be breathtakingly magnificent – for holiness is beautiful! [Exo. 15:11]. Huge images of cherubim were fashioned of gold and placed over the Ark of the Covenant in the holiest place within the tabernacle of Moses. In this Ark were the tablets given to Moses, written by the Lord. On top of the Ark was the "mercy seat." Two gold cherubim were on either side of the mercy seat, covering it with their wings. It was there the Lord God spoke with the high priest. [Exo. 25:18-22; 37:7-9] This same Ark (and images of cherubim) was brought into Solomon's temple (built in Jerusalem about 950 B.C.). Also, images of cherubim were embroidered on the tabernacle curtains and later put on the temple walls. [Exo. 26:1; 1 Kings 6:29.]

REPRESENTATIVES OF ANIMATE CREATION

The origin of the Hebrew word for "cherub" is unknown. So, its meaning is unclear.[18] However, *Vine's Complete Expository Dictionary* says something significant for our question, i.e., that

Cherubim *"are regarded by some as the ideal representatives of* **redeemed animate creation."** (Emphasis added)

Vines goes on to say the presence of cherubim at the gate of the Garden of Eden is a promise that "redeemed men, restored to God on God's conditions, would have access to the Tree of Life." As animals were sacrificed to spare Adam instant death, so representatives of redeemed creation guard and guide the way to the Tree of Life. How fitting! This is another piece of the answer to Mom's question.

John described living creatures in and around the throne of God which appear to be much like Ezekiel's cherubim. [Rev. Chapters 4 & 5] It is unclear whether John saw four different beings or one kind with four faces:

..And in the center and around the throne, four living creatures full of eyes in front and behind. And the first creature was like a lion, and the second creature like a calf, and the third creature had a face like that of a man, and the fourth creature was like a flying eagle. And the four living creatures, each one of them having six wings, are full of eyes around and within; ... [Rev. 4:6b-8a]

These beings are always heard saying, "Holy, Holy, Holy is the Lord God Almighty!" These being say "Amen" when "all creation praises Him Who sits on the Throne, together with the Lamb of God." [Rev. 5:13-14] These are the same living creatures or "beasts" which say, "Come!" to the four-horsemen of the Apocalypse which begins the final judgments, the end of this Age. [Rev. 6].

Think of it. This world began with animals. Adam was spared by the sacrifice of animals. God uses cherubim, the representatives of animate creation, both to guard the way to Life and to herald the End of this Age. That's a fit honor for "animate creation" which has suffered and been sacrificed for man. Beasts will announce the destruction of all that deals out suffering and death to man and to animals. Wow. Amen! Oliver B. Greene interpreted Revelation 4:9-11 as being related to Romans 8. [19]

Jesus (the second Adam) purchased redemption for the sinner when He died on the cross; but god's plan of redemption does not only include the soul, but also the whole creation. When Adam sinned, the whole creation was cursed .. And God promised deliverance. What God promises, God does. So – one day the whole creation will be delivered from the bondage of corruption that came with the curse six thousand years ago. . . . The four living creatures .. know that this redemption is about to occur. Therefore, they are exceedingly glad....

The six-winged seraphim, which stand above the Lord God, appear to be different beings, with different functions. [Isa. 6] Yet these living beings also proclaim: "Let everything that has breath praise the Lord!" [Ps. 150:6.] That's all creation, including you and me and our animals.

REAL OR MYTHICAL?
Some will say these cherubim (and seraphim) are mythical beings. No one in the Bible who saw them described them as such. Men may use metaphors to try to describe unearthly beings, but that does not mean they are not real. The Bible treats cherubim as real.

As I meditated on these cherubim, several things struck me. First, the images of human-animal combinations are found in other religions and cultures, like the Greek Pan and centaurs. Secondly, although cherubim appear similar to some mythical beings,, they differ greatly in character and purpose. There is nothing of the fickleness and cruelty of other gods, who care little for man. Cherubim are holy and loving servants of the living God.

ANIMALS, GOD'S COMPANIONS
What is relevant to our study is that the Lord of heaven is intimate with and enjoys other living beings, not just humans. Cherubim, as

"ideal representatives ... of redeemed animate creation," combine human and well-known animal attributes. The ox is strong, useful in work, and is domesticated. The lion is intelligent, regal, powerful, and beautiful. The eagle is smart, farsighted, and a magnificent master of the winds. God clearly likes to have more than just human types near Him. (You, too?) Amen!

To approach God is to approach cherubim. These servants of God are constantly in His presence. When I think of the Lord surrounded by cherubim, it reminds me of how my animals love to stay close to me. To visit my home is to visit my animals. They greet you, check you out, and stay with me, if permitted, while you visit. I've never had a loved animal which didn't follow me around. My cats have supervised the writing of this book. My stallion, Rebel, turned loose when we picked blackberries, would follow us and eat handfuls of berries! Pete, our parakeet, flew around the house following us. Of course, the dogs and cats follow, too.

If cherubim are heaven's animals, then they seem just like our earthly animal friends. Cherubim stay as close to the Lord God as possible, serving Him and loving Him. Sounds like heaven to me.

PETER'S VISION OF HEAVEN

Are you good at taking a hint? The apostle Peter had an interesting vision of animals which may hint at the answer to Mom's question.

> *Then he became very hungry and wanted to eat; but while they made ready, he fell into a trance and saw **heaven opened** and an object like a great sheet bound at the four corners, descending to him and **let down to the earth**. In it were **all kinds of four-footed animals of the earth, wild beasts, creeping things, and birds of the air**. And a voice came to him, "Rise, Peter; kill and eat." But Peter said, "Not so, Lord! For I have never eaten anything common or unclean." And a voice spoke to him again the second time, "What God has cleansed you must not call*

*common." This was done three times. **And the object
was taken up into heaven again.***

Acts 10:10-16 (NKJ) (Emphasis supplied)

The main purpose of Peter's vision was to prepare him to accept non-Jews as disciples of Jesus the Messiah. But is there more to learn here? Why did the Lord show Peter "animals of the earth" brought from and taken back up into heaven? Why didn't the Lord simply show Peter various animals on earth in the vision?

Is it possible these animals had once known life on earth and were now residents of heaven? That is implied by the vision. Was Peter's vision metaphor or reality? If real, then heaven already has earthly animals of all kinds.

THE EVIDENCE BUILDS

Now we have Biblical evidence that animals are already in heaven — horses, cherubim, beings like oxen, lions, and eagles. Also, there are Peter's animals: *"all kinds of four-footed **animals of the earth,** wild beasts, creeping things, and birds of the air"* which came down from heaven and were taken up there again.

In the preceding chapters, we have examined 1) creation 2) naming of the animals, 3) the Fall and its implications, 4) the covenant God made with Noah and all land animals of every species; (5) Job and other passages; and (6) Jesus relationship with animals. The Scriptures in these chapters more than hint at a hereafter for animals. What else is there? Lots more!

ISAIAH'S VISIONS OF NEW HEAVENS AND EARTH

The prophet Isaiah, who lived some 27 centuries ago, had several relevant visions. Isaiah's visions are Messianic prophesies which Christians believe refer to the Lord's Second Coming, the end of this age. Consider this passage:

*For behold, I create **new heavens and a new earth**;*
And the former things shall not be remembered or come to
mind. ... The wolf and the lamb shall graze together, and
the lion shall eat straw like the ox; and dust shall be the
*serpent's food. They shall do no evil or harm **in all My***
***holy mountain,** says the Lord.* Isa. 65:17 & 25

Note that there are **new** heavens and **new** earth, but not new
animals. Isaiah saw familiar animals – wolf, lion, serpent – with
changed natures and metabolisms. In a later passage, Isaiah repeats
almost the same thing:

And the wolf will live with the lamb, the leopard will lie
down with the goat, the calf and the lion and the yearling
together; and a little child will lead them. The cow will feed
with the bear, their young will lie down together, and the
lion will eat straw like the ox. The infant will play near the
hole of the cobra, and the young child will put his hand into
the viper's nest. They will neither harm nor destroy on all
my holy mountain, for the earth will be full of the knowl-
edge of the Lord as the waters cover the sea.
Isa. 11:6-9 [NIV]

Eternity contains earth's animals. This is confirmed by several
modern Christian leaders. Billy Graham quotes Rebecca Springer's
book [20] where she told of a kitten which predeceased a child,. The
kitten greeted the child when the little girl died just weeks later.
Rev. Jesse Duplantis reports seeing horses, dogs and large cats in
heaven.[21]   Roberts Liardon, taken to heaven by Jesus as an eight-
year-old, wrote: [22]

Jesus and I continued walking. As we went over a few hills,
I noticed more things. I saw all kinds of animals, every
kind you could think of, from A to Z. Sometimes people
have questioned this, but if you think about it, why should
there not be animals in heaven? The Bible talks about
horses in heaven, so why would God only have one kind of
animal?

How can one argue with that logic?

A dear friend of mine told me of a similar vision of heaven. Some years ago Mozelle saw a vision of Jesus beside a stream of bubbling water. There were trees and a grassy bank. Around Jesus were animals of various sorts. The animals were on Jesus' right, a place of honor. Included was a snake! The snake surprised Mozelle, since she didn't like snakes. Soon after receiving the vision, she shared it with someone. It turned out that person had a deep need to know that there are animals in heaven. Mozelle felt she was given that vision for that person. Perhaps it was for readers of this book as well.

Since the Fall of Adam, the earth has known nothing like Isaiah's harmony. Few have tasted such harmony since, although remnants of it are all around us. Areas of untouched wilderness seem to reflect great harmony at times. Yet there are death and disease. Many species feed off of other life forms. Some even will kill and eat their own species. Cats and bears have sharp claws and teeth designed to tear flesh. Vipers are dangerous to children. Isaiah's prophesy is yet to be fulfilled.

Some may be bothered by the thought of wild animals going to heaven. Wolves, snakes, lions and tigers injure or kill people and domestic animals. Others don't like dogs, because they or someone they love was badly hurt by a dog. Bulls, pigs and horses have injured and killed also. Chimpanzees have cannibalistically attacked their own.[23] I don't care to see centipedes in heaven – at Jesus' feet or anywhere else. However, dogs, wild animals, snakes and centipedes will be in the new earth. It will be good, because the Lord will change all of us — animals and people — so we will get along. God will remove our fear of such animals, and theirs of us. Heaven is harmony and love. However difficult that is to imagine, it's true.

It should not surprise us that there is redemption for snakes and other "dangerous" animals. The loving Lord is able to redeem anything He created (if they'll let Him). The choice lies with each creature, both human and animal. That should give us hope! We will all be changed. It is not clear what we'll be like in heaven – only that we will recognize one another. Since God can change human natures, reforming snakes should be easy.

Some theologians call Isaiah's vision "millennium" passages – referring to a thousand-year period described in Revelation 20. This isn't supported by Scripture. The passage in Isaiah 11 follows a description of the Messiah – full of the Spirit, judging the earth in righteousness and faithfulness. Isaiah's prophesies track Revelation 21, covering the advent of a new heaven and earth. Logically, the description of the animals returning to the pre-Fall vegetarianism and harmony would follow that last judgment.

Isaiah foresaw a "new heaven and earth" – God's promise that animals will be restored to an Eden-like state. I'll bet heaven is better than the original Garden. God's always doing new good things. [See Isa. 42:9; 43:19; Jer. 31:22 & 31; & Ezek. 36:26]

CREATION'S EAGER EXPECTATION

Next to the Isaiah passages, Romans 8 is the best known "proof text" that animals go to heaven. Let's take a look:

> **The creation waits in eager expectation** *for the sons of God to be revealed. For the **creation was subjected to frustration**, not by its own choice, but by the will of the one who subjected it, in hope that the **creation itself will be liberated from its bondage to decay** and brought into the **glorious freedom** of the children of God. We know that the **whole creation has been groaning** as in the pains of childbirth right up to the present time. Not only so, but we ourselves, who have the firstfruits of the Spirit, groan inwardly as we wait eagerly for our adoption as sons, the redemption of our bodies. For in this hope we were saved.*
>
> Rom. 8:18-24a [NIV] (Emphasis supplied)

What does this passage mean? It is clear that the sons of God must be revealed for all creation to be free, gloriously free. In Adam's fall, death, disease and everything bad affected all this earth. Why would we omit all creatures affected by death from Christ's redemption and restoration?

> *This earth's poets, philosophers, scientists, face to face*
> *with death with a capital D, – in every crushed ocean shell,*
> *in every rotten log, in the very minor keys in which the*
> *voices of beasts and birds are pitched, seem never to get a*
> *glimpse of the bondage of corruption in which all creation*
> *is groaning; but talk in sprightly ways of "progress," of*
> *"evolution"! How far from understanding the creation*
> *around them are human beings all, – except Spirit-taught*
> *Christians!* [24]

The groaning of creation started with human sin. The war between good and evil continues as long as men sin. Technology and the increase in knowledge (predicted by Daniel 12) has served two extremes: one enables us to better care for humans and animals, while the other give us greater abilities to destroy each other and creation.

It takes righteousness to heal and bless a land and its life forms.[25] [Deut. 28; Prov. 14:34; 2 Chron. 7:14]. Francis and Edith Schaeffer believed Christian stewardship over this earth means our gardens and lands should be the most artistic, beautiful and fruitful.[26] Agnes Sanford taught that our daily prayers should include the earth and all life around us.[27] Righteousness treats all life as a sacred trust, deserving of care and prayer. This has been the practice of many great Christians.

DO ANIMALS CEASE TO BE?

If animals cease to be after they die, then what does the passage from Romans 8 mean? Where is their freedom? Their restoration? What logic or reason could separate man from animals after death? How can it be that our animals might never know liberation from frustration and decay? Is that God's Truth or man's lie? If animals cease to be after death why would all creation be "groaning for the revelation of the Sons of God"?

> *Now although we who are in Christ are new creatures, yet God has left our bodies as the link with the present "groaning" creation. Meanwhile, how "the bondage of corruption" appears on every side! ... Every decaying carcass of poor earth-creatures speaks of the "bondage of corruption." What ruin man's sin has effected throughout the creation, as well as upon himself! It was God's good pleasure that, when man sinned and became estranged from his God, all creation, which was under him, should be subjected to the "bondage of corruption" along with him, in decay and disease, suffering, death, and destruction, everywhere, – of bondage, with no deliverer.[28]*

KING SOLOMON'S WISDOM

King Solomon was both the enormously wealthy "playboy" of ancient Israel, and a wise man. Solomon contemplated what the difference was between humans and animals.

> *I said in my heart with regard to human beings that God is testing them to show that they are but animals. For the fate of humans and the fate of animals is the same; as one dies, so dies the other. They all have the same breath, and humans have no advantage over the animals; for all is vanity. All go to one place; all were from the dust, and all turn to dust again.* **Who knows whether the human spirit goes upward and a spirit of animals goes downward to the earth?**   Eccles. 3:18-21 (NRSV)

God does test us to see what is in our hearts. [Deut. 8]. Will we treat all God's creation as our disposable toys? Or respect other living things as equal to us? It is a test, which each human faces. What is the answer to Solomon's last question? Is it rhetorical? The Spirit of the Lord inspired Solomon's question for a reason. I think the answer is implied.

Paul's words in Romans 8 answers Solomon's question, don't they? All creation was "subjected to futility" or "frailty" (Amplified), and "bondage to decay" or "corruption." John Wesley, founder of the Methodism, said:

> *But will the creature, will even the brute creation, always remain in this deplorable condition? God forbid that we should affirm this; yea, or even entertain such a thought! While "the whole creation groaneth together" (whether men attend or not) their groans...enter into the ears of him that made them.... [H]e knoweth their pain, and is bringing them nearer and nearer to the birth which shall be accomplished in its season. ...* **the whole animated creation ...'shall be delivered'** *(not by annihilation; annihilation is not deliverance) 'from the' present 'bondage of corruption, into' a measure of 'the glorious liberty of the children of God.'* [29]

Wesley and Newell's beliefs are further substantiated by the Apocryphal Book[30] of Wisdom: *"... because God did not make death, and he does not delight in the death of the living."* [1:13] "Living" is a term not limited to humans, as the next verse proves: *"For He created all things that they might exist."* [Wis. 1:14]

Modern writers agree that each animal is "a masterpiece" and "too valuable to be carelessly discarded." God's sentiments entirely.

> *Each species, to put the matter succinctly, is a masterpiece. It deserves that rank in the fullest sense: a creation assembled with extreme care and genius. ... If DNA helices in one cell of a mouse ... were placed end on end and magically enlarged to the same width as a piece of wrapping string, they would extend for about 600 miles... How all that genetic information translates into a fully functioning*

*organism is still partly a mystery. The lesson to be drawn
is that the life-forms around us are too old, too complex,
and too valuable to be carelessly discarded.*[31]

What the Lord created in delight has not ceased to be His. *The
earth is the Lord's, and everything in it.* Ps. 24:1a. Why would it be
surprising for our Great God to restore creation, with all the animals,
than to extinguish their existence? Why would anyone think that
loving God would not want all His masterpieces to be returned to
their former glory throughout eternity? What foolishness! I begin to
understand why Paul said that the wisdom of men is foolishness to
God! [1 Cor. 1:18-30]

*Every creature in the forest is mine, the wild animals on all
the mountains. I know every mountain bird by name; the
scampering field mice are my friends. ... All creation and
its bounty are mine. Do you think I feast on venison? Or
drink draughts of goats' blood? Spread for me a banquet of
praise, serve High God a feast of kept promises.*

Ps. 50:10-14 [TMB].

REDEMPTION AND RESTORATION

The good news is that God plans to redeem and to heal all His
creation — not just mankind. While man bears the responsibility for
this earth, we are powerless to cleanse our own sin, let alone sin's
effects – which have contaminated the earth like a massive plague.
Our need for a savior, a redeemer, extends beyond human need and
out to the whole earth. Only our Creator has the ability and will to
redeem, restore, and recreate all man has messed up.

Luke's record of the Apostle Peter's sermon given soon after
Jesus' ascension back to heaven puts "the cure" in simple terms:

*Repent, then, and turn to God, so that your sins may be
wiped out, that times of refreshing may come from the
Lord, and that he may send the Christ, who has been appointed for you – even Jesus. He must remain in heaven*

until the time comes for God to restore everything, as he
promised long ago through his holy prophets.
[Acts 3:20-21 [NIV]] (Emphasis supplied)

Peter's sermon is a wonderful promise, isn't it? We can do something! Repentance and turning to God will bring the Messiah, the Christ, who will *"restore everything."* The Greek word for "restore" is *"apokatastasis."* It means "reconstitution" or "restoration" in health, home or organization. Thayer's Greek-English Lexicon of the New Testament says it is *"the restoration of not only the true theocracy but also of that more perfect state of (physical) things which existed before the fall, Acts iii.21."* The New Revised Standard Version calls it *"the universal restoration that God announced"* and Weymouth says it will be *"the reconstitution of all things."* The term means restoring of a thing to its former state or place.[32] I like that. Don't you?

Jesus said that the prophet Elijah will return (as Malachi 4 says), and God *"will **restore all things**."* [Matt.17:11; Mark 9:12] This is from the same root word for "restoration" used in Acts 3:21. What does "all things" mean? Just mankind? That's not logical. "All" is everything? It is reasonable to believe all animals will be restored or "reconstituted" in the new earth. "Restored" does not mean "replaced." I've restored furniture, not replaced it. It's different. So "restoration" must mean God will take the scattered DNA of each life form, and remake each being anew. Hallelujah! There is hope for creation in its futile fragility. It will be set free in new life.

Regardless of how both the Church and her enemies have
ill-treated or been ignorant of the message of the Bible, one
*thing is certain. **The whole tenor and thrust of the***
***Bible is toward salvation and healing**, not only of in-*
dividuals, but of families, nations, and countries – indeed,
***of the very land itself.** The Bible demands personal*
responsibility on all levels of life and calls for a level of
commitment to care for life unmatched by any other major

religious writing in history.

* * *

*As a matter of fact, the sixth Commandment says, "You
shall not murder" (Exodus 20:13, NIV). It does not say,
"Do not murder people," but, "Do not murder," which
includes any selfish taking of life. .... including an animal,
flower or tree.... Every act of cruelty to animals, as well
as to other human beings, is offensive to the Creator of all
beings.[33]*

Wow, what a concept! Why is cruelty to animals wrong? God
loves them. That should be enough to correct one's thinking. Even
so, look at the phrase in Roman 8:21:

*"because creation itself also shall be delivered from the
bondage of corruption, into the liberty of the glory of the
children of God."*

*The "liberty of the glory of the children of God" awaits
Christ's second coming. How blessed it is to know that
into that glorious liberty, creation, which has shared "the
bondage of corruption," will be brought along with us! . . .
Contrast the state of creation now with the Millennial order described in Isaiah 11.6-9: The wolf dwelling with the
lamb, the leopard with the kid; the calf, the young lion, and
the fattling together, and the little child leading them.[34]*

Isn't strange that many Christian theologians believe that
redemption extends to all creation, but still aren't sure if the animals
we know and love have an afterlife. Consider these statements about
creation:

*Redemption extends to the furtherest corner of the physical
realm. ... this earthly kingdom is the same as the kingdom
of heaven, the world of the coming age, the coming redeemed creation[35]*   (Rom. 8:21).

This is echoed in Eastern Orthodox circles. Consider the words
of Vladimir Lossky:

Man is not a being isolated from the rest of creation; by his
very nature he is bound up with the whole of the universe
... In his way to union with God, man in no way leaves
creatures aside, but gathers together in his love the whole
cosmos disordered by sin, that it may at last be transfig-
ured by grace.[36]

It is difficult to reconcile these two positions, isn't it?

GROANING IN TRAVAIL

Paul's statement in Romans 8:22, that all creation "groans in travail" is not new. The prophet Jeremiah spoke of the earth and of a land mourning, and as a result, humans, animals and everything living in them suffering and disappearing.[37] [Jer. 4:27-28; 12:4 & 11; Hosea 4:3] God gave creation, i.e., all the animals, creeping things, birds, fish and flowers, the task of groaning in "travail." So all living things join with human believers to groan "and travail" together. Travail speaks of pregnancy, of childbirth. Those in natural childbirth do groan! Such travail is to produce LIFE, ETERNAL LIFE! Paul travailed until Christ was formed within the disciples. [Galatians 4:19] We need to join Paul and creation, don't you think! God's servants have this privilege. [Ps. 48:6; Isa. 53:11; 66:7-8; Micah 5:2-5; John 16:21-22]

> *... the Spirit does not take us out of sympathy with groan-*
> *ing creation, but rather supports us in such sympathy!*
> *.... No one should feel as tender as should the child of God*
> *toward suffering creation. No one should be as gentle.*
> *Not only should this be true about us as concerns unsaved*
> *people: as Paul says, "Be gentle, showing all meekness to-*
> *ward all men," but, I say, we should be tender and patient*
> *toward all animals, for they are in a dying state – until our*
> *bodies are redeemed.*
>
> * * *
>
> *Thus, then, does the Christian become the true connection*
> *of groaning creation with God! He is redeemed, heavenly;*

*but his body is unredeemed, earthly. ... Thus the believer
and the whole creation look toward one goal – the liberty
of the coming glory of the sons of God!³⁸*

"Groaning in travail" is unfamiliar to many Christians as a spiritual exercise. I dare say it is incomprehensible to a nonbeliever. Yet, it is a part of true intercessory prayer. Jesus groaned in the spirit before He raised Lazarus from the dead. [John 11:33] Saints through the ages wrote of groaning in prayer. I believe Mother Theresa of Calcutta understood such groaning.

I am willing to groan with creation until Christ is formed in myself and others. Until we bring down God's glory. Until my Lord Jesus returns in the flesh bringing in the new heaven and earth. Until all are free from the death and decay of this world! How about you? Are you willing to travail with creation? If so, tell the Lord about it. He'll teach and empower you to do His will. Together we can bring down heaven on earth!

THAT PLAN AND ORDER OF REDEMPTION

Is it not logical and reasonable that the Creator would include in His plan of redemption all that was subject to death at human hands?

*For since by a man came death, by a man also came the
resurrection of the dead. For as in Adam all die, so also in
Christ all shall be made alive.*   1 Cor. 15:21-22

God's plan of redemption is for the restoration of all creation: *"For as in Adam all die"* included, not just man, but all living creatures. *"In Christ all shall be made alive"* is inclusive. Jesus Christ is the resurrection and life! [John 11:25] Jesus alone has the power of indestructible life! [Heb. 7:16 NASV & Weymouth] Think about that! Glory!

In Romans 8, Paul made three points about creation. First, God Himself subjected all creation to the effects of Adam's sin. Second, God will liberate creation from decay when His purpose is fulfilled.

Third is that this is a "saving hope." A hope which is not given for us alone, but given to all creation. In the "revelation" of us as "sons of God," we get to go with creation into glory. It pays to be a child of God.

Restoring something well takes careful planning, skill, and time. God's plan and order of redemption are found in the Bible. It is most fully detailed in the New Testament letters to the early church. (Remember to ask the right questions or it won't be easy to see the plan.)

In I Corinthians, Paul addressed the issues of resurrection. Apparently, some in Paul's time challenged whether there is a resurrection of the dead — including Jesus' resurrection. (Things haven't changed.) What Paul wrote is relevant to Mom's question:

> *But each in his own order: Christ the first fruits, after that*
> *those who are Christ's at His coming, Then comes the end,*
> *when He delivers up the kingdom to the God and Father,*
> *when He has abolished all rule and all authority and*
> *power. For He must reign until He has put all His enemies*
> *under His feet. The last enemy is death.*   1 Cor. 15:23-26

Paul left us great insights into God's plans for His creation. I always read 1 Cor. 15 as referring exclusively to humans. Is that what 1 Cor. 15 really means? Paul's own words belie the assumption it's meant only for humans. Paul was instructed by Jesus Himself. [See Acts & Paul's Epistles.] Paul was "caught up" into heaven and heard unspeakable things. [II Cor. 12:2] Compare these two translations of Ephesians 1:7-10:

> *It is in Him, and through the shedding of His blood, that*
> *we have our deliverance – the forgiveness of our offenses*
> *– so abundant was God's grace, the grace which He, the*
> *possessor of all wisdom and understanding, lavished upon*
> *us, when He made known to us the secret of His will. And*
> *this is in harmony with God's merciful purpose for the*

government of the world when the times are ripe for it –
the purpose which He has cherished in His own mind of
restoring the whole creation to find its one head in
Christ; *yes, things in heaven and things on earth, to find*
their one Head in Him.
[Weymouth] (Emphasis supplied)

For by the blood of Christ we are set free, that is, our sins
are forgiven. How great is the grace of God, which he gave
to us in such large measure! In all his wisdom and insight
God did what he had purposed, and made known to us the
secret plan he had already decided to complete by means of
Christ. This plan, which God will complete when the time
is right, is **to bring all creation together, everything**
in heaven and on earth, with Christ as head.
[Good News Translation] [Emphasis supplied)

God's awesome plan is to restore everything in and through
Christ Jesus. We are destined for a huge celebration. The universe
will explode with restoration. There will be no death, corruption or
decay. Life will fill everything with pure glory. The beauty of restored
creation will dazzle us. God's great plan will be revealed. God will be
most happy when His precious creation is restored in full!

We belong to the natural world; it does not belong to
us. The interconnectedness of life, in the present instant
as well as through time, illuminates our place and our
rightful relationship with other species here are on earth.
Can we find our place in the world as human beings if we
devalue the rest of life? It is part of who we are.[39]

Can we find our place in heaven if we "devalue the rest of life"?
If we do not become fully "Sons of God," doing our part in the
restoration of all creation, don't we lose "part of who we are"? Being

part of the Body of Christ means doing our part to carry out God's plan in restoring creation, doesn't it?

OUR PETS

Does the Scripture say anything about the resurrection of animals we've known? Yes, I believe it does.

> And He is the image of the invisible God, the first-born of **all creation.** For by Him **all things were created,** both in the heavens and on earth, visible and invisible, whether thrones or dominions or rulers or authorities — **all things have been created by Him and for Him.** And He is before/existed prior to **all things,** and in Him **all things** hold together. He is also the head of the body, the church; and He is the beginning, **the first-born of the dead;** so that He Himself might come to have first place **in everything.** For it was the Father's good pleasure for all the fulness to dwell in Him and through Him to reconcile **all things to Himself,** having made peace through the blood of His cross; through Him, I say, **whether things on earth or things in heaven.**
>
> [Col. 1:15-20] (Emphasis supplied)

I have read Colossians hundreds of times, yet never before considered its application to animals going to heaven. I did the same with other Scriptures. I know I am not alone. All the ministers I've heard preach appear to do the same. Yet, "all creation" and "all things" cover more than the human race. The entire animal kingdom (and possibly more) is covered by this phrase.

Considering the marvelous complexity of life, the variety and inner-connectedness of it all, it makes more sense that God would restore, rather than wipe out creation. To make an analogy, an art or antique collector would never think of discarding any damaged piece that could be restored. Why would God discard precious living animals when He is well able to restore?

The plain words of Colossians include "all creation" and "all things." Just as Noah took every kind of animal into the Ark, so Jesus will restore, reconcile, and raise from death "all things." All were made in, by, for and through Him. Nothing is impossible for our God. "All" covers humans and animals, from insects to elephants, trees to flowers, springs and oceans, mountains and meadows, amoebae and atoms, sun, moon and stars. The Living Lord will restore the damaged DNA of each thing in His marvelous universe in a glorious new creation. The blood that Jesus shed on the cross is for all created things. Things both on earth and in heaven. Wow! That's enough to shout about. I have a Bible-based hope that my horses, dogs, cats and birds will be there, along with new friends of the animal sort. What an awesome God!

ENDNOTES:

1.   Luarentius Abstemius, Italy 16th century, *The Great Fables of All Nations* (Tudor Publ. Co. 1928), p. 205

2.   See Jeffrey Moussaieff Masson, *Dogs Never Lie About Love,* [Crown Publ. 1997], especially the chapter "Being Alone: the Sadness of Dogs"; Stephanie Laland, *Animal Angels; Amazing Acts of Love and Compassion,* [Conari Press; 1998], pp.188-189 (about a pet cougar who refused to eat and died after the couple who'd had him his first five years, abandoned him).

3.   Robert Byrne & Teressa Skelton, *Cat Scan; All the Best From the Literature of Cats,* (1983), p. 11.

4.   "The Hippo and the Antelope" is from Jeffery Moussaieff Masson, *Dogs Never Lie About Love,* [Crown Publ. 1997], quoted in *Listening to the Animals; Best Friends,* [Guideposts, 1999], p. 38. Also, see film at http://www.youtube.com/watch?v=ENWpoQ2RkTA

5.   Bert Clompus, "Cat with No Name," *Listening to the Animals; Best Friends,* [Guideposts, 1999], p. 195.

6.   *Dogs Never Lie About Love,* p. 177

7.   "Dr. Karen on behavior & beyond" *Pets,* Sept/Oct 1999, p. 10.

8.   Begun in 1233 A.D., the Inquisition continued until the 19th century. Originally the Roman Catholic pope commissioned a group of priests to investigate a heretical sect in France. Through the years, Inquisition became an instrument of corruption, and torture - even though such was frowned upon by the pope. The Spanish Inquisition, was begun by Ferdinand and Isabella of Spain, to spy out insincere Moorish and Jewish converts. Soon all feared the Inquisitors. Imprisonment was common. Burning at the stake made martyrs of many. Remember for centuries there were basically two Christian churches, Roman and Eastern Orthodox. Both have good and bad things, just as churches do today.

9.   Colleen McDannell & Bernhard Land, *Heaven, a History,* [Yale U Press 1988], p. 72

10.   *Heaven, a History,* pp. 84 & 118

11.   *Heaven, a History,* pp. 84-85

12.   *Heaven, a History,* pp. 154-155

13.   *Heaven, a History,* pp. 172-180

14.   *Sermons of John Wesley, Sermon 60 The General Deliverance and Sermon 64 New Creation*

15.   "Temple" *Pictorial Bible Dictionary,* supra, p. 831.

16.   #3742, "Cherub" Gesenius, supra, p. 413

17.   Icarus, in Greek mythology, escaped from the isle of Crete on wings fashioned from feathers. Exuberant with flight, he flew too close to the sun, which melted the wax which held the wings together. Icarus plunged into the sea and died.

18.   [Thomas Nelson, 1984, 1996], p. 98

19.   *Revelation, Verse by Verse,* (The Gospel Hour, Inc., 1963), pp. 163-165

20.   Rebecca Springer, *Within Heaven's Gates,* [Whitaker House, 1984]

21.   Heaven; *Close Encounters of the God Kind,* [Harrison House, 1996], p. 71

22.   *I Saw Heaven,* [Albury Publishing, 1983, 1991], p. 31

23.   Jane Goodall with Phillip Berman, *Reason for Hope,* [Warner, 1999], from review in Publishers Weekly, 8/2/99, p. 61.

24. William R. Newell, *Romans Verse By Verse*, [1938], p. 322

25. I recommend Winkie Pratney's *Healing the Land; a supernatural view of ecology*, [Chosen Book, 1993], especially chapter 11, for a short, thoughtful lesson in ecology from a Christian viewpoint. It's an eye-opener!

26. See Edith Schaeffer, *Hidden Art*, [London: Norfolk Press, 1971] & Francis A. Schaeffer, *Pollution and the Death of Man* [London: Hodder & Stoughton, 1970].

27. Agnes Sanford, *Creation Waits*, [N.J.:Logos International/Bridge Publishing, Inc.], p. 288-290

28. William Newell, Romans Verse by Verse, supra, p. 321

29. *Sermons of John Wesley, Sermon 60 The General Deliverance and Sermon 64 New Creation*, pp. 442-445

30. *The Apocrypha*, Revised Standard Version, [Thos. Nelson, 1957]

31. Introduction by E. O. Wilson, Witness; *Endangered Species of North America* by Susan Middleton and David Liitschwager [San Francisco: Chronicle Books, 1994], p. 17.

32. *The Analytical Greek Lexicon*, [Zondervan Publ. 1970, 1973], p. 42

33. Winkie Pratney, *Healing the Land*, supra., pp. 51-52

34. Newell, *Romans Verse by Verse*, supra, p. 321-322

35. *The Dictionary of New Testament Theology*, Vol. A-F, [1975] p. 518

36. *The Mystical Theology of the Eastern Church*, quoted in Andrew Linzey, *Animal Rights; a Christian Assessment of Man's Treatment of Animals*, [London: SCM Press Ltd, 1976] at p. 69

37. I am not alone in wondering if creation groaning for redemption from man's sin isn't part of what causes earthquakes and other natural disasters – just as a boil erupts to free the body from poison.

38. William R. Newell, *Romans Verse By Verse*, supra, pp. 323-324

39. Forward in *Witness; Endangered Species of North America* by Susan Middleton and David Liitschwager [San Francisco: Chronicle Books, 1994], p. 13.

CHAPTER 15

HOPE OF RESURRECTION

Her imagination made her wonder if in fact there were any animals to be found in Hades. . . .No, Heaven would be filled with animals, for it would not be Heaven without them, while in Hell it would be one of the things one longed for and could not have.[1]

Does the Bible say how the Lord will populate His new heaven and earth? Will He create new animals or resurrect some of the ones who have already lived? We have been seeing the pieces come together. For animal lovers, heaven just wouldn't be heaven without their animal friends. We have hope. *"Because of the hope laid up for you in heaven of which you previously heard in the word of truth, the gospel/good-news,"* were Paul's opening words in Colossians 1:5. The Scriptures we have examined already give us good news! These are pieces of the puzzle — pieces that give hope of a positive answer to Mom's question.

HEAVEN WILL MAKE US HAPPY

Mom's wisdom that "God is love, and if it isn't love, it isn't God" (in my experience) is a fair test of theological doctrines. An anecdote which the late William F. Buckley, Jr. (a giant of brilliant intellect), wrote about his faith as a Catholic, illustrates this test:

> *I would most like to visit Heaven because it was there I would be made most happy. I gave Fr. Sharkey's exegesis: He had been approached some weeks earlier, he told us, by a devout elderly woman who asked him whether dogs would be admitted into Heaven. No, he had replied, as there was no scriptural authority for animals getting Heaven. "In that case," the lady had said to him, "I can never be happy in Heaven. I can only be happy if Brownie is also there." I told her" – Fr. Sharkey spoke with mesmerizing authority – "that if that were the case – that she could not be happy without Brownie – why then Brownie would in fact go to Heaven. Because what is absolutely certain is that, in Heaven, you will be happy." That answer, I am sure, sophisticated readers of the Esquire dismissed, however intelligently, as Jesuitical. Yes. But I have never found the fault in that syllogism.[2]*

Neither have I, friend. Besides, there is far more scriptural authority for animals going to heaven than the good Fr. Sharkey realized. We could stop right now, I believe, and have proved our case. But there is yet more.

GLORIFIED BODIES

Bible teaches that believers (those in covenant relationship with God through their Messiah, Jesus) shall receive new "glorified" bodies and live with the Lord eternally "in glory." [Rom. 8:23; 2 Cor. 5:1-10; Col. 3:4]. Jesus described Himself as "the Resurrection and the Life," to Martha before raising her brother Lazarus from his grave. [John 11:25]. Consider this promise of heaven:

> *But there's far more to life for us. We're citizens of high heaven! We're waiting the arrival of the Savior, the Master, Jesus Christ, will transform our earthly bodies into*

glorious bodies like his own. He'll make us beautiful and whole with the same powerful skill by which he is putting **everything** *as it should be, under and around him.*

Phil. 3:20-21 (TMB)

FROM DEATH TO RESURRECTED LIFE

If human believers will be glorified, and get new immortal bodies, through Jesus Christ, what about animals? Will they get new bodies, too? Consider this statement from Psalms:

> *O Lord, how many and varied are Your works! In wisdom You have made them all; The earth is full of Your riches and Your creatures . . . When You take away their breath [ruwach], they die and return to their dust. When you send forth Your Spirit and give them breath [ruwach], they are created; and You replenish the face of the ground. May the glory of the Lord endure for ever; may the Lord rejoice in His works....* Psalm 104:24, 29b-31 [Amplified]

These verses (previously discussed in Chapter 4) concern animal life, not human.

Did you notice the order in which these statements are made: First, the death of animals; Second, "They are created;" and then "You replenish the face of the ground." I used to wonder if the Psalmist had things a little backward. Doesn't "die" come before "give them breath and they are created"? Why would the Lord inspire the psalmist to write in this order? The key must be in "replenish" "the earth." If this is a repeat of creation described in Genesis 1 & 2, it is not in the right order. But what if it is looking forward to the new heavens and earth? If Psalm 104 describes the restoration of all things in Christ Jesus in the next life, then it is written correctly! First death, then a new creation! First is the "taking away" and afterward comes the "restoration" or "resurrection" or "replenishing." This Psalm logically describes a progression from death to resurrection.

This interpretation fits with other verses. Consider Psalm 102:25-26, quoted in Hebrews 1:10-12:

> And, "Thou, Lord in the beginning didst lay the foundation of the earth, And the heavens are the works of Thy hands; They will perish, But Thou remainest; And they all will become old as a garment, And as a mantle Thou wilt roll them up; **As a garment they will also be changed [allasso]**. But Thou art the same, and Thy years will not come to an end.   (Emphasis added)

What will be changed? Who are "they?" What do the "foundation of the earth" and "the heavens" refer to? The earth and the heavens will perish. But that is not the end. They will be changed. Why would the Lord change the "foundation of the earth" and "the heavens" like an old garment? The only thing that makes sense is that God needs a new habitat for His creation – one that can bear His own Presence – those Psalm 104 recreated animal lives.

Is that what Ps. 102 is really saying? Read in conjunction with Psalm 104, Romans 8, Colossians 1 and other passages, it is a reasonable interpretation. The breath (or spirits) taken when animals die, are with God. [Eccl. 3] In the fullness of time, God will destroy this earth and its heavens with fire and create new ones. [2 Pet. 3; Isa. 66:15; 2 Thess. 1:7] Then, the Spirit of the Lord, which worked with God in the original creation, will breathe life into these dead animals and replenish the new earth and heavens. All animals, including extinct species, have hope. We have a glorious hope of our animals being included!

EVERY EYE SHALL SEE JESUS!

In the book of Revelation, John gives an interesting salutation to the churches which adds support to this thesis:

> John to the seven churches which are in Asia: Grace to you and peace, from Him who is, and who was and who is to come;... And from Jesus Christ, the faithful witness, **the**

first born from the dead, and the ruler of the kings of the earth. To Him who loves us and released us from our sins by His Blood,....to Him be glory and dominion forever and ever. Amen. Behold, He is coming with the clouds and every eye will see Him, even those who pierced Him... [Rev. 1:4-7 [NASV]] (Emphasis added)

Rev. Jack Van Impe discussed this Scripture on his television show.[3] The subject of discussion was whether or not animals go to heaven. Arguing that animals do go to heaven, Rev. Van Impe cited Rev. 1:7, stating the phrase "every eye" includes animals, because animals have eyes.

DEATH, WHERE IS YOUR VICTORY?

To me, the most powerful Scriptures to support our premise of animals being resurrected, are in Paul's writings. The Apostle Paul wrote his letters to the Corinthian church to address wrong teaching about the resurrection. Some leaders were stating there was no resurrection. If so Jesus Christ never rose from the dead, and we who believe in Jesus are deceived and without hope. Paul offered several arguments against this teaching in I Cor. 15. Ponder some of Paul's words with Mom's question in mind:

But someone will say, "How are the dead raised? And with what kind of body do they come?" You fool! That which you sow does not come to life unless it dies; and that which you sow, you do not sow the body, which is to be, but a bare grain, perhaps of wheat or of something else. But God gives it a body just as He wished, and to each of the seeds a body of its own.
All flesh is not the same flesh, but there is one flesh of men, and another flesh of beasts, and another flesh of birds, and another of fish. There are also heavenly bodies and earthly bodies, but the glory of the heavenly is one, and the glory of the earthly is another. There is one glory of the sun, and another glory of the

*moon, and another glory of the stars; for star differs from
star in glory. So also is the resurrection of the dead. It
is sown a perishable body/in corruption, it is raised an
imperishable/in incorruption; it is sown in dishonor, it
is raised in glory; it is sown in weakness, it is raised in
power; it is sown a natural body, it is raised a spiritual
body. If there is a natural body, there is also a spiritual.*
***So also it is written, "The first man, Adam, became
a living soul." The last Adam became a life-giving
spirit. However, the spiritual is not first, but the
natural; then the spiritual.*** *The first man is from the
earth, made of dust; the second man is from heaven. As is
the earthly, so also are those who are earthy; and as is the
heavenly, so also are those who are heavenly. And just as
we have borne the image of the earthy, we shall also bear
the image of the heavenly.*

*Now I say this, brethren, that flesh and blood cannot
inherit the kingdom of God; nor does the perishable inherit
the imperishable. Behold, I tell you a mystery: we shall not
all sleep, but **we shall all be changed (allasso)**, in a
moment, in the twinkling of an eye, at the last trumpet; for
the trumpet will sound, and the dead will be raised imperishable, and **we shall be changed (allasso)**. For this
perishable must put on the imperishable, and this mortal
must put on immortality.* ***But when this perishable
will have put on the imperishable and this mortal
will have put on immortality, then will come about
the saying that is written, "Death is swallowed
up in victory. "O Death, where is your victory? O
Death, where is your sting?"*** *The sting of death is
sin, and the power of sin is the law; but thanks be to God,
who gives us the victory through our Lord Jesus Christ.
Therefore, my beloved brethren, be steadfast, immovable,
always abounding in the work of the Lord, knowing that*

your toil is not in vain in the Lord.
[1 Cor. 15:35-58 [NASV -- plus Greek additions]

Why did Paul speak of God giving each living being a body as He chooses "and to each of the seeds a body of its own"? The meaning, taken in context, seems to be that seeds of immortality — of resurrection — are in all living beings. Is there any other rational explanation? This is at least a fair interpretation.

Paul does not limit the "dead" to humankind. Rather Paul describes how each kind of living thing has different "flesh." Both in Greek and Hebrew[4] the words most commonly translated "flesh" mean the "body" or by extension the "self." The Greek word used most in the New Testament, including in 1 Cor. 15, is "*sarx.*" It refers to meat stripped off an animal, as well as the "body" or "soul" or "spirit" of man or beast. In the New Testament, *sarx* is used also "a human being, with all our "frailty" or "human nature." When Paul wrote of "different kinds of flesh" (*sarx)* in I Cor. 15, he specifically mentions animals.

Some commentators say 1 Cor. 15 means that all animals are flesh so they will perish eternally. [Ps. 49:12 & Isa. 40:6]. I believe such commentators misread Paul's message. In truth, all flesh, both animal and human, will perish like dry grass in a prairie fire when the Lord returns. [Isa. 40:6 & 1 Pet. 1:24] Only those with the imperishable seed of regeneration will live again, i.e., be raised from the ashes of destruction to eternal life. [1 Pet. 1:22-25; 2 Pet. 3.] The Bible doesn't limit "flesh" to humankind. Why exclude animals? There is no Biblical basis to exclude animals from having "seeds of resurrection" so animals can receive spiritual, glorified bodies. Isn't it a better interpretation to ascribe to the Creator enough love and power to raise animals along with redeemed humans? God is love. Why would He exclude His living loving creatures?

In the above Scripture, Paul also contrasts the "glory of the heavenly" and the "glory of the earthly" bodies. Why? Does Paul wants us to understand that while the temporary, mortal body is perishable, weak, and dishonored, God's "glory" is heavy with splendor, like that of sun and stars? That the "seeds of glory" lie within every earthly body God created? It makes sense to me. This means each mortal thing — human and animal — can be raised in incorruption, in glory, in power, a spiritual body. This would never make sense if we did not know (as Paul knew) that both animals and humans have *nephesh*, i.e. souls, and *ruwach*, i.e. spirits. The flesh "returns to earth," but the spirit either "ascends" or "descends" — as Ecclesiastes 3:21 says.

PREACH THE GOSPEL TO ALL CREATION

Mark's Gospel ends with Jesus' commission to all His disciples to "*Go into the world and preach the gospel*" or good news to "*all creation.*" [Mark 16:15.] What did Jesus mean? Why was Mark inspired to write "*to all creation*"? Why not just "mankind" or all men? Always be careful in trying to interpret the Holy Bible. All Scripture is inspired by God. [2 Timothy 3:16; 2 Peter 1:20-21]. The Bible commands the readers not to "add to" or "to take away" from the Word of God. [Deut. 4:2; 12:32 and Revelation 22:18-19]. Remember Eve did both in one sentence! [Gen. 3].

By interpreting "all creation" as referring only to humans, are we not taking away from the full meaning of the term "all creation"? Doesn't "creation" include all living beings, from amoeba to zebras? What was God saying in Mark 16? It is reasonable to conclude that just as God ordered Noah to save animals from the Great Flood through the Ark, to include all creation in Jesus' sacrifice to redeem everything under Adam's dominion? St. Francis had something when he preached to the birds and his disciple preached to the fishes in the sea. Aren't we missing something, friends and animal lovers?

LIGHT — THE ENERGY FORCE

What are "spirits"? God is a spirit. [John 4:24] God is light, and He dwells in blazing light. [1 John 1:1; 1 Tim. 6:15-16; Ps. 104:2; Dan. 7:9] Jesus, Word of God, is Life in which is Light. [John 1:3]. People, dead in sin, are in darkness, as is the earth; but after rebirth or salvation, people become children of light. [Isa. 60:1-3; Acts. 26:18; Eph. 5:8; James 1:15] This light-energy has actually been measured in nonbelievers, "born-again" Christians, and Spirit-filled Christians.[5]

Remember the cherubim? Only pure spirits, purified by holy fire, are able to withstand the intense fire and light of God's being. Every living creature has a "glory" in the sense of "splendor" or "light."[6] "Light" is energy. All living creatures have an energy force we call "life." This energy leaves when they/we expire. When death extinguishes the light, where does that energy go? Do you think it goes back to God, its source? At least, such energy belongs to God (Ps. 24:1). If different kinds of natural flesh have their own "glory" then it makes sense that animals also have within them the "seed of glory," "the seed of resurrection."

We can interpret Corinthians 15 as including all creation without straining interpretive rules. 1 Corinthians 15:51 & 52 say "we" shall be "changed." Paul's "we" could include "all flesh" – just as Nivevah's judgment included all humans and animals. "Change" in this verse is the Greek word *"allasso."* It means to "make different, to change," "to exchange one thing for another," "to transform." If all the dead will be "raised imperishable" then animals change as well. It's a rational interpretation – perhaps the only one, in light of the whole Bible.

Paul's argument also addresses the issue of death. If animals are not resurrected, where is the full victory over death which the Bible's God promises? Death would be victor, if we who love them never see our animal friends in the hereafter. The swan's dying song would be for naught. God would violate His covenant with Noah and the animals. It maligns God character to limit Him to resurrection of humans alone. It limits His love, His compassion and His power. I'm sure no one can make a good case from the Holy Bible to so limit our Creator.

I believe these Scriptures fully answer Mom's question. It took me years of work and research to answer it, but it was worth every effort. Her question deserves a proper answer. It has blessed and changed me. I pray it blesses you as well.

TWO POSSIBILITIES; TWO CHOICES

Frankly, I did not start this book with any other design than to answer Mom's question. But the search has raised important issues. One is, how do you and I ensure our animals will get to heaven? Is anything required of us?

Ensuring that our animals get to heaven is something Scripture doesn't spell out clearly. I think that's very smart of God.[7] From what I have learned in this study, I believe there are two possible ways our animals get to heaven. One of them depends solely on you and me. Romans 8 and other Scriptures we have studied, support this theory — Sons of God take creation, those under their stewardship, with them.

One way is illustrated by C. S. Lewis in his novel, *The Great Divorce*, an allegory of heaven and hell.[8] In Chapter 12, Lewis described a lady in heaven, in her eternal body. She has a great entourage of spirits accompanying her and was greatly honored. Accompanying her were dozens of animals. When the visitor asked about the animals, the angel guide replied:

Every beast and bird that came near her had its place
in her love. In her they became themselves. And now the
abundance of life she has in Christ from the Father flows
over into them.[9]

C. S. Lewis further supports this when he wrote that: Because his dog and cat lived together and appeared to enjoy it, one of man's functions may have been to restore peace to the animal world. *The Great Divorce* may be more truth than fiction. Like the lady with her animal entourage, it may be our love, our salvation, our revelation as "Sons of God" (men and women) which determine whether our pets go. We may be their tickets to heaven!

If that is the case, then for our dog (or cat or horse or bird) to make heaven, we must become and behave like "Sons of God." Our rightness with God ensures that our animal goes with us. Our stewardship to our animals is to believe on Jesus, repent, and obey Him. If it depends on you for your pet to live in eternity, will you do it? Will you risk the alternative?

The second possibility is that, like humans, each animal has a choice. Noah's ark is an example. The animals came to Noah to enter the ark. Wild animals and tame, they gathered to God's call. No man captured them or forced them to come. They were chosen and they chose to come. I see this as an archetype of animals coming to Jesus to enter heaven. Because God calls all creation to redemption and to restoration, animals come voluntarily. Those who do not come perish.

I think of homeless strays, cats and dogs, or even wild animals, that have chosen human friends. Some have chosen us as companions and protectors. Some animals have protected and served us freely and willingly. My grandmother's dog chose her and protected her with its life. Others have served and protected their own and other species with apparent compassion and faithfulness. The living God is just and righteous. God must reward such good choices. The choice of heaven or hell is given to all flesh. God's will is that none perish. God, in His great love, leaves the choice to each of us. The call has gone out. We must answer or suffer the consequences. What if your dog (or other pet) is eligible for heaven, but you are not? If that animal loves you, won't it miss you? Will you cause your animal additional grief because you miss heaven? We must choose rightly or hurt those who love us.

FRESH WITNESSES

Now that we have Bible proof your dog (or cat, horse, lizard or bird) has a decent chance to go to heaven, let's look at a few anecdotes and some more questions.

The Tulsa newspaper reported that a three-year-old boy, Ben, had a near fatal accident. Ben's heart stopped on the way to the hospital. Ben was in critical condition with brain swelling, on a ventilator. When the awoke – and lots of folks were praying he would – Ben told his mommy that he saw Jesus, and that there were puppies in heaven. Ben got to play with those puppies. His mother was surprised, for they'd never had a dog, and Ben had always been afraid of dogs.[10] Heaven has puppies to play with — puppies which cure a little boy's fear of dogs. Isn't that like God! Ben's story is also a reminder of how fragile this life is. How quickly we can be gone!

"RAINBOW BRIDGE" ANECDOTES

When a pet dies, many people say they feel peace and a strong feeling the animal is in heaven. A man I knew said he experienced the Lord's comfort after his dog died. Jesus gave him a dream in which his dog was in heaven playing at the Lord's feet. This man was a coal miner, a family man, and a devout disciple of Jesus Christ. I have found his experience was not unique.

A little girl named Jennifer, from Nevada, wrote me about her puppy, Misty. Jennifer hopes her experience will "help those who have lost their beloved pets, to give them faith and hope." Jennifer wrote:

In October of '95, my puppy Misty died. She had drowned. I was so upset, ... I ... thought she would not go to heaven. So I prayed to God for peace. Well, after I cried myself to sleep, I dreamed a wonderful dream. I went up to heaven ... With me was my angel ... When I got up to heaven, I was greeted by God. I ran and gave him a big hug, and when he looked me in the eyes, I felt peace and he told me, "Everything is going to be all right." He then showed me around. It was so beautiful, flowers ... clear lakes... trees with fruit ... God and I passed over a big hill, ... There I saw what I wanted to see more than anything in the world

*— Misty. She ran from a group of other animals, which
all were playing... She ran into my arms, and kissed me
over and over again. I must have spent hours with her in
the flowers playing. While sitting there with her,... I saw
millions of animals. Everyone's dead pet was there. ... I
felt very peaceful and happy . . . So now I know that our
pets go to heaven. ... I said "good bye" to Misty and she just
looked me in the eyes ... like she was telling me, not good
bye but "see you soon." ... Yes, you feel sad for losing a lost
pet, but ... there's nothing to worry about. They're with
God in heaven.*

A few weeks after receiving Jennifer's letter, a client in North
Dakota told me her sister had lost her beloved cat in an accident.
Broken-hearted, this sister prayed for comfort. She too dreamt. Her
dream was remarkably like Jennifer's. She saw her cat in a field of
animals – animals awaiting the arrival in heaven of their human
friends.

Some argue dreams are mere subconscious longings. Ben's
case disproves that argument. The boy was not dreaming. He was
unconscious and afraid of dogs. He was clinically dead or dying.
There is only one logical explanation: it was real. Jesus and those
heavenly puppies actually appeared to Ben. These experiences are
like the popular "Rainbow Bridge" story:

*There is a bridge connecting Heaven and Earth. It is called
the Rainbow Bridge because of its many colors. Just this
side of the Rainbow Bridge, there is a land of meadows,
hills and valleys with lush green grass.*

*When a beloved pet dies, the pet goes to this place. There
are always food and water and warm spring weather.*

*The old and frail animals are young again. Those who are
maimed are made whole again. They play all day with
each other.*

There is only one thing missing. They are not with their special person who loved them on Earth. So each day they run and play until the day comes when one suddenly looks up! The nose twitches. The ears are up. The eyes are staring. And this one suddenly runs from the group.

You have been seen, and when you and your special friend meet, you take him or her in your arms and embrace. Your face is kissed again and again and again, and you look once more into the eyes of your trusting pet.

Then you cross the Rainbow Bridge together, never again to be separated[11]

Heaven is for animals, too. God gave them to us as gifts and teachers — as witnesses to the Lord's grace and glory.

But ask the animals, and they will teach you, or the birds of the air, and they will tell you; Or speak to the earth, and it will teach you, or let the fish of the sea inform you. Which of all these does not know that the hand of the Lord has done this? In his hand is the life of every creature and the breath of all mankind.   Job 12:7-10 [NIV]

SAMSON'S "HOMEGOING"

A few years after Mom passed on, her little poodle Samson started having seizures. Prayer and a special diet prolonged the little guy's life, but I knew his time with me was short. One evening he began having seizures again. The next morning Sampson could not walk with me to go outside. I had prayed for the Lord's grace and wisdom, and I knew He would help me. As I looked to the Lord, Jesus gave me a sense that Mom and Gretchen (Samson's German shepherd "best friend" who'd died years before) were coming to escort Samson home to heaven. This image gave me grace to take fifteen-year-old Samson to the vet for his last time.

Losing Samson was harder than any previous loss. Maybe it was because he was Mom's. I found myself very tearful. However, the "sense" of Mom and Gretchen coming for Samson gave me comfort. It also set up a longing for heaven within my own heart! I live in comfort and joy looking forward to what is ahead! My faith is doubly blessed, for it is grounded on the Bible and His personal word to me. Now I can say: Yes, Mom, dogs *do* go to heaven!

The Lord holds a special place in eternity for animals who have fulfilled His purpose in this life. Loving is the highest calling of God. The animals who have shown His unconditional love and forgiveness, His patience and faithfulness, surely have a place close to the throne room of God. Sampson loved us. He was a ray of sunlight all his days.

THE PUZZLE COMPLETED

As I was writing this book, I found these words in one of Mom's notebooks. I do not know if they are original or copied from another, but I wept as I read them for they are so like Mom:

Looking at Life Through Rain Spattered Glass

Rain spattered glass blurs the images into gentle shades.
It is like taking off a strong pair of eyeglasses.
Things become fused into each other.
Nothing is quite so clear.
The edges are not sharp.
(Perhaps that is the way we were meant to see things.)
And yet there is a beauty about un-blurred images —
a cleanness, a sharpness.
However painful reality may be,
it is somehow worth it to see one clear image,
than a thousand imperfect pieces.
Being shown the lumber and cement,
the paint and the candelabra,
and even the master plan,
is never quite the same
as seeing the cathedral.

Do you see how the pieces to Mom's question have come together? Do you see the "cathedral?"

Yes, Mom, dogs do go to heaven!

Perhaps not all dogs, but good dogs go. So do all the animals who have chosen or been chosen to grace God's new heavens and earth. God has a plan and place for them — just as He did on the Ark during the Great Flood.

Some may say that the idea of animals in heaven is like wearing "rose-colored glasses" – one big fantasy. However, God's reality is usually better than any dream. Life, real life, is something about which we can be joyously excited! The *joie de vivre* for a believer is a "joy-of-eternal-life!" Eternity with the Creator who Loves all creation is beyond comprehension. What a trip!

I want to be there. To be sure there is no chance of missing it, I keep my heart close to the Lord's heart, trusting Him and obeying His loving orders found in His Holy Bible.

I hope to take many people and animals along with me. Heaven would not be heaven without all of you. Please be sure you come, too.

Your pet's life may depend on it.

> *Old Blue died and he died so hard,*
> *I dug the ground in my back yard.*
> *Lowered him down with a silver chain,*
> *Every link I did call his name.*
> *Blue, oh Blue, You good dog, you.*
> *When I get to heaven, I know what I'll do.*
> *I'll take my horn, And I'll blow for Blue.[12]*

ENDNOTES:

1.   Barbara Cartland, *Lucifer and the Angel*, [1980, Bantam] p. 82

2.   *Nearer, My God; an autobiography of Faith*, [Harcourt Brace 1997], p. 13-14

3.   The date I saw this program was September 18, 1996. I don't know if it was live or pre-recorded.

4. Interestingly, the Hebrew word for flesh, "basar," comes from a root word meaning "to be fresh," i.e., "full" or "cheerful." So being "fleshy" can be a good thing, too.

5. Harold Hill, with Irene Harrell, *How Did It All Begin? From Goo To You By Way Of The Zoo*, [Logos International, 1976], pp. 81-84. Harold Hill was an engineer. He describes an experiment where light in these three groups of people were measured. The three emitted significantly different degrees of light energy! Frankly, it is usually apparent to the enlightened eye.

6. The Hebrew term most used for the Lord and heavenly things, translated "glory" is "kabowd." It means "weight" or "heavy" in a good sense. It is also translated "honor." Poetically the term is used of the "heart" or "soul," i.e. the noble part of man. [*Gesenius*, #3519, p. 382] The Greek word used in the New Testament is doxa whose root means to "think" or "seem," relating to reputation. So doxa signifies an opinion or estimate, and therefore the honor resulting from a good opinion.

Vine' Expository Dictionary (pp 267-268), glory or glorious is defined: "It is used (1)(a) of the nature and acts of God ... i.e., what He essentially is and does, ... (b) of the character and ways of God as exhibited through Christ to and through believers, 2 Cor. 3:18 and 4:6; (c) of the state of blessedness into which believers are to enter hereafter through being brought into the likeness of Christ, e.g., Rom. 8:18, 32; Phil 3:21 ... (d) brightness or splendor. (1) supernatural, emanating from God (as in the shekinah "glory," in the pillar of cloud and in the Holy of Holies, e.g., Exo. 16:10, 25:22) Luke 2:9, Acts 22:11; Rom. 9:4; 2 Cor. 3?7, Jas 2:1: in Titus 2:13 it is used of Christ's return ... (2) natural, as of the heavenly bodies, 1 Cor. 15:40, 41..."

7. The Lord, in inspiring Scripture, is very clever. The Lord knows me — and you! Getting to heaven is both very simple, and exceedingly difficult. It is as simple as choosing to love and live for God, to serve and trust Jesus, like a child trusts. It also requires dying daily to all our selfish, willful ways to get there. So getting to heaven is impossible without God's help. I like to take the easiest way, but I'll choose the hard way if that's the only one ensuring success. How about you?

8. While C. S. Lewis reserved his opinion as to whether our particular pets would actually populate the new earth, he clearly imagined such a possibility. See *The Problem of Pain*, "Animal Pain." — Chapter 9 [Macmillan Publ. Co., 1962]

9. *The Great Divorce*, [Macmillan Publ. Co. 1946, 1974], p. 106

10. *Tulsa World*, 12/11/93, p. 1 & 3

11.   Author unknown.   According to Wikipedia: http://en.wikipedia.org/wiki/Rainbow_Bridge_%28pets%29

12.   "Blue, oh Blue, I'm a' comin there, too".   U.S. (southern) folk song

TO GOD YOU GO

My furry friend
I cannot say "Goodbye!"
Through prayers,
Through our pain,
It must be "until we meet again."

When I first saw you, your eyes of love drew me.
I took you home. You made your home in my heart.
What life we shared! What frolicking great times you led me into!
Your joy in living fired my own.
God's emissary, you won my heart.
In life, you've been my strong friend and gentle companion.
Forgiving, faithful, full of healing hope and joy,
A masterpiece of the Lord of Creation and His grace you are.
Death can never steal an eternal friendship born in God.
We heard the Good News and believed, you and I.
Our God will preserve such forever! That's what Heaven's for.

My four legged friend,
I can not say "Goodbye!"
Through prayers,
Through the pain,
It's "'Til we meet again!"

Death cannot kill our love. Death's seeming victory is short.
Death and pain were conquered by the Sacrifice of
the Lamb of God.
The unbreakable promise of God,
Of redemption, of resurrection, of restoration of all creation,
Is our sure comfort.
Your too brief life is my rich treasure wrapped with memories.

What a gift of God you have been! You are!
I thank God for you and what you mean to me!
Sweet images of your life will sustain me while we are apart!

Go, friend, to our God! ,
Run to Jesus, the Great Shepherd born in a stable!
Into the arms of our Lord Jesus outstretched to bring us into
God's Heaven of delights!
Through Heaven's Gates, go now!
Into perfect meadows of eternal love, frisk in eternal life!
Await me there until my time! I'm coming, too!

My loving friend,
I need not say "Goodbye!"
Through prayers,
Through His pain
In God's heaven, we will meet again!

A P P E N D I X

OVERCOMING A LOSS

L osing a loved animal can be very painful. It is okay to grieve. It is losing a member of your family. If your pet was your constant companion or working partner, the bond can be deep. You may need help overcoming the loss. Healing and moving on may require knowledgeable counsel and prayer. Sometimes it requires forgiveness, too. You may feel anger at the pet, someone who caused or contributed to your loss or was callus toward your feelings, or even anger or disappointment that God let the animal be lost or die. Healing is not only good for you, but for the animals who wish to love you.

I am sure there are a number of grief recovery techniques and groups, you could find. I attended a grief recovery workshop offered by a local cemetery. The leader or facilitator was certified with the Grief Recovery Institute in California. Russell Friedman and John James started it and it is based on their book, The Grief Recovery Handbook. I found it very good when I choose to explore grief recovery about a favorite horse. I was amazed that my grief was still there after many years. The release brought a wonderful change in me. As this book and workshop suggest, grief is grief – whether it is loss by death, divorce, loss of a pet, or other thing that causes you sorrow. While we each grieve differently, even for the same person, pet or loss, the things that help follow a pattern. Check out their website: www.grief-recovery.com (If the Internet is not your cup-of-tea, ask for help or check whether your local library can get the book for you.)

Do your homework or get a friend to help. Check out what is available in your area. If nothing is, ask a partner or friend to go through a program like The Grief Recovery Handbook offers. Talking and doing the written assignments are keys to recovery from your loss.

Of course, I recommend spending time with God. The God of the Bible is the God of all comfort [2 Corinthians 1:2-4]. Jesus called the Holy Spirit "the Great Comforter" [John chapters 14, 16, 26] for good reason. I recommend "soaking" – which means putting on soft anointed Christian music (or classical music, like Beethoven or Mozart or Handel), get quiet and think about God or Bible verses which speak of Him, His love and grace. It helps me to say "Hallelujah" or "Praise the Lord" or to verbalize thanks for things God has done for me or others. It's the best medicine I've ever known when I'm hurting or down. Letting God comfort you is the best! Talk to Him. Listen, too. Try it.

25693424R00190